Deconstructing Morphology

Deconstructing Morphology

Word Formation in Syntactic Theory

Rochelle Lieber

The University of Chicago Press

Chicago and London

Rochelle Lieber is associate professor of English at the
University of New Hampshire.

The University of Chicago Press, Chicago 60637
The University of Chicago Press, Ltd., London
© 1992 by The University of Chicago
All rights reserved. Published 1992
Printed in the United States of America
01 00 99 98 97 96 95 94 93 92   5 4 3 2 1

Library of Congress Cataloging-in-Publication Data

Lieber, Rochelle, 1954–
    Deconstructing morphology : word formation in syntactic
theory / Rochelle Lieber.
        p.   cm.
    Includes bibliographical references and index.
    ISBN 0-226-48062-3. — ISBN 0-226-48063-1 (pbk.)
    1. Grammar, Comparative and general—Morphology.
    2. Grammar, Comparative and general—Syntax.
    3. Government-binding theory (Linguistics)   I. Title.
    P241.L53   1992
    415—dc20   91-23116
                                                CIP

Contents

Preface   vii

List of Abbreviations   ix

Prologue: On Productivity   1

1   The Interface between Morphology and Syntax   11

2   Head Theory and Principles of Construction   26

    2.1 Development of the Theories of Phrase Structure and Word Structure   26
    2.2 Revised Principles of X-bar Theory   33
    2.3 Tagalog Phrase and Word Structure   40
    2.4 English Phrase and Word Structure   49
    2.5 Comparison: English, French, Dutch   64
      2.5.1 French   64
      2.5.2 Dutch   68
    2.6 Conclusions   75

3   Feature Percolation and Inheritance   77

    3.1 Previous Treatments of Percolation   78
    3.2 What Features Percolate   80
      3.2.1 Diacritics   80
      3.2.2 Argument Structures   86
      3.2.3 The Categorial Signature   88
    3.3 Head and Backup Percolation   91
    3.4 Multiply Marked Features   93
    3.5 A Case Study: P/N Marking in Vogul   101
    3.6 Ramifications   111
      3.6.1 Inflection vs. Derivation   111
      3.6.2 V Movement to Infl Analyses   115
    3.7 Inheritance   116
    3.8 Conclusions   119

4   Binding, Barriers, and X^0 121

    4.1 Binding below Word Level   122
      4.1.1 Sublexical Indexing   124

4.1.2 Binding Theory and Anaphoric Islands   126
4.1.3 Binding below X^0: A Closer Look at the Data   129
4.1.4 Sublexical Anaphors   132
4.1.5 Permissive vs. Nonpermissive Dialects   139
4.2 Move Alpha, Barriers, and X^0 140
4.2.1 Movement into Words   140
4.2.2 Movement Out of Words   145
4.2.3 Movement of Morphemes within Words   147
4.2.4 ECP and Bracketing Paradoxes   147
4.3 The Lexicalist Hypothesis and the Notion
of Lexical Integrity   151

5   Beyond Affixation and Compounding   154

5.1 Circumfixation   155
5.2 Conversion   157
5.3 Mutation and Umlaut   165
5.3.1 Consonant Mutation   166
5.3.2 Umlaut   170
5.4 Reduplication   171
5.4.1 Reduplication as Affixation   172
5.4.2 Quantity Sensitive Reduplication and
the Parafixation Analysis   175
5.4.3 Against Head Operations: Affixation to Prosodic Structure   178
5.5 Templatic Morphology and the Morphemic Plane Hypothesis   185
5.6 Conclusions   195

6   The Interface with Phonology   197

Notes   205

References   219

Author Index   229

Language Index   233

Subject Index   235

Preface

This book is the outgrowth of a conviction I have harbored for a number of years that the forms of morphological rules within lexicalist theories of morphology have been too suspiciously similar to the forms of syntactic rules for this similarity to be coincidental. It is an attempt to take seriously the notion that the rules of word formation *are* in fact the rules of syntax and to work out this idea in some detail. Before I begin, I should clarify two points. The first is that although I have chosen as the syntactic framework in which to develop this idea the Government-Binding theory of Chomsky (1981, 1982, 1986a, 1986b), I believe my main thesis to be independent of any particular syntactic framework; I would hope it possible, in other words, to generate productively derived words within any theory of syntax that is sufficiently well articulated, and to achieve the same results I have achieved here using Government-Binding theory.

My second point concerns the title of the book. I have chosen to call this book *Deconstructing Morphology* in spite of the possible misunderstandings it may cause, because the literal sense of the verb "deconstruct"—"to take something to pieces"—so aptly expresses what I am trying to do in this book; in it I wish to take to pieces the morphological component of lexicalist theories and to reconstitute morphology as an integral part of the syntax. With apologies to my literary critic friends, I do not intend any similarity here to the use of the term 'deconstruction' by contemporary literary critics such as Derrida.

This book could not have been written without the help of a number of people. First I wish to thank Geert Booij for many hours of helpful discussion of an early draft of this book, as well as of issues concerning morphology in general. He is directly responsible for asking the questions that led to chapter 6. To him, and to the generosity of NWO, the Netherlands Organization for Scientific Research, I owe the opportunity to spend four months at the Free University of Amsterdam in the fall of 1989, during which I wrote several chapters. I also owe thanks to my other colleagues at the "VU"—Aafke Hulk, Ans van Kemenade, Martin Hietbrink, and Harald Baayen—for stimulating and helpful discussion; special thanks to Harald Baayen for long discussions of and help with issues related to productivity. I thank all my Dutch friends as well for their hospitality while I was in Amsterdam. I also wish to thank the linguists at Tilburg University, the University of Utrecht, and the Max Planck Institute for Psycholinguistics for the opportunity to talk about parts of this book during my stay in the Netherlands.

Thanks also to Carole Paradis for help with the French data, and for discussion of issues related to phonology, and to Laurie Bauer, Richard Sproat, and Harald Baayen for useful comments on the penultimate draft of the manuscript. Closer to home, I wish to thank the Graduate School of the University of New Hampshire for a Summer Faculty Fellowship during the summer of 1988 which allowed me to begin work on this project, Deborah Watson of the UNH Dimond Library and Barbara Cooper of the French Department for last minute help, and all my colleagues in the English Department of UNH for their support and interest. Finally, I thank Cliff Wirth and the beagle pack for support and too many other things to mention.

Abbreviations

Glosses

1	first person
2	second person
3	third person
ACC	accusative
COBL	complementizer oblique
DEF	definite conjugation
DET	determiner
DIMIN	diminutive
DS	different subject
DU	dual
ERG	ergative
GEN	genitive
IN	inclusive
INDEF	indefinite conjugation
INSTR	instrumental
LOC	locative
MABL	modal ablative
MASC	masculine
NEUT	neuter
NOM	nominative
NPAST	nonpast
OBJ	object
PL	plural
PRES	present
SG	singular
SS	same subject
SUBJ	subject
SUF	nominal inflectional suffix

Features

I	first person
II	second person

Act	active
C	case
Compl	completive
Cons	consonantal
Cont	continuant
D	arbitrary diacritic feature (Latin)
Def	definite
Du	dual
F_i, F_j	arbitrary morphosyntactic features
Fem	feminine
Hi	high
L	learned
Masc	masculine
Perf	perfect
Pl	plural
Poss	possessive
Pres	present
Pret	preterite
Rd	round
Sg	singular
Son	sonorant
Strid	strident
T	arbitrary diacritic feature (Latin)

Category Labels

A	adjective
Adv	adverb
Agr	agreement
AgrP	agreement phrase
AP	adjective phrase
Comp	complementizer
CP	complementizer phrase
Deg	degree
DegP	degree phrase
Det	determiner
DP	determiner phrase
Infl	inflection
IP	inflection phrase
MP	measure phrase
N	noun

NP	noun phrase
P	preposition
PP	prepositional phrase
QP	quantifier phrase
S	sentence
S′	sentence-bar
Spec	specifier
T	tense
TP	tense phrase
V	verb
VP	verb phrase
X^0	word level category
X^{max}	maximal phrase
XP, YP, ZP	arbitrary maximal phrases

Other Abbreviations Used in the Text

Af	affix
arb	arbitrary reference
BC	Blocking Category
BEC	Bracketing Erasure Convention
C	consonant
CFC	complete functional complex
Compl	complement
ECP	Empty Category Principle
F	foot
GPSG	Generalized Phrase Structure Grammar
HMC	Head Movement Constraint
LB	Learned Backing
LCS	Lexical Conceptual Structure
LF	logical form
μ	mora
MGC	Minimal Governing Category
minWd	minimal word
MOD	modifier
MPH	Morphemic Plane Hypothesis
N	token
n_1	a type showing only one token, i.e., a hapax
OCP	Obligatory Contour Principle
OE	Old English
P	productivity

PA	possessive adjective
PAS	Predicate Argument Structure
p.c.	personal communication
PF	phonetic form
P/N	person/number
QR	Quantifier Rule
r	root
RHR	Right-hand Head Rule
σ	syllable
σ_c	core syllable
σ_μ	light (monomoraic) syllable
$\sigma_{\mu\mu}$	heavy (bimoraic) syllable
SCC	Strict Cycle Convention
SMPH	Strong Morphemic Plane Hypothesis
t	trace
T/A	tense/aspect
U	phonological utterance
UTAH	Uniformity of Theta Assignment Hypothesis
V	type *or* vowel
Wd	prosodic word
WFR	word formation rule
Wd^{MIN}	minimal word
WMPH	Weak Morphemic Plane Hypothesis

Prologue: On Productivity

This book is an attempt to articulate a theory of word formation based on the premise that there is no separate component of morphology in the grammar. In its body I will be concerned with identifying what I mean by "component," and with what rules and principles can account for the formation of words in the absence of a morphological component. Before I embark on this enterprise, however, it seems appropriate to talk about the data that any theory of word formation should respond to. Certain things almost go without saying: that such a theory should be based on data from many unrelated languages, that it should be applied to at least some languages in some depth, and that it should be based on observations about living, productive patterns of word formation, rather than unproductive, or moribund patterns.

The first of these desiderata is relatively unproblematic; I will draw on examples not only from familiar territory (English, Dutch, French), but also from a good variety of other languages—Tagalog, Vogul, and Yavapai, among others. I will try to look at some of these languages in some depth. Achieving the last goal is much trickier, however, since we must have an idea of what we mean by productivity in order to delimit our subject matter in a reasonable way. Since I will concern myself in this book almost entirely with productive processes of word formation,[1] I will try to make clear at the outset what I mean by morphological productivity, and how productivity might be measured.

Aronoff (1976, 35) points out that although the notion of productivity is widely used in morphology, and although there is some intuition behind its use, the notion is often left rather vague. Productivity cannot, for example, be measured by counting up the number of words formed with an affix X and comparing it to the number formed with an affix Y. As he points out, the problem with this naive notion of productivity is that "it doesn't take into account the fact that there are morphological restrictions on the sorts of words one may use as the base of certain WFRs. Thus *#ment* and *+ion* both form nouns from verbs (*detachment, inversion*), but the latter is restricted to latinate verbs." Aronoff does, however, suggest a somewhat different notion of productivity:

There is a simple way to take such restrictions into account: we count up the number of words which we feel **could** occur as the output of a given WFR (which we can do by counting the number of possible bases for the rule), count up the number of actually occurring words formed by that rule, take a ratio of the two, and compare this with the same ratio for another WFR. In fact, by this method we could arrive at a simple index of productivity for every WFR: the ratio of possible to actual words. (1976, 36)

Productivity under this view is the degree to which the actually occurring output of a word formation process exhausts its pool of possible bases. Baayen (1989) suggests that Aronoff's index of productivity might be formalized as in (1), where V = the number of types and S = the population number, that is, the number of forms the word formation rule in question could have given rise to (note that by "words" in this passage, Aronoff seems to mean types rather than tokens):

$$(1) \quad I = \frac{V}{S}$$

But there are a number of reasons why this notion of productivity and the ratio proposed to measure it are not suitable for my purposes.

Note first that Aronoff's ratio of productivity is a relative rather than an absolute one. It gives no method of distinguishing morphological rules which are unproductive from those which are marginally or truly productive. For my purposes, then, such a measure would be inadequate, since it would not help to determine which processes of word formation the theory need not be responsible to.

A second problem concerning the measure in (1) is discussed in Baayen (1989). Baayen argues that it is not necessarily clear how to arrive at the figure S, the number of types which could **potentially** be created with a given affix. For example, as Williams (1981a) has pointed out, certain affixes "potentiate" certain others in the sense that the attaching affixes occur very productively with the base affix (e.g., *-ity* can be affixed to any word formed in *-able*). If the base affix is itself very productive, there may be no way of estimating how many forms there are with that base; dictionaries, after all, would not necessarily list all such forms. Baayen (1989, 30) in fact points out that "the index of productivity vanishes for productive word formation rules. . . . The index is, in fact, applicable to unproductive word formation rules only, and is perhaps better named an index of unproductivity." That is, as S approaches infinity, as it would be expected to do for a productive word formation rule, the index of productivity will approach zero.

A final problem is not particular to Aronoff's measure of productivity, but is shared by all potential measures of productivity: it has to do with the notion of counting "actually occurring" words. Words are not "actual" or "existing" in any objective sense. They exist only in the mental lexicon of some individual or other, or in a fixed list or corpus such as a dictionary produced at a certain time by certain lexicographers. The actual words of any mental lexicon or dictionary may coincide in large part with the actual words of another, but perhaps will never do so entirely. That is, the notion of "actual" words is a fiction, although perhaps an unavoidable one if we are to find some way of measuring productivity. So in order to use Aronoff's measure of productivity, or any other one, for that matter, we must first make clear what we are using as a data base. I will have more to say about this below.

   In this work I will assume an intuitive definition of productivity rather different from the one proposed by Aronoff. The particular definition I will adopt here is that proposed by Schultink (1961) (translation from van Marle 1985, 4):

Onder produktiviteit als morfologisch fenomeen verstaan we dan de voor taalge-bruikers bestaande mogelijkheid . . . unopzettelijk een in principe niet telbaar aantal nieuwe formaties te vormen.

By productivity as a morphological phenomenon we understand the possibility for language users to coin, unintentionally, a number of formations which are in principle uncountable.

There are two important elements in Schultink's definition: first, the notion that words formed by truly productive word formation processes are unintentional, and second, the notion of uncountability. By unintentionally formed words I mean those whose creation can go unnoticed. No English speaker would ever take note of the creation of a new noun in *-ity* from a base in *-able,* nor would a new noun in *-ness* attract attention.

   Schultink refers to the ability to consciously coin a new word on an unproductive pattern as "morphological creativity," in distinction to "morphological productivity." With unproductive processes a new word may sometimes be coined, but such coinages will always draw attention to themselves. They will be perceived by the native speaker as odd, amusing, repulsive, or otherwise remarkable. Such words are often coined by advertisers to draw attention to their products. They may show up in Safire's *New York Times* column, or on the back page of *The Atlantic,* or in the "Among the New Words" feature of *American Speech*. But they are not necessarily to be taken seriously by a theory of word formation.

   The second element of Schultink's notion of productivity is the idea of countability. Truly productive word formation processes can give rise to potentially unlimited numbers of new words. "Morphological creativity," in contrast, will give rise to a fixed, countable, and presumably small number of new forms.

Schultink does, of course, allow that there might be differences in the degree of productivity among productive word formation processes. Some affixes, for example, have phonological, syntactic, or semantic restrictions on the bases they attach to. The suffix *-ity* can attach only to latinate adjectives, and therefore would be expected to be somewhat lower in productivity than *-ness* which attaches to any adjective. Affixes which attach to verbs (e.g., agentive/instrumental *-er, -able, -ee*) frequently attach only to verbs with specified argument structures. Still other affixes attach only to bases having the requisite number of syllables (e.g., comparative *-er* in English), or a particular stress pattern (noun-forming *-al*). We would therefore want to be able to distinguish degrees of productivity.

I take Schultink's to be a reasonable intuitive notion of productivity, since it allows us to rule out some types of word formation as unproductive, even if it is conceivable that a few new formations in those types might be evidenced. To make his notion of productivity useful to my present enterprise, however, I must show that there is some reasonably objective way of measuring productivity in the Schultinkian sense. Baayen (1989), in fact, proposes a statistical measure of productivity which is somewhat more sophisticated than (1), and which is compatible with Schultink's intuitive definition of productivity in that it allows us to distinguish productive from unproductive word formation processes, and to differentiate degrees of productivity in those processes which are productive. It is to Baayen's measurement of productivity that I now turn.

Baayen (1989) shows that when one compares the ratio of tokens (N) to types (V) in a large corpus for various affixes, what one finds is that affixes which intuitively feel productive to native speakers show a relatively high proportion of hapax legomena (types which occur only once in the data base), and intuitively unproductive affixes a much lower proportion of hapaxes. Conversely, intuitively unproductive affixes show a large proportion of high-frequency types and intuitively productive ones a much lower proportion. The formula Baayen suggests for testing productivity is that in (2), where n_1 is the number of types which show only one token, i.e., the hapaxes:

(2) $P = \dfrac{n_1}{N}$

This measure can also provide us with a reasonable cutoff to separate productive from unproductive word formation processes. If the measure in (2) is applied to frequency data from simplex (underived) items of a given category, it gives us a measure of the probability of coining a new simplex item of that category. Baayen argues that if the P value for an affix falls below that of the simplex class, we can call it unproductive. In other words, if it would be easier to coin an entirely new simplex member of the class than to form a new item using that affix, we can take that affix to be unproductive. Affixes with a P value above that for simplex items can be called productive, and degrees of productivity can of course be distinguished.

Baayen's measure of productivity, like all such measures, must be applied to some fixed corpus of words. In the study of English derivation in Baayen and Lieber (1991), which I will describe below, we make use of a large English lexical database of 18 million wordforms of the Dutch Center for Lexical Information in Nijmegen, CELEX. The CELEX database was compiled on the basis of the corpus of the Cobuild project of the University of Birmingham (Renouf 1987), which consists of 75 percent written language and 25 percent spoken language from such categories as the following: "broadly general, rather than technical, language; current usage, from 1960, and preferably very recent; 'naturally occurring' text, not drama; prose, including fiction and excluding poetry; adult language, sixteen years or over; 'standard English,' no regional dialects; predominantly British English, with some American and other varieties" (Renouf 1987, 2). We could perhaps wish for a corpus with more spoken language and more language from technical areas where we would expect more novel word formation, but we take the Cobuild corpus to be a reasonably representative slice of the language on which to base our frequency studies.

Note incidentally that a database like CELEX is superior in a number of ways to the list of words one would find in a dictionary. First, dictionaries offer no information on frequency, and frequency is of vital importance in the calculation of P. Secondly, dictionaries often do not list all words formed with a given affix. In fact, for highly productive affixes like *-ness*, dictionaries tend not to list exhaustively the forms which occur with that suffix. Dictionaries, moreover, tend not to list words which have a very low frequency in actual use. But it is these words which give the best indication of productivity, according to Baayen.

Baayen and Lieber (1991) investigate the following derivational affixes of English: (1) **Noun-forming affixes**—the patient noun affix *-ee* (*employee*), the agentive/instrumental suffix *-er* (*baker, sweeper*), the process/ result noun-forming suffixes *-ation* (*representation*), *-ment* (*commitment*), and *-al* (*refusal, societal*), the abstract noun-forming suffixes *-ness* (*happiness*) and *-ity* (*purity*), and the suffixes *-ian* (*comedian, civilian*), and *-ism* (*Marxism, purism*); (2) **Adjective-forming affixes**—the suffixes

-able (*washable*), *-ive* (*impressive*), *-ish* (*clownish, reddish*), *-ous* (*monstrous*), and *-esque* (*picturesque*), and the prefixes *un-* (*unsure*) and *in-* (*impure*); (3) **Verb-forming affixes**—the prefixes *re-* (*rewash*), *be-* (*beset, behead, belittle*), *en-* (*enchain*), and *de-* (*debug*), and the suffixes *-ize* (*finalize, hybridize*) and *-ify* (*codify, purify*). Tables 1–3 show the values for N (number of tokens), V (number of types), P (productivity), n_1 (number of types occurring once), and n_2 (number of types occurring twice), for the affixes listed above, as well as for simplex nouns, verbs, and adjectives. Within each table, the affixes have been sorted according to the category of item they attach to. Where a particular affix, for example *-ish* or *-ize*, can attach to bases of different categories, it will appear twice in the appropriate table. Within each table, affixes are listed in order of decreasing P.

Here I will make only general observations about the data in tables 1–3. The reader is referred to Baayen and Lieber (1991) for further details and in-depth discussion of particular affixes.

Note first that affixes may exhibit a relatively large number of types (V), and yet be ranked fairly low in productivity (P), and vice versa. Good ex-

affix	N	V	P	n_1	n_2
	18,000,000				
from verbs					
-ee	1213	23	0.0016	2	2
-er	57683	682	0.0007	40	40
-ation	74466	678	0.0006	47	37
-ment	44419	184	0.0002	9	7
-al	7317	38	0.0001	1	3
from adjectives					
-ness	17481	497	0.0044	77	54
-ian	505	16	0.0040	2	0
-ity	42252	405	0.0007	29	21
-ism	3755	82	0.0005	2	4
from nouns					
-ian	2898	27	0.0007	2	0
-ism	3290	50	0.0006	2	1
-al	29445	45	0.0001	2	0
simplex nouns	2781258	6582	0.0001	256	257

TABLE 1   Noun-forming Affixes

affix	N	V	P	n_1	n_2
18,000,000					
from verbs					
-able	15004	187	0.0007	10	8
-ive	21337	179	0.0003	6	8
from adjectives					
-ish	290	16	0.0034	1	2
un-	11952	184	0.0005	6	9
in-	14426	237	0.0004	6	6
from nouns					
-ish	1602	67	0.0050	8	4
-ous	21861	264	0.0006	13	10
-esque	238	3	0.0000	0	0
simplex adjectives	994716	1659	0.0001	60	32

TABLE 2 Adjective-forming Affixes

affix	N	V	P	n_1	n_2
18,000,000					
from verbs					
re-	23591	96	0.0000	1	3
be-	41210	26	0.0000	0	0
from adjectives					
-ize	14083	61	0.0001	1	0
-ify	7764	17	0.0000	0	0
en-	6705	11	0.0000	0	0
be-	82	1	0.0000	0	0
from nouns					
de-	1887	32	0.0016	3	1
-ize	12491	85	0.0002	2	2
-ify	9815	33	0.0000	0	1
en-	20961	40	0.0000	0	0
be-	628	4	0.0000	0	0
simplex verbs	3660693	2581	0.0000	24	24

TABLE 3 Verb-forming Affixes

amples of this are *-ee* versus *-al* and *-ment* in table 1. Affixes may be quite productive even if they show up relatively infrequently in a corpus, since P is more directly a function of n_1 (number of hapaxes) than of V.[2]

Table 1 indicates that of the noun-forming affixes, all but *-al* are at least somewhat productive. The P value for *-al*, however, either falls below that of simplex nouns, or is not significantly greater than that of simplex nouns, as can be seen if we carry the P calculation out to six places (simplex nouns P = 0.000092, *V-al* P = 0.000136, *N-al* P = 0.000068). We can also observe in table 1 that the P values for rival affixes (that is, affixes which attach to and form items of the same category, and which have the same semantic effect) are very much in accord with native speaker intuitions. The noun-forming affixes *-ness* and *-ity* both appear to be productive, but *-ness* exhibits a far higher P value than *-ity*. The noun-forming affixes *-ation*, *-ment*, and *-al* all form process/result nominals from verbs, and of the three *-ation* has the highest P value, which accords with my intuition that it is much easier to form new nouns in *-ation* than new nouns in *-ment* or *-al*.

Of the adjective-forming affixes investigated, the only one which appears to be thoroughly unproductive is *-esque*, which has a P value of 0.0000. The P values for rival affixes *-ish* and *-ous* again accord well with intuitions; *-ish* shows a far higher P value than *-ous*, although even the latter is marginally productive. One pair of affixes in table 2 is worth looking at in more detail. The negative prefixes *un-* and *in-* are rival affixes which both appear to be productive, and which show up in the CELEX database with roughly equal P values (0.0005 for *un-*, 0.0004 for *in-*). Does this suggest that for any given new adjective there is roughly an equal chance that a negative form in *un-* or one in *in-* could be formed? In fact, it is possible to show that this is not the case. Baayen and Lieber (1991) determine that *un-* and *in-* in fact divide up the domain of possible bases into sets which overlap very little. They both attach to simplex bases, with *un-* being productive with predominantly native bases and *in-* with latinate bases. Also, *un-* is productive with complex adjectives formed with native suffixes like *-ed, -ing, -ful,* and *-y,* while *in-* takes complex adjectives in *-able/-ible/-uble,* and predominates with *-ous*. In fact, the pattern of productivity exhibited by these affixes illustrates the sort of paradigmatic characteristic discussed by van Marle (1985).

The verb-forming affixes in table 3 are perhaps the most interesting cases studied in Baayen and Lieber (1991). Here it is possible to determine that a number of verb-forming affixes are truly unproductive. The P values for the prefixes *en-* and *be-* and the suffix *-ify* fall below the P value for simplex verbs. The productive verb-forming affixes in synchronic English are *de-* and *-ize*. Table 3 shows *re-* with a P value of 0.0000, but carrying the calculation out to six places reveals that it too shows some productivity (P = 0.000042, as compared to 0.000000 for *be-, en-* or *-ify,* or 0.000007 for simplex verbs). Baayen and Lieber (1991) discuss this case in some detail, and also provide some explanation for the fact that the P values for productive verb-forming affixes appear in general to be much lower than the P values for productive noun- and adjective-forming affixes.

My point in this brief Prologue is not to give a full account of which word-formation processes in English are productive and which unproductive, much less to give such an account for the word-formation processes of the other languages that will figure in this study. At present this is impossible, since suitable corpora on which to carry out the productivity calculations are not available for all the languages in question. My point is rather to suggest that a reasonable decision process is available, so that the goal of constructing a theory of word formation that accounts for all and only productive word formation processes is at least in principle a realistic one. What this means is that it is, or will be, possible to determine whether particular sorts of data stand as reasonable evidence for or against the theory to be developed in this book. Potential counterevidence can be counted as significant only if it passes the test of productivity. Positive evidence for the theory must also be taken seriously only insofar as it comes from productive sorts of word formation. In effect, a theory of word formation is not responsible for accounting for every complex word which has been or will be coined, but only for a carefully delimited subset of these. With this in mind, I turn now to the theory itself.

1   The Interface between Morphology and Syntax

The starting point for this theory of word formation is a somewhat odd one—the fringes of morphology, so to speak, where the syntax of words and that of phrases seems to converge. Occasionally in the morphological and syntactic literature one finds reference to constructions in which a phrase appears to occur within something which otherwise looks rather like a compound or derived word. I have in mind first items like the so-called phrasal compounds in English, Afrikaans, Dutch, and German in (1):

(1) a. English
        the Charles and Di syndrome
        a pipe and slipper husband
        a floor of a birdcage taste
        over the fence gossip
        in a row nests
        off the rack dress
        an ate too much headache
        a slept all day look
        a pleasant to read book
        God is dead theology
        a who's the boss wink
        a connect the dots puzzle
    b. Afrikaans (data from Savini 1983)
        Charles en Di sindroom   'Charles and Di syndrome'
        op 'n ry neste   'in a row nests'
        vies vir die wêreld uitdrukking   'cross for the world
                                           expression'
        liewer vas mense   'preferably together people'
        gou baklei spelers   'quickly fight players' (i.e.,
                                           players who are known to
                                           be free with their fists)
        God is dood theologie   'god is dead theology'
    c. Dutch (Hoeksema 1988)
        lach of ik schiet humor   'laugh or I shoot humor'

blijf van mijn lijf huis   'stay off my body house' (i.e., shelter
                                    for abused women)
d. German (Toman 1983, 47)
   die Wer war das Frage   'the who was that question'
   die Rund-um-die-Uhr-Rennen   'the round the clock racing'
   die Muskel-für-Muskel-   'the muscle for muscle muscle
      Muskel-Methode   method'
   Hoch-wasser alarm   'flood alarm'

The items in (1) consist of a phrase, arguably a maximal phrase, plus a lexical noun. That the left-hand phrasal element is maximal is suggested, first of all, by the possibility of having CP in this position, with a wh-word occupying Spec of CP, as, for example, in *a who's the boss wink*. Specifier of PP may also be filled in phrasal compounds—e.g., *a right off the rack dress*. If the phrasal element of the phrasal compound is what is traditionally referred to as a noun phrase, it is true that no determiners are allowed: **a the floor of a birdcage taste, *the the king and the queen syndrome*. But, as Hoeksema (1988) points out, there is independent reason for ruling this out. It has been argued, for example in Abney (1987), that what is traditionally called a noun phrase should actually be called a determiner phrase (DP), which is headed by a determiner. The determiner takes as its obligatory complement what Abney calls a "nominal phrase" (NP), which is the maximal projection of the noun. If the DP analysis is correct then, Hoeksema points out that what can occur as the first element of a phrasal compound is any maximal phrase that belongs to an open class, that is, VP, AP, NP (in Abney's sense), arguably PP, and, I would add, CP. Open classes are of course the classes that typically take part in word formation. DPs cannot occur in the nonhead position of the phrasal compound because determiners belong to a closed class.[1]

Phrasal compound data have been discussed in a number of places in the morphological literature, for example, in Botha (1980), Savini (1983), Toman (1983), Fabb (1984), Hoeksema (1985, 1988), Sproat (1985), Lieber (1988), and Kiparsky (1982). Let me first review some of the evidence which suggests that the data in (1) are indeed compounds. I will then go on to discuss the question that these data raise for morphological theory.

It is well known that there are no unequivocal criteria for identifying compounds in English; see Levi (1977) and Bauer (1978) for extensive discussion of this issue. A characteristic stress pattern—heaviest stress on the leftmost stem—frequently serves to pick out compounds, but not all compounds exhibit this pattern; *bláckboard, fíle cabinet* do, but *ice créam, apple píe* do not, at least for many speakers. Comparison to syntactic phrases is sometimes used to distinguish compounds. That is, compounds frequently have items as their first elements which could not occur prenominally in a noun phrase, preadjectivally in an adjective phrase, and so on. For example, nouns do not occur in the pre-head position either in NPs or APs, so where they do appear in these positions it must be within compounds (e.g., *file cabinet, sky blue,* etc.). But this criterion would not identify *blackboard* and *greenhouse* as compounds. Finally, some appeal to inseparability of elements can be made to distinguish compounds from phrases; elements of compounds cannot be separated—*a black heavy board.* This is perhaps the most reliable of the criteria for compoundhood in English. In other languages compounds can be distinguished from phrases by the fact that the nonhead element appears uninflected, where such an element in a phrase would require inflection. This is the case, for example, in Danish, according to Bauer (1978). But the poverty of inflection in English prevents this criterion from being useful for English compounds. Nevertheless, one or more of the first three criteria will usually allow us to identify items which are intuitively felt to be compounds in English.

Similarly, although there is no one foolproof criterion for identifying phrasal compounds as compounds, one or more of the tests described above will usually work for the items in (1). First, some speakers do get compound stress on such items, that is, heaviest stress on the rightmost primary-stressed syllable in the phrasal element of the compound (for example *a [[floor of a **birdcage**][taste]]*). Second, the phrasal elements preceding the noun are generally not the sort of items that occur in prenominal position in NPs. Maximal phrases of all types are in fact explicitly ruled out in the position before the head of NP in English (see chapter 2). Third, the first elements of these compounds are just as inseparable from the second element as first elements in ordinary compounds are (for example, *a floor of a birdcage salty taste*). All of this suggests that these items are compounds. Note further that I know of no explicit arguments for these items *not* being compounds.[2]

It is also significant that these phrasal compounds appear to be productive. Although to date no database available allows a systematic study of the frequency distributions of phrasal compounds, Baayen (p.c.) observes that when they do turn up in the Dutch corpus of 40 million wordforms, they tend to show up as hapaxes (e.g., *bijna-eigenlijk-ook-meester* 'almost-in fact-also-master', *in-het-wilde-wegmanier* 'in-the-wild-way-manner' occur only once each), or with very low frequency (*glas-in-loodvensters* 'glass-in-lead-windows' occurs twice), indicating that the P value is likely to be quite high for them.

Assuming then that the items in (1) are compounds, they constitute important data for morphological theory, for they raise the question of what the proper relationship is between morphology and syntax. Specifically, phrasal compounds call into question the strict separation of components countenanced by lexicalist theories of morphology. The Lexicalist Hypothesis (Chomsky 1970; Lapointe 1980) states roughly that rules of morphology and rules of syntax cannot interact.[3] The Lexicalist Hypothesis has been the foundation of a number of the influential morphological theories of the 1980s, including Lieber (1980), Williams (1981a), Selkirk (1982), DiSciullo and Williams (1987), among others. But any theory which acknowledges that compounds such as those in (1) can be generated productively must allow for some degree of interaction between morphology and syntax. Rules of word formation must at least be allowed to refer to phrasal categories which are presumably generated as part of the syntax. In other words, if morphological theory is to account for phrasal compounds, the strict form of the Lexicalist Hypothesis must be abandoned. And this abandonment leads inevitably to the question of how much interaction between word formation and syntax needs to be allowed, and what sort?

Other phenomena at the fringe of morphology raise the same questions. Consider the cases described in (i)–(v):

i. **English Possessive Marking:** It has frequently been noted that the possessive morpheme *'s* in English attaches to the end of an NP rather than to the end of a lexical noun:

(2) $_{NP}$[a friend of mine]'s book
    $_{NP}$[a man I know]'s hat

This fact is somewhat puzzling from the point of view of a morphological theory with strictly lexicalist assumptions, since it is not possible in such theories to state a word formation rule in which an affix attaches to a phrasal category.[4]

ii. **Case Marking in Warlpiri:** Simpson (1983) argues for a phrasal constituent N' as the maximal projection of N in Warlpiri. Although it has been argued that Warlpiri contains no phrasal constituents at all (Nash 1980), Simpson shows that a sequence of nominal elements can precede the Auxiliary constituent. Since the Auxiliary must be the second element in a Warlpiri sentence, this suggests that the preceding nominals form a single constituent, which Simpson calls an N'. Simpson notes that a sequence of nominals may each be marked with the same case, as illustrated in (3a), or that the sequence can consist of one or more caseless nominals followed by a casemarked one, as illustrated in (3b):

(3) a. Kirri-ngka　　　　wiri-ngka　　rlipa　　　nyina-ja
　　　large camp-LOC　　big-LOC　　1.PL.IN　sit-PAST
　　　'We sat in the large camp.'
　　b. Maliki　　wita-jarra-rlu　　ka-pala　　　wajili-pi-nyi
　　　dog　　small-DU-ERG　PRES-3.DU　chase-act on-NPAST
　　　'The two small dogs are chasing it.'

In (3a) each nominal before the auxiliary has morphological case, but in (3b) it appears that the entire N′ is marked only once. Simpson notes that in this case the ergative marker has scope over the entire phrase. This suggests that the structure of the preauxiliary nominal in (3b) is one in which the case morpheme has attached to the whole N′, as in (4):

(4)

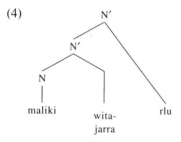

Again, this structure would be problematic from the point of view of lexicalist theories of word formation, since it entails that an affix can attach to a phrasal category.

iii. **Adjectival Possessives in Upper Sorbian:** Corbett (1987) discusses the case of what he calls Adjectival Possessives in Upper Sorbian, a West Slavonic language spoken in the eastern part of east Germany. An example of the adjectival possessive is given in (5) (Corbett 1987, 300):

(5) mojeho　　　　　　　bratrowe　　　　　dźěći
　　my(GEN.SG.MASC.)　brother's(NOM.PL)　children(NOM.PL)
　　'my brother's children'

Corbett explains the problem with the example in (5) (1987, 300):

Bratrowe is a PA [possessive adjective], formed from the noun *bratr* 'brother'. The adjectival stem *bratrow-* takes the ending *-e* to show agreement with the head noun *dźěći*. The problem is the form *mojeho*, which has no apparent head; clearly it does not agree with *dźěći*, since it carries the wrong features. It seems rather that its agreement controller is a form of *bratr*, which is masc. sg. and which underlies the adjective *bratrowy* . . .

Nominal modifiers in Slavic typically agree with the head noun. In (5), the head of the whole NP is *dźěći*, and we would expect all modifiers to bear the case, gender, and number features of this noun. Yet the possessive *mojeho* appears to be agreeing with the base of the possessive adjective *bratrowy*. A simple explanation of the agreement pattern in (5) exists, if we assume that the phrase in (5) has the structure in (6):

(6)

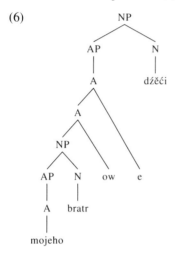

In other words, the possessive adjective ending actually attaches to an NP, rather than to a lexical noun. Within the inner NP, agreement of the nominal modifier with the head proceeds as expected. Of course, this analysis is again problematic if one assumes the strict lexicalist model in which word formation and syntax comprise rigidly separated components.

iv. **Verbal Derivations in Tagalog:** Schachter and Otanes (1972) describe a means of word formation in Tagalog which seems to take phrases of various sorts—PPs, locative adverbial phrases, negative phrases, NPs—and derives lexical verbs from them. Examples are shown in (7):

(7) a.

nasa akin	'in my possession'	pumasa-akin	'come into my possession'
nasa Maynila	'in Manila'	pumasa-Maynila	'go to Manila'
walang bisa	'having no effect'	magpawalang-bisa	'render ineffective'
walang halaga	'having no value'	magpawalang-halaga	'render valueless'

b.	sa ayos	'in order'	magsaayos	'put in order'
	sa dula	'in a play'	magsadula	'put into dramatic form'
	ibang bayan	'another country'	magibang-bayan	'go abroad'
	magandang gabi	'good evening'	magmagandang-gabi	'wish (someone) good evening'

In (7a) verbs are formed from the phrases in the left-hand column first by prefixing *pa-* to the phrase, and then adding the appropriate Subject Topic affix (for these examples, either the infix *-um-* or the prefix *mag-*).[5] The examples in (7b) possess no overt verbalizing affix. They appear to be "zero-derived" from phrases, with the Subject Topic marker adding to the phrase as a whole. Again, facts such as these could only appear as a puzzle to a strictly lexicalist theory of word formation.

v. *Tal* **Nominalizations in Tamil:** Subramanian (1988) discusses a process of nominalization in Tamil which appears to bear similarities to the cases discussed above. She contrasts two sorts of nominalization in Tamil. The first, illustrated in (8), is what Subramanian calls *VU* nominalization. Examples of *-tal* nominalization are given in (9).

(8) VU nominalizations[6]

peecu	'speak'	peeccu	'speech'
vaLai	'bend'	vaLaivu	'curve'
tura	'renounce'	turavu	'renunciation'
mara	'forget'	marati	'forgetfulness'

(9) TAL nominalizations (intransitive verbs)

| peecu | 'speak' | peecutal | 'speaking' |
| vaLai | 'bend' | vaLaital | 'bending' |

(10) TAL nominalizations (transitive verbs)

a.

| tura | 'renounce' | *turattal |
| mara | 'forget' | *marattal |

b.

illaram	tura	illaram	turattal
family	renounce	leaving	home
'become a hermit'		'becoming a hermit'	

| nanri | mara | | |
| gratitude | forget | nanri marattal | |

c.

uNmai-yai	marai	'ingratitude'	
truth-ACC	hide	uNmai-yai marai-ttal	
		'hiding the truth'	

	nilatt-ai	uRu	
	land-ACC	plow	nilatt-ai uRu-tal
c.	kaTinamaaka	uRai	'plowing the land'
	hard	work	kaTinamaaka uRai-ttal
			'working hard'

As the examples in (8) show, -VU nominalizations can be formed on either intransitive or transitive verbs. -TAL nominalizations can be formed on intransitive verbs, as shown in (9), but not on transitive verbs (10a), unless they have their internal subcategorized arguments present. In (10b), the base of the -TAL nominalizations appears to be a compound, but in (10c), as indicated by the case marking on the nouns, the base appears to be an entire VP. The last example in (10c) contains what Subramanian calls a VP adverb, which suggests as well that the scope of the -TAL nominalization is the whole VP. In contrast, the -VU nominalizing suffixes cannot attach either to compounds or to verbs accompanied by case marked arguments or VP adverbs.

Subramanian points out that these facts cause problems for strictly lexicalist theories, and even for those theories which allow inflection to be done in the syntax. -TAL nominalization cannot be accomplished in the lexicon, since lexical processes cannot refer to phrasal constituents. But -TAL nominalization is not like inflectional processes either, since it is a category-changing word formation process. I would suggest that the solution to the dilemma that Subramanian raises is to give up any form of the Lexicalist Hypothesis. The suffix -TAL in Tamil is a derivational suffix that attaches to VPs and forms from them Ns, as illustrated in (11):

(11)

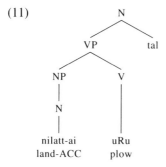

Cases like those in (i)–(v) are not terribly hard to find, and they suggest the same conclusion that the phrasal compounds do. The Lexicalist Hypothesis is clearly too strong. Some measure of interaction between morphology and syntax must be allowed, at least enough to allow compounds or derived words to be formed from phrases in some cases. The only solution available to a Lexicalist theory is to allow some sort of loop from syntax to morphology which feeds phrases back into the word formation component (see Kiparsky 1982 for a suggestion of this sort). But such a loop effectively undermines the Lexicalist Hypothesis. Still, if we abandon the Lexicalist Hypothesis, the question remains open, how much interaction between syntax and morphology should be allowed, and interaction of what sort? This is the major question with which this book will concern itself.

This question has indeed been the focus of much recent research into word formation. Even when many theories of word formation were basing themselves on the Lexicalist Hypothesis (Allen 1978; Lieber 1980; Williams 1981a, 1981b; Selkirk 1982), Anderson (1982) was arguing that at least inflection had to be done as part of the syntax. More recent works such as Toman (1983), Fabb (1984), Sproat (1985), Baker (1985, 1988a), and Borer (1988) all argue for some degree of interaction between morphology and syntax. Fabb (1984), for example, agrees with Anderson (1982) that inflection is a syntactic process, and argues as well that certain sorts of productive compounding and derivation should be accomplished in the syntax, using a modified form of X-bar theory, a version of Williams's Right-hand Head Rule, and an expanded system of licensing and case marking. Less than fully productive word formation processes are still consigned to a separate lexical component, however. Baker (1985, 1988a) is most concerned with those aspects of compounding and affixation that have to do with grammatical function-changing syntactic processes: incorporation, passivization, formation of applicative and causative constructions, and the like. Such processes are performed as part of the syntax, subject to precisely the same principles that syntax is subject to. Other sorts of word formation, however, are done in a separate component, presumably subject to different principles. Borer (1988) assumes that there is a lexical component as well with principles distinct from those of syntax, but that this component does not simply precede or follow the syntax. Rather, it runs alongside or "parallel" to the syntax, interacting with the syntax in well-defined ways. Certain sorts of word formation process (e.g., compounding and formation of construct state nominals in Hebrew) can apply at more than one level of the syntax, resulting in forms with slightly different properties. Category-changing morphology, however, does not interact with the syntax. None of these theories allows or accounts for the sort of interaction between syntax and morphology suggested by the examples above, where syntactic phrases seem to be the input to processes of derivation and compounding.

Toman (1983), Sproat (1985), and Walinska de Hackbeil (1986) take a much stronger position than Baker, Fabb, and Borer on the interaction of syntax and morphology, namely that word formation is not to be segregated into a separate component from the syntax, but rather that the same general principles should be able to account for both. Sproat (1985), for example, seeks to derive the properties of complex words from general principles of grammar. His theory is perhaps the best known attempt to construct a model of the grammar in which there is no separate morphological component.[7] His theory, however, is not without problems. Most prominently, in his theory the actual putting together of words—at least the linear ordering of morphemes—is attributed to the phonology (1985, 77). But Sproat actually says very little about how this is to work. It is not clear how his theory would derive phrasal compounds and the like, nor is it clear, since he does not develop a theory of headedness for words, whether separate principles of headedness would be needed for syntax and word formation.

Walinska de Hackbeil (1986) also suggests that there are no separate rules of word formation, just general principles of grammar that constrain both word formation and syntax. Her dissertation confines itself, however, to an analysis of a very few word formation processes (*en-* prefixation, *over-* prefixation, and certain zero affixation processes in English), without working out how this unification is to be accomplished. Again, it is not clear how her theory could account for data like the phrasal compounds or the material in (i)–(v).

Toman (1983) comes closest to giving an account of these odd phenomena. He argues that the principles of what he calls "word syntax," roughly the putting together of morphemes to form words, are simply the general principles of grammar assumed in Government-Binding theory (Chomsky 1981, 1986a), that is, the principles of X-bar theory, Theta theory, and so on. He allows for a separate morphological component, but only to account for such phenomena as the morphologically conditioned distribution of affixes, rules of truncation, reduplication, and allomorphy. The actual concatenation of morphemes is performed as part of the syntax, however. Toman even allows for the presence of maximal phrases before the head of a word, which is the first step in being able to derive phrasal compounds. What Toman does not succeed in doing, however, is in unifying X-bar theory so that the parameter settings for a given language define simultaneously both the head of the word and the head of a phrase. As we will see shortly, this is a necessary prerequisite for doing away with separate principles of morphology.

To summarize, although the interaction of morphology and syntax has been a topic of much concern among morphologists recently, and although some have suggested that there should be no distinction between the theory of morphology and the theory of syntax, no one has yet succeeded in deriving the properties of words and the properties of sentences from the same basic principles of grammar.

My reason for wanting to do so is simple. In order for phrasal categories to be the input to processes of derivation and compounding, at least some construction of words must be done in the syntax. The conceptually simplest possible theory would then be one in which all morphology is done as a part of a theory of syntax. I take as my model here recent work in Government-Binding theory (Chomsky 1981, 1982, 1986a, 1986b), as Toman did. In Government-Binding theory we have at least a rough idea of the workings of some of the subsystems of the theory of grammar: X-bar theory, Theta theory, Case theory, Binding theory, and so on. A truly simple theory of morphology would be one in which nothing at all needed to be added to the theory of syntax in order to account for the construction of words.

It is unlikely that Government-Binding theory as it is now constituted would give this result. What I hope to show in this book, however, is that with minimal, and perhaps trivial changes to X-bar theory and other subsystems as they now stand, it will be possible to derive not only the phrasal compounds and forms such as those in (i)–(v), but also to derive other, less exotic sorts of word structures as well. I try to show as well that this approach has explanatory advantages, since it allows us to predict correlations between headedness in phrases and headedness in words in particular languages.

I therefore assume that syntax and morphology are not separate components of the grammar, either in the sense of being two separate "places" where words and sentences respectively are derived, or in the sense of being two (at least partially) distinct sets of principles (Sproat 1985; Baker 1988a). We will strive for one general set of principles within a modular framework that allows the generation of both well-formed words and well-formed sentences.

At the outset the theory of word formation to be developed here will share certain assumptions with other recent theories of word formation. Like Sproat (1985) and DiSciullo and Williams (1987), I assume the existence of a lexicon which lists all idiosyncratic information about listemes. I assume, with DiSciullo and Williams (1987), that this repository of listemes is not structured, but I also assume that each listeme has a lexical entry, as described below. The lexicon, here, will be roughly equivalent to what I called the "permanent lexicon" in Lieber (1980). It lists all morphemes, both free and bound. The lexical entry of each morpheme contains a phonological representation and a semantic representation (which I call, following Levin and Rappaport 1986; Jackendoff 1987, 1990; and Rappaport and Levin 1988 a Lexical Conceptual Structure [LCS]), as well as an indication of the syntactic category to which that element belongs.[8] In addition many entries will also contain a Predicate Argument Structure (PAS), which will give the mapping between LCS and syntactic structure. Bound morphemes have, in addition to their own category information, an indication of their morphological subcategorization, that is, the category of the items to which they attach. In other words, affixes like *-ize* will be regarded as bound verbs, with all of the properties to be expected of verbs (e.g., having an argument structure, possessing the morphosyntactic features of verbs). The notation for lexical entries that I adopt here is basically that developed in Lieber (1980). A number of sample lexical entries are illustrated in (12):

(12) a. words   run $[_V \rule{1cm}{0.4pt}]$
                    [rʌn]
                    LCS: $[_{Event}$ GO $([_{Thing} \rule{1cm}{0.4pt}], [_{Path} \rule{1cm}{0.4pt}])]$
                    PAS: x^9

                    enter $[_V \rule{1cm}{0.4pt}]$
                    [ɛntr̩]
                    LCS: $[_{Event}$ GO $([_{Thing} \rule{1cm}{0.4pt}] [_{Path}$ TO
                        $([_{Place}$ IN $([_{Thing}])])])]$
                    PAS: $x \ \underline{<y>}$

                    cat $[_N \rule{1cm}{0.4pt}]$
                    [kæt]
                    LCS: $[_{Thing} \rule{1cm}{0.4pt}]$

   b. affixes   -ize $]_{N,A} \rule{1cm}{0.4pt}]_V$
                    [ayz]
                    LCS: [CAUSE $([_{Thing} \rule{1cm}{0.4pt}]$, [BE (LCS of base)])]
                    PAS: x

                    un- $[\rule{1cm}{0.4pt} {}_A[$
                    [ʌn]
                    LCS: negative

   c. roots   path $[X [_N \rule{1cm}{0.4pt}]]$ or $[[_N \rule{1cm}{0.4pt}] X]$
                    [pæθ]
                    LCS: ...

   d. lexicalized   transmission $[_N \rule{1cm}{0.4pt}]$
      words   [trænsmɪšən]
                    LCS: $[_{Thing}$ part of a car]

e. lexicalized phrases and sentences
    to kick the bucket
    The cat is out of the bag.

Here I will follow Pesetsky (1985) in assuming that the negative prefix *un-* does not itself bear category features; *un-* will receive its category by percolation, as is discussed in chapter 3.[10] In addition, I assume that bound roots such as *path* (as in *psychopath* or ***pathology***) have lexical entries as any other morphemes do. For convenience I represent the fact that they are bound as in (12c), although nothing of consequence hinges on the notation I have used. Finally, I follow DiSciullo and Williams (1987), among others, in assuming that idiosyncratic items consisting of more than one morpheme also have entries in the lexicon. Among these idiosyncratic items I include multimorphemic words like *transmission* 'part of a car' whose meanings are not compositional, as well as lexicalized phrases and sentences such as those in (12e).

From this point on, however, my theory of word formation diverges substantially from those of Lieber (1980), DiSciullo and Williams (1987), and other lexicalist theories. In chapter 2 I work out in detail the mechanisms for projecting word structures. I argue that the means made available for parameter setting in X-bar theory are sufficient, with a few minor modifications, to account for word structure as well as syntactic structure. Much of my initial support for this position comes from a close examination of the word structure and phrase structure of Tagalog, a language whose word structure defies much current dogma about headedness in morphological theory, since it is predominantly left-headed. I try to show that given the phrase structure of Tagalog and my assumptions about the nature of word structure, it is no accident that Tagalog has predominantly left-headed morphology. I then examine the word structure of English, French, and Dutch to see whether my assumptions about modified X-bar parameters suffice to account for word formation in these other languages. The focus of chapter 2 is on the notion of headedness in morphology, and whether it needs to be defined differently than the notion of headedness in syntax.

Chapter 3 focusses on another aspect of the mechanics of word formation, that is, on the mechanism which has been called **feature percolation.** There I argue that accounts of feature percolation in current morphological theory are far too vague; theories of feature percolation such as those in Lieber (1980), Selkirk (1982), and Williams (1981a) fail to determine exactly what features percolate and exactly how percolation occurs. I argue first that only morphosyntactic features percolate, and that percolation occurs only within what I call the **categorial signature,** a frame which determines what features are syntactically relevant in a particular category in a particular language. Other sorts of features, such as diacritic features, do not percolate. I try to show as well that argument structures are not to be encoded in features, and indeed that the passing of argument structures from node to node is not the same as feature percolation, but rather is an entirely different process, which I call, following Toman (1983), Randall (1988), and others, **inheritance.** I attempt to show that inheritance is the effect of combining the Lexical Conceptual Structures of morphemes and of projecting them to the level of Predicate Argument Structure. Finally, I try to work out in some detail how feature percolation takes place in languages in which a single feature, for example, case, person, or number, can be marked more than once on a single lexical item. This discussion will shed some light on the conditions under which one value for a morphosyntactic feature overrides another, and will lead us in the end to a consideration of the difference between inflectional and derivational word formation within the present theory.

Chapter 4 considers the extent to which the principles of other modules of Government-Binding theory apply in structures smaller than the word. I first discuss Binding theory and suggest, along the lines of Lieber (1984a), that the principles of Binding theory explain the possibilities of coreference and obligatory disjoint reference in the set of data that has been called "anaphoric islands" in the literature (Postal 1969; Ross 1971; Lakoff and Ross 1972; Corum 1973; Browne 1974). I show that Binding theory also explains the interpretation of words in *self-* (*self-contempt, self-deception*). I then go on to discuss the extent to which Move-Alpha can affect morphemes inside words, arguing that this movement rule applies freely below X^0, just as it does above X^0, and that illicit movement of morphemes into and out of words is constrained by the Empty Category Principle (ECP). At the end of chapter 4 I return to the Lexicalist Hypothesis and argue that the theory developed here captures some of the insights of this principle, although in a rather different way.

Chapters 1–4 are concerned with the analysis of conventional concatenative word formation, that is, with affixation and compounding. Chapter 5, however, is devoted to the sorts of word formation that appear not to fit comfortably under the rubric of word syntax: circumfixation, conversion, umlaut and consonant mutation processes, reduplication, and templatic morphology. I suggest that all of these seemingly problematic sorts of word formation are in fact consistent with the theory developed in chapters 2–4, if close attention is paid to the nature of lexical entries, and if insights of current phonological theory are taken into account. I rely in this chapter on some of the results of autosegmental morphology that have been achieved in the last ten years (e.g., McCarthy 1979, 1981, 1989; Marantz

1982; McCarthy and Prince 1986, among others). In chapter 6, finally, I briefly discuss the implications for the phonological component of the model of morphology-syntax developed in this book. In particular, I try to determine how compatible this theory is with the principles of Lexical Phonology.

2   Head Theory and Principles of Construction

As indicated in chapter 1, the starting point for any theory of word formation is the lexicon, that is, the list of idiosyncratic items—affixes, roots, words, and so on—that form the atomic particles of language. In this chapter we will be concerned with how the grammar works to put together these atomic particles into productively derived complex words—not only conventional derived words and compounds, but also the phrasal compounds and derived words discussed in the previous chapter. Both morphological theory and syntactic theory have been much concerned in recent years with the principles by which word structures on the one hand and sentence structures on the other are generated, and to some extent the development of the former has shadowed the development of the latter. I begin in section 2.1 with a brief historical overview of the development of structural principles (phrase structure and X-bar theory) in the fields of syntax and morphology. In section 2.2 I suggest what a logical next step in this development might be. Specifically, I argue that it is possible to merge the two theories so that in fact there is only one set of structural principles with parameters that are set only once for each language. I show that such a theory can account for ordinary derived words and compounds and their phrasal counterparts, and also that it yields an interesting prediction about the relationship between the morphology and the syntax of particular languages. The key to the convergence of structural principles in morphology and syntax is the redefinition of the notion "head of a word." Sections 2.3–2.5 are devoted to detailed case studies, showing how the theory can account for both word formation and basic phrase order in four languages: Tagalog, English, Dutch, and French.

2.1 Development of the Theories of Phrase Structure and Word Structure

The notion that hierarchically structured trees are generated by some set of rules or principles, and that lexical items are inserted into those structures has long been a part of the theory of generative syntax. In the standard theory of Chomsky (1965) the base component consisted of a lexicon and a set of phrase structure rules like those in (1):

(1) NP → (Det)(A) N (PP)
      VP → V (NP)(NP)(PP)
      PP → P NP
          etc.

The notion that each phrase had a head was at most implicit in the phrase structure rules, and the idea that different phrase types in a single language showed structural parallels was not yet considered an issue of the base component.[1] Chomsky (1970) first raised the possibility that such cross-categorial similarities should be stated in the phrase structure component of the grammar, and an early version of what has come to be called X-bar theory was worked out in Jackendoff (1977). Important in even the early versions of X-bar theory were the notions that each phrase has a head of the same category as the phrase as a whole, but with one less bar level as in (2), and that cross-categorial similarities in structure not only exist, but are to be expected. The latter sort of generalization was encoded in the generalized phrase structure template in (3) (where Spec = Specifier and Compl = Complement).[2]

(2)

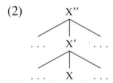

(3) X″ → Spec X′
      X′ → X Compl

Works such as Chomsky (1981) and Stowell (1981) brought to X-bar theory further refinements; from the former the Projection Principle and from the latter the idea of parameterization of X-bar theory. The Projection Principle, as stated informally in (4), requires that the subcategorization properties of lexical items be met at all syntactic levels:

(4) Chomsky (1981, 29)
      Representations at each syntactic level (i.e., LF, and D- and
          S-structure) are projected from the lexicon, in that they observe
          the subcategorization properties of lexical items.

The Projection Principle removes from X-bar theory the necessity for stipulating particular sequences of categories in the rules since the nature and sequence of categories are determined once and for all in lexical entries. Parameterization of X-bar theory suggests that each language makes a choice as to the position of the head with respect to its complements and specifiers. Very roughly, each language chooses consistently across categories whether the head precedes or follows its complements and whether the head precedes or follows its specifiers.

Further refinements were added to X-bar theory in the works of Stowell (1981) and Travis (1984, 1990), where it was argued that the ordering of head and complement need not be a parameter of X-bar theory itself, but rather may be determined by the direction of Theta-role assignment and Case marking. The most recent developments in X-bar theory concern the treatment of functional categories like Det, Infl, and Comp. Abney (1987), following Chomsky (1986a), proposes that functional categories are actually heads of phrases—Det of DP, Infl of IP, and Comp of CP. Det takes NP or AP as its complement, Infl VP, and Comp IP. Abney does not concern himself with the parameterization of the X-bar system, but presumably in his system, too, the ordering of specifiers and modifiers with respect to the head must be set, or must follow from some other principles of grammar.[3]

The history of the theory of phrase structure in generative grammar is thus one in which the principles of ordering and hierarchical structure have come increasingly to be derived from other principles of grammar, rather than being stipulated as part of individual rules. In a sense, the theory of word formation has followed a parallel development from a stipulative and particularistic theory in which a separate rule was required for determining the hierarchical structure and linear order of each individual morpheme towards a theory in which rules of word structure are made to follow from more general principles of grammar.

Aronoff, in his groundbreaking (1976) monograph on morphology, states word formation rules as in (5):

(5) Aronoff (1976, 63)
    Rule of negative un#
    a. $[X]_{Adj} \rightarrow [un\#[X]_{Adj}]_{Adj}$
       semantics (roughly) $un\#X = $ not X
    b. Forms of the base
       1. $X_V en$ (where *en* is the marker for the past participle)
       2. $X_V \#ing$
       3. $X_V \#able$
       4. $X+y$ (worthy)
       5. $X+ly$ (seemly)

6. X#ful (mindful)
7. X-al (conditional)
8. X#like (warlike)

Word formation rules, as the rule for attachment of negative *un-* in (5) illustrates, were stated separately for every affix; each rule included along with the syntactic and semantic information in (5a) a series of morphological restrictions on possible bases, as shown in (5b). Cast in this way, word formation rules appear to be very different from phrase structure rules in any form. Selkirk (1982) and Williams (1981a) propose, however, that word formation rules be recast in a more general form which makes them look more like the *Aspects* style phrase structure rules in (1). Selkirk states some of her word structure rules as in (6), where *Af* stands for affix and *r* for root.

(6) Selkirk (1982, 82)

a. $N^r \rightarrow \begin{Bmatrix} N^r \\ A^r \\ V^r \end{Bmatrix} N^{Af}$

$A^r \rightarrow \begin{Bmatrix} N^r \\ V^r \end{Bmatrix} A^{Af}$

$V^r \rightarrow \begin{Bmatrix} N^r \\ A^r \end{Bmatrix} V^{Af}$

b. $N \rightarrow \begin{Bmatrix} N \\ A \\ V \end{Bmatrix} N^{Af}$

$A \rightarrow \begin{Bmatrix} N \\ A \\ V \end{Bmatrix} A^{Af}$

$V \rightarrow \begin{Bmatrix} N \\ A \\ V \end{Bmatrix} V^{Af}$

As in *Aspects*-style phrase structure, items from the lexicon are inserted into the trees generated by the rules in (6). In the theories of Selkirk (1982) and Williams (1981a), affixes have lexical entries just as roots, stems, and words do. Each affix has a listing of the syntactic environment in which it can be inserted, as well as information about its own syntactic category, semantic representation, and so on. Rules such as those in (6), then, obviate the need for a particular word formation rule for each affix.

Lieber's (1980) treatment of word structure is similar in spirit to that of

Selkirk and Williams,[4] since it eschews the use of particular rules for each affix. However, it follows the progress of X-bar theory in syntax one step further. Lieber argues that affixes and free morphemes alike have lexical entries which indicate their syntactic category, semantic and phonological representations, etc. Affixes differ from free morphemes only in that their lexical entries contain in addition to the information mentioned above, a subcategorization frame indicating the environment in which they can be inserted into word structure trees. Lieber does not make use of actual word structure rules, however. She proposes that morphemes be inserted into unlabeled, binary-branching trees according to their subcategorization frames. Category and other information is then percolated up the structure in accordance with a series of Feature Percolation Conventions.[5] Lieber's theory of word formation incorporates, albeit implicitly, a notion somewhat like that of Chomsky's (1981) Projection Principle. Word structures like base structures of sentences in Government-Binding theory, are projected from the lexicon. There is no need to repeat lexical information in a separate set of word structure rules such as those in (6).

There is one area, however, in which the theory of word structure has not paralleled developments in the theory of phrase structure, namely in the treatment of heads. As mentioned above, the notion of head of a phrase in syntax has always been a relatively straightforward one. In a structure like that in (2), the head is simply the item which has the same category as, but one less bar-level than the category which dominates it. From the start, however, the notion of head of a word has been controversial and problematic. Williams (1981a) introduced the notion to morphology as follows:

(7) Williams (1981, 248)
     In morphology we define the head of a morphologically complex
     word to be the righthand member of that word. . . . Call this
     definition the Right-hand Head Rule (RHR).

Thus, in the words below, the element in bold in each is the head:

(8)

         instruct **ion**   re **instruct**

Williams bases his RHR on the morphology of English, where (in general) suffixes determine the category of the complex word, but prefixes do not.

Selkirk for the most part accepts Williams's notion of head, but modifies it to account for those few cases in English in which the right-hand member of the word does not seem to determine the category and other features of the word as a whole, for example, verb-particle sequences such as *grow up* or *step out*. She proposes the revised version of the RHR in (9):

(9) Selkirk (1982, 20)
Right-hand Head Rule (revised)
In a word-internal configuration,

where X stands for a syntactic feature complex and where Q
contains no category with the feature complex X, X^m is the head
of X^n.

In other words, a word may have a head which is not the rightmost morpheme just in case all morphemes to the right of it lack the relevant features
to determine the category of the word as a whole. Selkirk (following Lieber
1980) points out as well that the RHR even in its revised form is not a
universal rule, since there are languages in which a left-hand morpheme
determines the category of the word as a whole even though category features are available on a morpheme further to the right. Although she does
not elaborate on the idea, she suggests that headedness in morphology is
parameterized. Presumably languages choose either the left- or the rightmost morpheme as the head.

Lieber (1980) rejects Williams's RHR on the basis of two sorts of data.
First, she points out that English has at least a few prefixes which determine the category of the word as a whole, for example the prefix *en-* which
makes verbs from nouns (*encase, entomb*) or adjectives (*endear, ennoble*).
Furthermore, there are languages which have much more robust left-
headed morphology, for example, Vietnamese, which has left-headed
compounds such as those in (10):

(10) a. nguòi ò' 'person be located' = servant
     b. nhà thuong 'establishment be wounded' = hospital
     c. làm viêc 'do-make matter-affair' = to work
     d. làm ruông 'do-make rice field' = to engage in farming

Lieber proposes a symmetrical system of feature percolation which allows
the outermost affix at any stage of word formation, whether prefix or suffix,
to determine the category and features of the word as a whole. In a sense
the head of the word may be either the leftmost or the rightmost element.
For compounding, the direction of headedness must simply be stipulated.
English has right-headed compounds and Vietnamese left-headed ones.

None of these three accounts of headedness in morphology is entirely
satisfactory, however. Williams's RHR is too rigid. As Selkirk points out,
the RHR as he states it could not be a universal rule. On the other hand,

Lieber's symmetrical definition of head is probably too loose. Although it is true, for example, that English has a small amount of left-headed morphology, the bulk of English word formation is indeed right-headed. Yet the symmetrical theory of Lieber (1980) would lead one to expect a roughly equal amount of left-headed and right-headed morphology for English and for other languages. Selkirk's (1982) proposal falls somewhere in between these two in terms of restrictiveness. It is potentially possible in her theory to stipulate that a language has predominantly left- or right-headed morphology.[6] Still, there is reason to believe that Selkirk's definition of head of a word can be improved upon.

There has in fact been a good deal of discussion in recent literature about the appropriate characterization of the head of a word. Trommelen and Zonneveld (1986) defend Williams's strict Right-hand Head Rule for Dutch, arguing that Dutch prefixes which change category (that is, those which are the counterparts of English *en-* and *de-*) are subject to separate redundancy rules: "a. Dutch prefixes are verb-forming, except for noun-forming *ge-* and other marginal cases. b. All existing prefixed nouns from any source are neuters" [1986, 165]). They do not, however, broach the problem of languages with robustly left-headed morphology. DiSciullo and Williams (1987) also modify Williams's RHR; they adopt a revised RHR which, like Selkirk's version, allows for features to come from a morpheme which is not rightmost just in case the morpheme to the right lacks those features. Again, languages with strongly left-headed morphology are not accommodated. Scalise (1988) and DiSciullo (1988) offer further modifications to the positional head rules of Williams (1981a) and Selkirk (1982). Scalise suggests that in Italian, suffixes are heads but not prefixes, and that the position of the head in compounds is simply stipulated; Italian compounds are left-headed. DiSciullo (1988) (as reported in Brousseau 1989) similarly suggests that the position of the head can be stipulated independently for each sort of word formation; derivation in French is right-headed, whereas compounding is left-headed. Brousseau (1989), finally, suggests that the definition of head in morphology is at base intrinsic and semantic. The head of a word is simply that item of which the word is a hyponym.[7]

Aside from the last suggestion, which simply denies that there is any independent way of determining the head of the word, none of these recent proposals is free of the following difficulty: with any of the proposed modifications, the direction of headedness in morphology must still be stipulated (sometimes more than once for a single language), whereas more and more in syntax the direction of headedness has come to follow from parameter settings in other modules of the grammar such as Theta theory and

Case theory.[8] And as long as the direction of headedness in the morphology of a language must be stipulated as a language-particular matter, there must still be principles of morphology distinct from other principles of grammar. That is, as long as the direction of headedness must be determined separately for word formation, we must still allow a distinct word formation component to the grammar, and we will not yet have attained the simplest theory described in chapter 1, the one in which there are no principles of word formation that are not also general principles of grammar. As mentioned in chapter 1, the most attractive theory for dealing with phrasal compound data and the like would be one in which all principles of grammar apply both above and below word level. For the issue in question this would mean that the head element is defined once and for all for each language—for word formation and for phrasal syntax. In the next section we will begin to explore whether this goal is achievable.

2.2 Revised Principles of X-bar Theory

The goal of this section is to modify the present principles of X-bar theory minimally so that the same set of principles allows us to generate both well-formed phrases and well-formed complex words in languages. Remember that we would like as an outcome of this theoretical merger to be able to generate the sort of phrasal compounds and derivations discussed in chapter 1.

Stowell (1981, 87) sets out a number of notions which he believes form the foundation of X-bar theory:

(11) a. Every phrase is endocentric.
      b. Specifiers appear at X'' level; subcategorized complements appear within X'.
      c. The head always appears adjacent to one of the boundaries of X'.
      d. The head term is one bar-level lower than the immediately dominating phrasal node.
      e. Only maximal projections may appear as nonhead terms within a phrase.

We will consider each of these in trying to arrive at a statement of the fundamental X-bar principles of Government-Binding theory.

Note first that Stowell himself doubts that (11b) should be considered one of the primitives of X-bar theory; he argues that in fact, "languages such as Japanese and German allow specifiers to appear within the X' level, situated between the head and its complements . . ." (1981, 87). If so, the placement of specifiers and complements within the hierarchy of the

phrase is subject to parametric variation; the placement of specifiers under
X″ and complements under X′ is not a primitive of the system, and indeed
need not be the case at all in particular languages. We will therefore abandon (11b) as part of X-bar theory. We will also put aside (11e) for the moment, and return to it in our discussion of word structure below.

Principles (11a, c, and d) form the basis of most versions of X-bar theory. Principles (11a) and (d) together are the basis for the X-bar template—
$X^n \rightarrow \ldots X^{n-1} \ldots$—that is familiar within all versions of X-bar theory.
We will adopt it as one of our basic principles at least for the moment.

What most needs to be fleshed out is how the primitive in (11c) is to be
incorporated into X-bar theory. Travis (1990) notes that (11c) is usually
referred to as the Head Initial/Final parameter—roughly, heads always
occur first or last in their phrase—and that this primitive is in fact too
strong to accommodate all attested word orders. Languages such as Chinese and Kpelle have the head of V′ adjacent to neither the left nor the right
boundary of V′. What Travis proposes is that the primitive notion in (11c)
be instantiated in X-bar theory by a number of parameters: direction of
Theta-marking, direction of Case assignment, and the Head Initial/Final
parameter itself. Some languages, such as English, simply set the Head
Initial/Final parameter: in English heads are initial with respect to their
complements. Other languages, such as Chinese, set a more specific parameter. Since in Chinese objects and argument PPs appear to the right of
the verb but other adjunct members of the VP appear to the left, Travis
proposes that Chinese sets the Theta-marking parameter (Theta-roles are
assigned rightwards), and that all other VP constituents are positioned by a
default setting of the head parameter (heads are otherwise final). In Kpelle,
only objects precede the verb; all PPs, whether argument or adjunct, follow
the verb. Here Travis argues that the relevant parameter is one of Case assignment. Kpelle sets Case assignment leftwards. A default setting of the
head parameter (heads are otherwise initial) covers the positioning of non-
object constituents. Travis stipulates that only one of the subdomain parameters (Theta-marking or Case assignment) can be set in a language, and
that the default head parameter must be set once for all categories if a subdomain parameter is set. If no subdomain parameter is set, then the headedness parameter must itself be set, and may be set differently for different
categories. The reader is referred to Travis (1990) for justification of these
proposals. What is important for our purposes is that Travis's theory offers
us the beginning of a concrete working proposal for instantiating primitive
(11c) that is restrictive, but also sensitive enough to account for the word
orders that seem to be attested in natural languages.

I say that Travis's proposal is just the beginning for us because in fact

her parameters pertain only to the position of complements and adjuncts
with respect to heads. Since it is possible in a language for specifiers and
modifiers to appear on one side of the head and complements on the other
(the case in English, as we will see in section 2.4), or for specifiers to occur
on one side of the head and both complements and modifiers on the other
(the case in French, cf. section 2.5), it appears that in fact we need three
separate Head Initial/Final parameters, one concerning the position of
complements, a second concerning the position of specifiers, and a third
concerning the position of modifiers. What I propose, then, is that primitive (11c) be fleshed out in our theory as the Licensing Conditions in (12):

(12) Licensing Conditions
    a. Heads are initial/final with respect to complements and adjuncts.
      i. Theta-roles are assigned to the left/right.
      ii. Case is assigned to the left/right.
    b. Heads are initial/final with respect to specifiers.
    c. Heads are initial/final with respect to modifiers.

Although I know of nowhere in the literature of Government-Binding theory where the Licensing Conditions are stated exactly in this way, I believe
that (12) represents the minimal set of parameters needed to fix the linear
order of heads with respect to nonheads. It is of course possible that one or
more of the Licensing Conditions could be made to follow from other principles of grammar, but it is beyond the scope of the present work to explore
this issue further.

    The basic X-bar template ($X^n \rightarrow \ldots X^{n-1} \ldots$), the Licensing Condi-
tions in (12), and the stipulation that only maximal projections appear as
nonheads are the X-bar principles that we will start with here. It is immediately obvious that as they stand these principles will not yield word structures in addition to phrasal-level constituents. The question that we raise
next is whether there is any way of changing them so that we can achieve
this result.

    Consider first the X-bar template. Although in phrases the head charac-
teristically carries one-bar level less than the phrasal node which dominates
it, this is not true in words. That is, complex words (X^0s) typically are said
to have the recursive structure in (13b) rather than the structure in (13a):

(13) a.

Although structures like (13a) have been proposed in the literature on morphology (cf. Scalise 1984 for a proposal something like this and Lieber 1987a for a discussion of Scalise's proposal), significant difficulties arise in working out a system in which the head of a word bears one less bar-level than the category which dominates it. For cases of suffixation in English where the affix is head, giving the affix the negative bar-level seems relatively plausible. But consider the case of prefixation in (14):[9]

(14)

If sublexical structure is to conform to the X-bar template, and if the stem *happy* is the head in (14), as is usually assumed, then *happy* must be an A^{-1} in (14). But where it is not head, e.g., in (13a), it is surely not an A^{-1}. Rather, since *happy* is otherwise a free morpheme, it is most likely an A^0. There is in fact no evidence to suggest that *happy* is ever anything but an A^0.

The attempt to apply the basic X-bar template below word level becomes even less tenable when we consider words that are somewhat more complex in structure. Take, for example, the verb *relegalize,* where -*ize* attaches to the A^0 *legal* to create a verb and *re*- to the verb *legalize.* As with most other prefixes in English, *re*- does not change category, and it does not alter the argument structure of the items to which it attaches. Indications are, then, that *re*- is not the head of *relegalize.* If not, then the head in the complex word must be the form *legalize,* as illustrated in (15):

(15) a.   b.

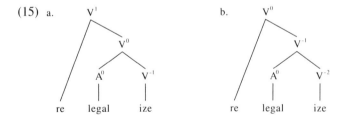

If the structure of *relegalize* is to conform to the X-bar template in (12a), then the word must have either structure (15a) or (15b). In (15a) the category dominating the word *relegalize* is V^1. But V^1 is a *phrasal* category, which is surely incorrect. The only alternative would be to call the suffix -*ize* a V^{-2}, as in (15b). The problem here would be that -*ize* would be a V^{-2}

in the word *relegalize*, but a V^{-1} in the word *legalize*, again a result that is surely incorrect. We must conclude, then, that recursion is necessary in complex words, so that a word like *relegalize* has a structure like that in (16):[10]

(16)

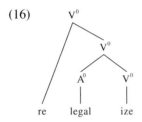

To permit the generation of lexical structures such as those in (13b) or (16), we must loosen the basic X-bar template to allow recursion at least at the X^0 level. I therefore propose to replace (12a) with (17):[11]

(17) $X^n \rightarrow \ldots X^{\{n-1,n\}} \ldots$; recursion allowed at least for n = 0[12]

Let us now consider whether we want to maintain (11e), the principle that nonheads must be maximal phrases, as part of our generalized X-bar theory. Note that although Stowell (1981) and Baker (1988a) assume that (11e) is a tenet of X-bar theory, this assumption is not universally accepted. Emonds (1985), for example, proposes that specifiers preceding heads are nonphrasal (that is, not maximal phrases), and Baltin (1990) proposes that only the heads of complements are subcategorized for, so that in essence an X^0 can be complement of a head. Clearly, if we are to use the basic principles of X-bar theory to generate words as well as phrasal constituents, we must side with Emonds and Baltin, and abandon (11e) as a principle of word structure. Adopting (11e) would in fact prevent us from generating the basic lexical structures in (18):

(18)

I therefore propose that (11e) be modified to allow the generation of either maximal phrases (X^{max}) or lexical forms (X^0) in pre- or post-head position. We will see below that other principles of grammar rule out the occurrence of bare lexical forms either before or after the head of a phrase.

To summarize, (19) contains the basic principles of X-bar theory as we have revised them in this section:

(19) a. $X^n \rightarrow \ldots X^{\{n-1,n\}} \ldots$, where recursion is allowed for n = 0.
    b. Licensing Conditions
       i. Heads are initial/final with respect to complements.
       —Theta-roles are assigned to left/right.
       —Case is assigned to left/right.
      ii. Heads are initial/final with respect to specifiers.
     iii. Heads are initial/final with respect to modifiers.
    c. Pre- or post-head modifiers may be X^{max} or X^0.

The major question that we must now raise is whether the Licensing Conditions in (19) are specific to syntax, or whether they apply both above and below word level. I will argue below that the Licensing Conditions in (19b) fix the position of the head in words as they do in phrases, and that the parameters are set just once for each language. The novelty of my proposal in fact lies in the suggestion that the principles in (19b) can and should apply to sublexical structure.[13]

To apply the Licensing Conditions in (19b) below word level, we must first explore whether it makes sense to categorize sublexical elements as specifiers, modifiers, and complements, and in order to do this, we must clarify as much as possible what we mean by these terms. It is relatively clear what is meant in the literature by the term **complement:** complements are internal arguments ("internal" in the sense of Williams 1981b) obligatorily selected by a verb. What is meant by the term **modifier** is somewhat less clear, since, as mentioned above, modifiers are rarely distinguished from specifiers in the literature on X-bar theory. In his brief discussion of modifiers, Stowell proposes that by modifiers we mean restrictive modifiers, that is, those that limit the reference of the modified item:

> We can think of a head noun as having an indeterminate scope of reference, ranging over entities or classes of entities. The function of a restrictive clause is to fix the scope of reference of the phrase, narrowing the reference to a specific subset of the referents allowed by the head. (1981, 278)

Since, according to Stowell, the scope of reference of categories other than N is usually fixed, it is typically only Ns that have restrictive modifiers, although under special circumstances other categories may have them as well. Following Stowell then, we will use the term **modifier** here to refer to a constituent which limits potential reference, typically, of a noun.[14]

Most problematic for us is what is meant by the term **specifier,** since this term has been applied to a rather heterogeneous group of items. Among the items classically considered to be specifiers are determiners (*the, a*), demonstratives (*this, that,* etc.), quantifiers (*all, some, no,* etc.), and modals (*will, would, can,* etc.). Subjects of NP and IP are often considered to be specifiers as well (Stowell 1981).[15] Of course, of these disparate cases, several have been argued not to be specifiers at all. Abney (1987) suggests that determiners are not specifiers of NP, but rather are heads of DP, with NP as their obligatory complement. Similarly, he argues that degree words are not usually specifiers of APs, but instead are typically heads of DegPs (degree phrases), which take APs as their obligatory complements. Still, Abney does allow certain DegPs and QPs to be specifiers of DegPs (1987, 304). If this is correct, this leaves us with quantifiers, degree words, subjects, and perhaps modals as plausible candidates for specifiers. As Emonds (1985) points out, this is not a class that can be characterized in any simple, coherent fashion.

Having made as clear as possible what we mean by complement, modifier, and specifier in phrasal syntax, we can begin to explore whether it makes sense to categorize sublexical elements as complements, modifiers, and specifiers. That there are sublexical complements seems relatively uncontroversial. The first elements in English synthetic compounds like *cat lover* and *pasta-eating* are surely functioning as complements in the sense that they are interpreted in the same way that syntactic complements would be in phrases like *a lover of cats,* or *the eating of pasta.*[16] Similarly, in the Tagalog compound *magbigay-galang* 'give respect', the second element functions as the complement of the first.

That there are sublexical modifiers also seems relatively uncontroversial. The initial element in English root compounds like *file cabinet* or *rowhouse* is surely restricting or limiting the reference of the head of the compound. Similarly in Tagalog, the second element in the compound *amoy-isda* [smelling-fish] 'fishy-smelling' is modifying or restricting the first element.

The question of whether or not there are sublexical specifiers is of course made more difficult by our inability to characterize the class of syntactic specifiers in any coherent fashion. To the extent that sublexical specifiers exist, we would expect them to fill some of the same semantic functions as phrase-level specifiers. They might be morphemes expressing negation (***unable, impossible, nontoxic***) or quantification (***biweekly, semicoherent***), for example (cf. also Walinska de Hackbeil 1986). But sublexical specifiers might include other classes as well. I shall leave this issue for the time being, and return to it in section 2.4.

We assume, then, that it makes sense to use terms like specifier, modifier, and complement to refer to sublexical elements. The proposal that I make here then is that the Licensing Conditions in (19b) are set just once for each language and that they apply both above and below word level.

From this follows a very strong prediction, namely that the location of heads in phrases and the location of heads in words must be the same. The position of the head of a word is inextricably linked to the position of the head of a phrase, and vice versa. We will explore in the sections that follow the extent to which this prediction seems to be borne out by empirical data.

2.3 Tagalog Phrase and Word Structure

In the last section, I proposed that the revised principles of X-bar theory might be adequate as they stand to account for both phrase structure and word structure in languages; it remains to be seen whether this proposal is a reasonable one. The Philippine language Tagalog provides an especially good test case for this claim for two reasons. The first is that the parametric settings for the Licensing Conditions in (19b) are reasonably straightforward. And secondly, Tagalog word formation, being predominantly left-headed, provides a challenge to most other theories of word formation. We will see below, however, that it is no accident that Tagalog has so much left-headed word formation.

I begin with a brief review of Tagalog phrase structure which will allow us to determine what the settings of the parameters in (19b) should be for this language. My data is taken from Schachter and Otanes (1972). Word order in Tagalog NPs, PPs, and APs is fairly clear. Generally, complements, modifiers, and specifiers all follow their heads. The data in (20) illustrates the ordering of complements with respect to heads:

(20) a. NP   mambabasa ng **diyaryo**
                  'reader (of) newspapers'
                  sulatan ng **liham**
                  'writing one another letters'
       b. AP   bigay **para sa bata**
                  'suitable for the child'
                  kapos ng **pera**
                  'lacking in money'
       c. PP   nasa **kusina**
                  'in the kitchen'
                  para sa **bata**
                  'for the child'

It seems clear from the data in (20) that heads are initial with respect to complements.

Modifiers also seem most likely to follow heads:

(21) NP libro-ng **nasa mesa**
       book   on   table   'the book on the table'
      libro-ng binasa ko
      book   read   I   'the book that I read'

Schachter and Otanes (1972, 118) point out that modifiers sometimes do precede their heads—"Thus 'new book' may be either *bagong libro* or *librong bago . . .* ,"[17]—but acknowledge (1972, 120) that "the **preferred** ordering of nouns within a simple modification construction is: head-linker-modifier [emphasis mine]." I assume then that the basic order is head-modifier, and that the modifier-head order is the result of low-level stylistic rules. I also assume that this basic order is valid for APs. As with NPs, some modifiers appear either before or after the head: *lubhang kawawa* 'terribly pitiful' or *kawawang lubha* 'pitiful terribly'. Schachter and Otanes make no comment in this case as to which order is preferred. I assume, however, that APs may be treated as parallel to the NPs, with the head-modifier order as basic and the opposite order as a result of low-level stylistic rules.

As for specifiers, their ordering is relatively clear. In NPs, subjects generally follow the head. This is strictly true of the possessive construction in (22a). The alternative construction in (22b) appears to be more or less equivalent to the NP modification construction discussed immediately above in that the possessor phrase can either follow or precede the head. That is, the possessor in an NP in Tagalog can sometimes be treated as a modifier rather than as a specifier. Where this is the case, the preferred order is the first one in (22b), with the possessor again following the head. In any case, where the possessor is clearly a specifier, as in (22a), it follows the head.

(22) a. lapis **ng**   **bata**   'the child's pencil'[18]
        pencil SUBJ child
     b. lapis na   **sa bata**   'the pencil of the child'
        pencil LINKER child
        sa bata -ng   lapis   'the child's pencil'
        child   LINKER pencil

AP specifiers also tend to follow the head:

(23) gutom   **nang kaunti**
      hungry   rather   'rather hungry'
      magugulo   **nang kaunti**
      troublesome rather   'rather troublesome'

Cardinal and ordinal numbers, however, typically precede the head.

(24) **dalawang** bata
'two children'
ikalawang bata
'the second child'

As very little hinges on the position of the specifier, I will assume here that specifiers generally follow heads in Tagalog, and that cardinal and ordinal numbers are moved to pre-head position.

Thus far, I have not discussed word order in VP or IP. Sentences in Tagalog are usually verb initial, but the order of NP arguments, both internal and external, can vary according to which argument is topic. The topic argument generally occurs in the sentence final position, preceded by the particle *ang* (*si* for a personal noun). Nontopic arguments follow the verb and precede the topic argument; they are marked *sa* if they are directional or locational, and *ng* otherwise (*ni/kay* respectively with personal nouns).[19] The verb is marked with one of a number of affixes that mark which argument is the topic, in (25) *mag-* for the Subject Topic form, *i-* for the Object Topic form, and *-an* for the Location Topic form. The topic constituent is in boldface in (25) (example from Schachter and Otanes 1972, 79):

(25) a. Maglalakip ng kuwalta   sa sulat   ang istudyante.
       enclose   some money in the letter the student
       '**The student** will enclose some money in the letter.'
    b. Ilalakip ng istudyante sa sulat   ang kuwalta
       enclose the student   in the letter some money
       'The student will enclose **some money** in the letter.'
    c. Lalakipan ng istudyante ng kuwalta   ang sulat
       enclose   the student   some money in the letter
       'The student will enclose some money **in the letter**.'

There are at least two plausible ways of dealing with data like that in (25). The order of elements in VP and IP could perhaps be treated in the same way that underlying order is treated in Clark (1985) for the Austronesian language Toba Batak. Toba Batak appears to have sentence forms that are like those in (25) in that different arguments, internal or external, are focussed depending on the verbal morphology, with the focussed argument always occuring in sentence final position.

(26) Clark (1985, 664)
    a. mang-allang sassing i   dengke i
       voice-eat   worm   DET fish   DET
       '**The fish** ate the worm.'[20]

b. di-allang dengke i   sassing i
   voice-eat fish   DET worm   DET
   'The fish ate **the worm**.'

Clark suggests that Toba Batak sentences are strictly head initial, with the structure in (27):

(27)

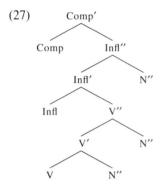

In sentences in which the verb bears the *mang-* prefix, the patient Theta-role is associated with the lower N″, the agent role with the upper N″. If the verb bears the *di-* prefix, the agent role is associated with the lower N″, the patient with the upper one.

   Alternatively, we might assume, as Carrier-Duncan (1985) does, that sentences are verb initial, but have a somewhat flatter structure than that in (27). That is, sentences would lack a VP constituent, with NP arguments following the verb in any order. Even on this view it would be possible to assume that complements and specifiers follow the verb. After all, since the verb is initial this will be true even if the structure is flat.

   If either of these analyses can be made to work for Tagalog, then we can say that order in IP and VP (if it exists) can be made consistent with the ordering that appears in other phrasal categories. Complements, modifiers, and specifiers all follow heads. Following the format of (19b), the X-bar system for Tagalog will be stated as in (28):

(28) Licensing Conditions: Tagalog
   a. $X^n \rightarrow \ldots X^{\{n-1,n\}} \ldots$, where recursion is allowed for $n = 0$
   b. i. Head **initial** with respect to complements.
      ii. Head **initial** with respect to modifiers.
      iii. Head **initial** with respect to specifiers.
   c. Pre- and post-head constituents are either X^{max} or X^0.

   What does the X-bar system of Tagalog predict about possible word formation in Tagalog? Consider the structures in (29), which represent all the logically possible lexical structures that can be generated in accordance with (28a) and (28c):

(29) a.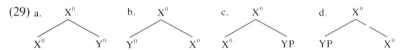

The Licensing Conditions in (28b) lead us to expect that certain of these structures will occur in Tagalog word formation and others not. Structure (29a), for example, should be one that is well represented. Since heads are initial with respect to modifiers, complements, and specifiers, we should expect to find many word formation processes in Tagalog which are head-initial, that is, **left**-headed. On the other hand, (29b) should be a structure which is rare or nonexistent in Tagalog. Structure (29c), like (29a), should be attested, at least if Tagalog allows some sort of phrasal derivation or compounding. That is, if Tagalog allows phrasal derivation or compounding at all, it should follow the left-headed pattern in (29c), rather than the right-headed one in (29d). We shall see that Tagalog word formation fulfills these predictions to a remarkable extent.

First, as predicted by our theory, Tagalog has a significant amount of word structure that fits the pattern of (29a). Much of Tagalog category-changing derivational word formation is prefixal, as the examples in (30) illustrate (all data, again, is from Schachter and Otanes 1972):

(30) a. mang-dup$_1$ $[_N ——— [_{\{N,V\}}$
     awit   'song'   mangaawit   'singer'
     tanggol 'defend' manananangol 'lawyer'

  b. pa- $[_N ——— [_V$
     abot 'hand over' paabot 'something caused to
                               be handed over'
     luto 'cook'   paluto 'something caused to
                               be cooked'

  c. taga- $[_N ——— [_V$
     b-um-ili 'buy'   tagabili 'buyer'
     mag-luto 'cook'   tagaluto 'cook'

  d. ma- $[_A ——— [_{\{N,A\}}$
     bigat   'weight'   mabigat   'heavy'
     bundok 'mountain' mabundok 'mountainous'

  e. pa- $[_A ——— [_V$
     b-um-ulong 'whisper' pabulong 'in a whisper'
     d-um-abog 'move   padabog 'with motions
                 angrily'   of anger'

f. pang- $[_A \text{——} [_N$
kamay 'hand'   pangkamay 'for the hand'
kape 'coffee'   pangkape 'for coffee'

g. ka-dup$_2$ $[_A \text{——} [_N$
galang 'respect'   kagalang-   'inspiring great
                                      galang   respect'
tawa 'laughter'   katawa-tawa 'hilarious'

h. maka- $[_A \text{——} [_N$
ama 'father'   makaama   'close to father'
Hapon 'Japan'   maka-Hapon 'pro-Japanese'

i. na-dup$_A$-ka- $[_A \text{——} [_N$
na-ka-dup$_A$-

        antok 'sleepiness'   nakakaantok
                                   nakaaantok 'causing
                                            sleepiness'

Some of the examples in (30) require comment. First, Schachter and Otanes list the verbal bases in (30c,e) in their Subject Topic form, i.e., with the verbal morphology that indicates that the subject is in topic position, marked with the case particle *ang*. Other verbal bases, such as those in (30a,b) are listed in stem form. There is no particular reason for this inconsistency, as far as I can see. Second, I list the reduplicative morphemes as dup$_1$, dup$_2$, dup$_A$, following the notation used by Schachter and Otanes. In terms of current theory, the actual reduplicative prefixes would be CV skeletons or syllable templates of various kinds, following Marantz (1982), Steriade (1988), and similar work. The exact nature of each template is of no particular consequence here.[21] Next, note that (30) does not contain an exhaustive list of prefixes in Tagalog; in addition to the prefixes in (30), there are a number of prefixes which are noncategory-changing, but which nevertheless are arguably heads in their words. A list of these is contained in (31):

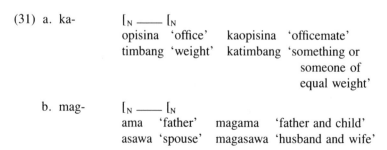

(31) a. ka- $[_N \text{——} [_N$
opisina 'office'   kaopisina 'officemate'
timbang 'weight'   katimbang 'something or
                                            someone of
                                            equal weight'

b. mag- $[_N \text{——} [_N$
ama 'father'   magama   'father and child'
asawa 'spouse'   magasawa 'husband and wife'

c. mag-dup₁   [N —— [N
baboy   'pig/pork'   magbababoy   'pig/pork
                                     vendor'
bulaklak 'flower'   magbubulaklak 'flower
                                    vendor'

d. taga-   [N —— [N
Maynila   taga-Maynila 'person from Manila'

One of the facts that has been used to suggest that prefixes in English are not heads is that, in addition to not changing the category of the base they attach to, they sometimes attach to bases of different categories. The prefix *counter-* in English, for example, attaches to Ns (*counterweight*), to As (*counterintuitive*), and to Vs (*countersign*), and the resulting word in each case has the category of the word to which it attaches. None of the prefixes in (31) has this characteristic. Since they attach only to nouns, and uniformly form nouns, there is no reason to believe that they are not marked for category. It seems reasonable to assume that they are indeed heads of the words that they form, just as the prefixes in (30) are.[22]

All of Tagalog compounding fits the left-headed structure (29a) as well, as the examples in (32) illustrate:

(32) a. N[N-N] compounds
        matang-lawin
        eyes hawk   'keen eyes'[23]
        ngusong-baboy
        upper-lip pig   'protruding upper lip'
        isip-lamok
        mind mosquito   'weak mind'
     b. A[A-N] compounds
        amoy-isda
        smelling fish   'fishy smelling'
        lasang-isda
        tasting fish   'fishy tasting'
     c. V[V-N] compounds
        magbigay-galang
        giving respect   'show respect'
        magbangong-puri
        raise honor   'redeem one's honor'
     d. Deverbal (synthetic) compounds
        pamatid-uhaw
        cutter-thirst   'thirst quencher'
        panawag-pansin

caller-attention   'attention getter'
pantawid-gutom
bridger-hunger   'hunger appeaser'

The compounds in (32b,c) are clearly left-headed, since the category of the compound as a whole is determined by the category of the left-hand stem. Examples (32a,d) are also left-headed. Although both stems in these compounds are nouns, the semantic head is clearly the left-hand stem. Tagalog in fact has no compounds which are either syntactically or semantically right-headed.

The Licensing Conditions in (28b) also predict that if Tagalog has phrasal compounds or derivations they too will be left-headed, i.e., will exhibit structure (29c) rather than (29d). We saw in chapter 1 that Tagalog indeed does have phrasal derivations and that these derivations are formed by prefixation of *pa-* to phrases of different categories including locative NPs marked with *sa* and negative phrases:

(33) (na)sa akin [24]   p-um-asa akin [25]
      'in my possession'   'come into my possession'

      (na)sa bata   p-um-asa bata
      'in the child's possession'   'come into the child's possession'

      (na)sa Maynila   p-um-asa Maynila
      'in Manila'   'go to Manila'

      walang bisa   magpawalang-bisa
      'having no effect'   'render ineffective'

      walang halaga   magpawalang-halaga
      'having no value'   'render valueless'

In the word formation process illustrated in (33), the verbalizing prefix *pa-* attaches to the locative NP or negative phrase to create a verb which is then inflected. Illustrated in (34) is the structure I am attributing to such examples:

(34)

Tagalog has no cases of phrasal derivations or compounds which are right-headed, just as predicted by the Licensing Conditions in (28b).

The only structure in (29) that we have yet to discuss is (29b). The Licensing Conditions in (28) predict that we should find no examples of structure (29b) in Tagalog, that is, no compounds or derived words which are right-headed. We have seen that there are in fact no right-headed compounds in Tagalog. But, contrary to the prediction, there are a few suffixes which change the category of the stems to which they attach, and which therefore would appear to be heads:

(35) a. -an $]_{\{N,V\}}$ ——$]_N$
               giik 'thresh'   giikan 'threshing place'

     b. -an $]_V$ ——$]_N$
               umaway   'fight'   awayan 'fighting one another'
               magbigay 'give'   bigayan 'giving one another'

     c. -in $]_V$ ——$]_N$
               magalaga 'take care of'   alagain 'something to take of'
               magaral   'study'   aralin 'something to study'

     d. -an $]_N$ ——$]_A$
               dugo 'blood'   dugoan 'covered with blood'
               putik 'mud'   putikan 'covered with mud'

     e. -in $]_N$ ——$]_A$
               antok   'sleepiness'   antokin   'given to sleepiness'
               bulutong 'smallpox'   bulutungin 'susceptible to smallpox'

Contained in (35) is an exhaustive list of the category-changing suffixes in Tagalog that are mentioned by Schachter and Otanes. Note that they are of only two kinds: three of the five create nouns from verbs, and the other two adjectives from nouns. There are a number of possible explanations for the occurrence of these category-changing suffixes. One might be that the five processes in (35) are not particularly productive. Schachter and Otanes do not mention the productivity of any of the word formation processes that they catalogue, but if these suffixes were not productive, then the particular examples listed in (35) might be listed in the lexicon, and not derived by the processes that give rise to word structure.

Another possible explanation for this apparent right-headed residue is that the Licensing Conditions in (28) do not strictly rule out right-headed structures—they do so only if the item that occurs to the left of the head is a specifier, a modifier, or a complement. Since verbs do not generally function as either modifiers, specifiers, or complements, but rather as predicates, right-headed structures such as those that would be needed for (35a–c) would be not be ruled out. As for (35d,e), it is less clear that the N which serves as base of these structures is not specifier, modifier, or complement of the head, but perhaps the previous explanation might hold here too. If the base noun is a predicate rather than a modifier or specifier, then the Licensing Conditions would not rule out a right-headed structure.

In any case, the examples in (35) are the only ones which pose any challenge to the predictions made by the Licensing Conditions. It is clear that these conditions come remarkably close to characterizing the sort of word formation that we do find in Tagalog. This is an especially noteworthy result, since a theory like that of Williams (1981a) predicts that extensive left-headed morphology should not exist at all. Note further that the data from Tagalog strongly support the claim that the position of the head of the word and of the head of the phrase are not independent of one another, but rather can and should be linked. We will see below that this claim can be supported for other languages as well.

2.4 English Phrase and Word Structure

In this section I try to show that there is also a nonarbitrary connection between the position of the head in words and its position in phrases in English, in spite of the existence of prima facie evidence which contradicts this hypothesis. We will start below with a discussion of the parameter settings necessary for English phrase structure, and then return to the subject of lexical structure.

The position of specifiers and complements with respect to the head in English is relatively uncontroversial. Complements uniformly follow their heads, as the examples in (36) show:

(36) a. NP   the destruction of **the city**
     b. AP   fond of **ice cream,** proud of **their daughter**
     c. PP   in **the hole,** up **a tree**
     d. VP   devoured **the pizza**

Complements of functional categories such as Comp, Infl, Det, and Deg also follow their heads. IP is the complement of Comp, VP of IP, NP of Det, and AP of Deg in the theory of Chomsky (1986a) and Abney (1987). The first of the Licensing Conditions is therefore set as in (37):

(37) Heads are **initial** with respect to complements.

Specifiers, on the other hand, uniformly precede their heads in English. For example, subjects of IP and NP come before Infl and N respectively:

(38) **The children** devoured the pizza.
     the children's destruction of the treehouse

Other specifiers such as quantifiers and measure phrases also precede their heads in NPs.

(39) examples from Abney (1987)
     two parts steel
     one half garbage
     two dozen roses
     a million stars

In other categories as well, specifiers uniformly precede heads:

(40) a. PP   **just** down the road
             right in the box
     b. AP   **rather** good
             quite soft

The setting for the third Licensing Condition in English is therefore as in (41):

(41) Heads are **final** with respect to specifiers.

What is somewhat more difficult to determine, however, is the position of restrictive modifiers with respect to the head; surface position can be either before or after the head, depending on the category of the restrictive modifier and its internal structure:

(42) a.   a **large, gray** dog
          *a dog **large, gray**
     b.   *a **fond of his daughter** father
          a father **fond of his daughter**
     c.   *an **on a bicycle** bear
          a bear **on a bicycle**
     d.   *a **running for president** candidate
          a candidate **running for president**
     e.   *a **that I saw** man
          a man **that I saw**

The examples in (42) show that any modifying phrase which itself has a complement cannot occur prenominally. Certain sorts of APs, however, do occur, and indeed are preferred prenominally. In a category neutral X-bar theory such as the one developed in Stowell (1981), we must determine that only one of these modifier positions is basic. The question of course is which one, and how to derive the placement of those modifiers whose surface position differs from the base order.

The position of restrictive modifiers with respect to the head in English has received relatively little discussion in the literature on phrase structure.

Jackendoff (1977) argues that restrictive modifiers like relative clauses are generated in a position after the head (we will review his argument for this claim shortly), but he also provides a structural position for a prenominal AP. Since an X-bar theory incorporating parameters requires a single underlying base position, we will avoid Jackendoff's ordering unless absolutely necessary. Stowell (1981) also devotes relatively little attention to the position of modifiers with respect to the head, although he does briefly sketch a treatment of modifiers in a category neutral X-bar theory. I will outline his theory, and then argue that the ordering which he suggests is incorrect.

Stowell (1981) proposes that restrictive modifiers in English always follow the head; specifically, he positions them after X′ as daughters of the maximal projection of X: $[_{X''}\text{SUBJ-X}'\text{-MOD}]$. Certain sorts of modifiers, specifically bare adjectives, are then "cliticized" to the head noun. That is, to account for the position of prenominal adjectives, Stowell suggests a movement rule which repositions adjectives before the head. In support of the underlying post-head position for restrictive modifiers, Stowell refers to Jackendoff's (1977) arguments. Jackendoff argues against a very early analysis of relative clauses in Smith (1964) in which restrictive relatives are generated prenominally as part of the Determiner position in NP. In her article, Smith notes that cooccurrence restrictions exist between relative clauses and determiners in NPs:

(43) a.   the Paris that I knew
         *the Paris
     b.   the manner in which he spoke
         *the manner

Proper nouns and certain common nouns like *manner* and *way* can take a restrictive relative clause only if there is a determiner present. With only the resources of early generative grammar, Smith chose to express this cooccurrence by actually generating the relative clause in the determiner, and moving it to the posthead position by transformation. Jackendoff points out, however, that similar cooccurrence restrictions also exist between determiners and other restrictive modifiers:

(44) a. the old Paris
        the Paris of my dreams
     b. a cold manner
        the manner of his arrival

The inference that he draws is that Smith's analysis would be forced to generate PP and adjectival restrictive modifiers under the determiner as well, an analysis which he dismisses as implausible. From this in turn Jackendoff concludes that PP modifiers and restrictive relative clauses should be generated after the head, and that the relevant cooccurrence restrictions must be stated on discontinuous items.

Note that Jackendoff's conclusion does not follow from his argument, however. The argument from cooccurrence restrictions between determiners and restrictive modifiers merely shows that **all** restrictive modifiers behave alike, regardless of what category they belong to, and that the cooccurrence restrictions should be stated uniformly across categories. This is just what we would expect to be the case given a category-neutral theory of the base. It is also clear that within the terms of the present theory of syntax, restrictive modifiers should not be generated as part of the determiner. However, this does not force us to the position that Stowell adopts, that modifiers must uniformly follow their heads, as in (45a). Also possible is a theory in which all restrictive modifiers occur before their heads as daughters of X″, as illustrated in (45b):

(45) a.

Stowell, following Jackendoff's conclusion, chooses (45a). But since the structure in (45b) is also consistent with Jackendoff's arguments, we must base the choice between the two on other grounds. I suggest that those grounds have to do with the nature of the rule necessary to derive the surface order in each case.

As mentioned above, since Stowell (1981) chooses to position modifiers after the head, he is obliged to provide a rule to reposition some adjectives before the head. He suggests that the adjectives that end up prenominally are not maximal projections (1981, 283), that the rule responsible for moving them to prenominal position is one of cliticization, and that cliticization is indeed a matter of word formation, and not the concern of syntax at all. The result of cliticization of the adjective to the head noun is the structure in (46):

(46) [_N A-N]

Stowell notes further that since more than one prenominal adjective is possible, this rule of cliticization must be allowed to apply iteratively to its own output.

There is good reason to believe, however, that prenominal adjectives are **not** like clitics. First, bona fide clitics, like the pronominal clitics in Romance, are closed class items. They are limited in number, and become phonologically a part of the words to which they cliticize. Prenominal adjectives, on the other hand, are members of an open class and do not become part of the phonological word which follows them. Furthermore, it is not at all clear that prenominal adjectives are less than maximal phrases. Conjoined adjectives are permitted prenominally as are adjectives with a full array of adjectival specifiers:

(47) a. a **very big and unbelievably dirty** dog
      b. a **not too surprisingly tall** woman

Since specifiers like *very,* and *not too* are daughters of the maximal phrase, the data in (47) suggest that prenominal adjectives are APs, contrary to Stowell's claims. The rule moving adjectives to prenominal position cannot then be a rule of word formation, but rather must be a syntactic rule. Moreover, it must be able to pick out just those APs which lack complements to move them to prenominal position. Since this sort of rule does not seem otherwise necessary within versions of Government-Binding syntax with which I am familiar, the theory incorporating structure (45a) no longer seems so attractive.

Let us now consider the possibility that all modifiers begin in prehead position, as shown in (45b). Specifically, let us assume that the underlying structure of noun phrases (now DPs, following Abney 1987), is that in (48):

(48)

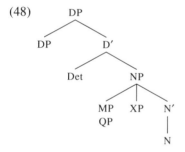

All restrictive modifiers are maximal phrases, and any sort of maximal phrase can be a restrictive modifier. Cooccurrence restrictions between determiners and restrictive modifiers of whatever category are stated on items which may be discontinuous, just as in Jackendoff's and Stowell's analyses. What this analysis requires now is some sort of rule which takes heavy modifiers and moves them to the position under NP after N′. What counts as a "heavy" modifier can be left somewhat open. Surely anything with a complement should count as heavy, but also some sorts of complementless adjectives, as the examples in (49) (taken from Abney 1987, 236) suggest:

(49) a man **alone**
      a man **bruised and battered**
      a fish **this big**

Since at least one other rule moving heavy constituents to the right (Heavy NP Shift) appears to be necessary in the grammar of English, this analysis of restrictive modifiers has the virtue of not needing a new and ill-defined sort of rule like Stowell's cliticization rule. I therefore adopt the position here that modifiers precede their heads in English.

To summarize, the Licensing Conditions needed for English phrase structure are the ones in (50):

(50) Licensing Conditions: English
   a. Heads are **initial** with respect to complements.
   b. Heads are **final** with respect to specifiers.
   c. Heads are **final** with respect to modifiers.

Let us consider now the sorts of word formation that we might expect to find in English given the parameter settings in (50). We will start again from the four logically possible word structures in (29), repeated below as (51):

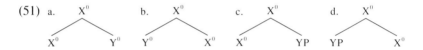

(51) a. X^0 b. X^0 c. X^0 d. X^0
         X^0 Y^0 Y^0 X^0 X^0 YP   YP X^0

First, since heads follow both specifiers and modifiers in English, we should expect to find examples of right-headed word formation, that is, of structures (51b) and (51d). Indeed, the majority of category-changing derivation, of prefixation, and of root compounding in English does fit the right-headed pattern of (51b), as the examples in (52) illustrate:

(52) a. Category-changing Suffixes
       i.   -ness $]_A$ —— $]_N$ happiness
            -ity $]_A$ —— $]_N$ curiosity
            -ian $]_A$ —— $]_N$ civilian
            -ism $]_A$ —— $]_N$ purism

       ii. -y $]_N$ —— $]_A$ fruity
            -ish $]_N$ —— $]_A$ monkish
            -ous $]_N$ —— $]_A$ monstrous

       iii. -er $]_V$ —— $]_N$ baker
            -ee $]_V$ —— $]_N$ employee
            -ation $]_V$ —— $]_N$ restoration

       iv. -able $]_V$ —— $]_A$ washable
            -ive $]_V$ —— $]_A$ impressive

v. -ify $]_{\{N,A\}}$ ——$]_V$ glorify, solidify
   -ize $]_{\{N,A\}}$ ——$]_V$ standardize, unionize

b. Prefixes
  counter- $[$——$[_{\{N,A,V\}}$ counterweight, counterintuitive, countersign
  un- $[$——$[_A$ unhappy
  re- $[$——$[_V$ rewrite
  pre- $[$——$[_{\{V,N\}}$ precook, preschool
  mis- $[$——$[_V$ misjudge
  ante- $[$——$[_N$ anteroom
  co- $[$——$[_N$ co-conspirator
  ex- $[$——$[_N$ ex-governor

c. Root Compounds
  $[A\text{-}N]_N$ greenhouse, hardhat
  $[N\text{-}A]_A$ sky blue, ice cold
  $[N\text{-}N]_N$ file cabinet, towel rack
  $[A\text{-}A]_A$ red hot, worldly wise
  $[V\text{-}N]_N$ drawbridge, pickpocket

The suffixes in (52a) are clearly heads of their words, since they provide the category and other morphosyntactic features of those words. Whether we should consider the stems to which these suffixes attach as specifiers, modifiers, or perhaps as neither is of course a vexing question, and my remarks here are necessarily tentative. I am inclined to consider the stems in at least (52a-i,ii) as specifiers for the following reason. The relationship between *happy* and *-ness*, or between *fruit* and *-y*, or between *curious* and *-ity* is not transparently one of restrictive modification. Since the class of specifiers is so heterogeneous in any case, it seems preferable to consider the stems as specifiers in this case. For the suffixes which attach to verbs in (52a) (that is, (52a-iii,iv)), I will make a different choice. As mentioned in the discussion of Tagalog in section 2.3, verbs are typically not specifiers, modifiers, or complements in the phrasal syntax. Rather they are predicates, and as such are not covered by the Licensing Conditions. Strictly speaking, the hypothesis that I am testing does not predict that deverbal nouns and adjectives must be right-headed then, but neither is it inconsistent with the fact that they are right-headed. Finally, I will set aside discussion of the verb-forming suffixes in (52a-v) for a moment, and will return to them in the discussion of verb-forming prefixes below.

Before I come to the problem of verb-forming affixes, however, I want to discuss the data in (52b) and (52c). It has been noted frequently (Williams 1981a, Selkirk 1982, among others) that most prefixed words in English are right-headed, that is, that they exhibit structure (51b). Pesetsky (1985) has argued that this is because prefixes are unmarked for category. The fact that *counter-* attaches to Ns, Vs, or As and that the resulting word maintains the category of the stem suggests that the prefix has no category of its own. (The subcategorization frames in (52b) reflect this assumption.) But it is equally consistent with the theory being developed here that some of the prefixes in (52b) are adjectival (*ante-, co-*) or adverbial (*re-, mis-*), as suggested by Marchand (1969, 134), and therefore are modifiers. Note that as modifiers they precede their heads, as would be the case in phrasal syntax. Similarly, it may be that negative prefixes like *un-* in English are specifiers, and thus naturally precede their heads. Whichever of these hypotheses is correct, the words which result from the attachment of these prefixes exhibit the right-headed structure (51b).

Also exhibiting structure (51b) are English root compounds, as illustrated in (52c). Even where both stems bear the same category features, as in N-N or A-A compounds, it is possible to tell that they are right-headed, since semantically the right-hand stem determines the object or quality denoted by the compound as a whole. And here the relationship between nonhead and head is transparently one of modification. In a root compound like *towel rack,* the left-hand stem restricts or limits the reference of the right-hand head. We can conclude that structure (51b) is indeed abundantly attested in English word formation.

Similarly, to the extent that English allows words to be formed using phrasal bases, the resulting words exhibit the right-headed structure (51d). These are the phrasal compounds discussed in chapter 1, some of which are repeated in (53):

(53) Phrasal Compounds
    [$_N$[$_{NP}$ floor of a birdcage][$_N$ taste]]
    [$_N$[$_{PP}$ over the fence][$_N$ gossip]]
    [$_N$[$_{VP}$ ate too much][$_N$ headache]]

Here too the Licensing Conditions make accurate predictions for English.[26]

According to the Licensing Conditions, however, English word formation ought to exhibit another pattern, as well. That is, since heads precede their complements (i.e., since Theta-roles are assigned to the right), we ought to find words with the structure (51a), where the head occurs on the left and is a Theta-assigner. Let us first consider more closely the sorts of derived words we might expect to find. Note first that there are limited possibilities for such a structure. For an affix to assign a Theta-role, it must belong to a category of Theta-role assigners, that is, to V or P. We would not expect a nominal prefix to be a Theta-assigner, since nouns typically have Theta-roles to assign only when they are derived from verbs (e.g., *destruction*) and therefore inherit the Theta-assigning property from the verbs. Assuming that prefixes are underived items, they have nothing to inherit the Theta-role from. Furthermore, of the two remaining Theta-assigning categories, we would not expect to find any affixal Ps at all. P is virtually a closed class, which is to say that it is impossible, or nearly so, to derive new members of that category. What remains to look for then are category-changing prefixes in English which create verbs having the structure of (51a).

In fact, we find that the **only** category-changing prefixes that exist in English are verb-forming ones. Specifically, they are the prefixes *en-* and *de-* which attach to nouns (also to adjectives for *en-*) and form verbs:[27]

(54) Category-changing Prefixes

    de- $[_V$ ——— $[_N$ debug, dethrone, defuzz

    en- $[_V$ ——— $[_N$ encase, enrage, enthrone

It is plausible to claim that the prefixes *de-* and *en-* are in fact Theta-assigners. The theory being developed here assumes that affixes have all the properties of free members of the categories to which they belong. Since verbs typically are Theta-role assigners, we would expect to find that affixal verbs are Theta-role assigners as well. Furthermore, it appears that *de-* and *en-* do assign an obligatory Theta-role word internally (to the right). Semantically, the base noun to which *de-* attaches bears the theme role; for example, to *defuzz* X is to remove *the fuzz* from X. It can be argued that *en-* assigns an obligatory locative role to its stem; to *encase* Y is to put Y *in a case,* and to *enthrone* Z is to put Z *on a throne.* In comparison, verb-forming suffixes like *-ize* or *-ify* do not assign Theta-roles to their stems, but rather assign their obligatory Theta-roles **outside** the derived word. So to *unionize* X is to make X a union, and to *purify* Y is to make Y pure. If anything, the stems to which *-ize* and *-ify* attach are predicates rather than obligatory arguments of the affix.[28] This is a pattern which seems so far to have gone unnoticed in the literature of morphology, but it is exactly what we would expect under the theory being developed here. Since Theta-roles are uniformly assigned to the right in English, only verbalizing **prefixes** can assign Theta-roles word-internally to their stems. Verbalizing suffixes like those in (52a-v) are obliged to go outside the word to assign Theta-roles, leaving the word-internal noun or adjective stem to be a predicate.[29]

We have arrived at an important result here. The status of category-changing prefixes in English has long been a problem for morphological theory. A theory using Williams's RHR predicts that category-changing prefixes should not exist at all. On the other hand, in the theory of Lieber

(1980), it is puzzling that there are so few category-changing prefixes in English. If headedness were really symmetrical, as that theory claims, then we would expect to find more category-changing prefixes, and ones of different categories. The present theory of headedness, in contrast, comes fairly close to predicting the kinds of word formation that we find in English; the only sort of category-changing prefixes we expect to find is the only sort that we do find.

The Licensing Conditions in (50) predict the kinds of word formations we find in English quite accurately, but not perfectly accurately. That is, in addition to derived words with the left-headed pattern of (51a), we might expect also to find left-headed compounds in English in which the left-hand head element assigns a Theta-role to the right-hand element:

(55) a. $*[_V \text{ V X}]$ e.g., to pushcart (meaning 'to push a cart')
      b. $*[_P \text{ P X}]$ inbox (meaning ???)
      c. $*[_N \text{ N X}]$ destruction city (meaning 'destruction of the
                      city')

As the examples in (55) suggest, however, no such left-headed compounds exist in English. I would like to argue that there are independent reasons why this gap occurs.

Consider, first, the case of left-headed compound verbs. It is true that no such thing occurs in English word formation, but it is also the case that virtually no **right-headed** verbal compounds occur in English either. The few that do occur (*babysit, typewrite, aircondition*) are usually said to be backformations from nominal synthetic compounds (*babysitter, typewriter,* and *airconditioner,* respectively) (Marchand 1969; Selkirk 1982), and are plausibly just listed in the lexicon. We might assume, then, that there is some sort of constraint in English which prevents verbal compounds of any sort from being created. The exact formal nature of that constraint need not concern us here. For our purposes, it is sufficient to note that this constraint would rule out all verbal compounds, left- as well as right-headed.

The compounds in (55b) are easily ruled out as well. As mentioned before, the category P is a closed category. New prepositions are not usually derived by any morphological means. It is no surprise, then, that there are no left-headed prepositional compounds.

Left-headed noun compounds require a bit more thought, though. Note that we are probably talking here about left-headed N-N compounds in which the left-hand stem is deverbal (it must be a Theta-assigner) and the right-hand stem a noun (it must be able to receive a Theta-role). The problem that arises here is most likely one of structural ambiguity: a compound of the structure [$_N$ N-N] is clearly also interpretable as a right-headed root compound. What seems to be the case is that English disallows such structural ambiguity. All N-N compounds **must** be interpreted as right-headed, although the mechanism which does this must remain an open question for now.

At this point we come to the most serious problem for the theory being developed here. English has an abundance of one kind of compound that does **not** seem to be predicted by the Licensing Conditions in (50), namely the so-called synthetic compounds. Synthetic compounds are those in which the second stem is deverbal, and the first stem is interpreted as an argument of the verbal base, e.g., *thirst-quencher, truck driving, flea-bitten.* What makes these unexpected under our present assumptions is that the complement of the verb appears to the left of its head, contrary to Licensing Condition (50a). I will argue here, however, that there is an analysis of synthetic compounds available within our framework that not only explains the unexpected position of the complement, but also explains the fact, noted by Roeper (1988) and by Safir (1987), that there are no **phrasal** synthetic compounds in English: **apple on a stick taster, *flea on the couch bitten.* I will argue further that synthetic compounds are a residue that has remained productive since an earlier stage of English in which Theta-roles were assigned to the left. The derivation of synthetic compounds has changed in the course of the history of English, but the actual word order in synthetic compounds has not.

The analysis that I propose for synthetic compounds is the following. Remember that the Licensing Conditions permit either X^{max} or X^0 to be generated in pre- or post-head position. We have seen the results of this within lexical items, but we have not yet seen the consequences of this move for the syntax. As the theory stands, then, there is nothing in X-bar theory that would rule out a structure such as (56):

(56)

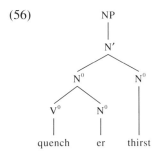

In (56) an N^0 has been generated as complement to the deverbal noun *quencher.* The Theta-role of *quench* is inherited by the N^0 formed by suffixation of *-er,* and is assigned to the right. However, if we assume that Case can be assigned only to maximal projections, the representation in (56) will be blocked as it stands. At this point Head Movement (Travis 1984; Baker 1988a; Roeper 1988) is forced so that the Visibility condition—the condition that requires that NPs must be Case-marked (Chomsky 1986a, Baker 1988a)—is not violated (we will assume that Case marking is not required inside words). The N^0 *thirst* moves leftward and adjoins to the N^0 *quencher* forming a synthetic compound. This is illustrated in (57):

(57) a.   b.

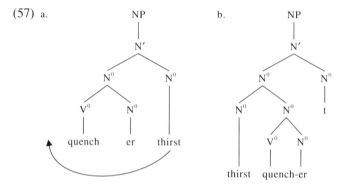

This analysis not only accounts for what looks like aberrant left-hand complements in synthetic compounds, but also provides a natural explanation for the observation made by Roeper and Siegel (1978), Safir (1987), and Roeper (1988) that a phrase never occurs as the first element in a synthetic compound. In (58) below the complement is an NP rather than an N^0.

(58)

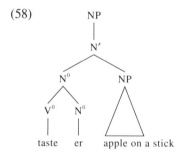

The NP will be Theta-marked by the N^0 *taster,* but it will also be assigned Case since it is a maximal projection (and the Case marker *of* must of course be inserted). We will assume that movement does not occur unless it is forced, and since the NP in (58) has received Case, it does not need to move. Phrasal synthetic compounds can therefore be ruled out.[30]

Notice that a movement analysis of synthetic compounds allows us to maintain Baker's (1988a, 46) Uniformity of Theta Assignment Hypothesis (UTAH) for English:

(59) The Uniformity of Theta Assignment Hypothesis (UTAH)
  Identical thematic relationships between items are represented by identical structural relationships between those items at the level of D-structure.

The complements of *thirst quencher* and *quencher of thirst* are represented in very similar structures at D-structure. The former, as we have seen, comes from (56). The latter is minimally different in that the N^0 *thirst* is part of a maximal phrase, and therefore can be Case-marked:

(60)

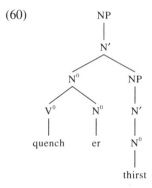

If we assume that Theta-marking does not distinguish between X^0 and X^{max}, then structures (56) and (60) will count as the same with respect to Theta-marking.

A final advantage of the analysis proposed here is that it makes sense in terms of what is known about the acquisition of synthetic compounds by English-speaking children. Clark, Hecht, and Mulford (1986) report that children learning to produce agentive or instrumental synthetic compounds like *truckdriver* and *thirst quencher* go through three stages. At the first stage they form only primary (root) V-N compounds like *washman* and *openmachine,* and use no affixes at all. During the second stage, they begin to add the *-er* affix to forms like *kick-ball* or *build-wall.* Significantly, the synthetic compound forms that they produce at this point are forms like *kicker ball* and *builder wall,* which maintain the Verb-Complement order of sentences. Only at the third and final stage of development do they get the order *ballkicker* and *wall builder,* as in adult language. The analysis proposed here in fact incorporates something like the second stage of development as one of the derivational stages of synthetic compounds.

The analysis I have sketched here is in fact very close to that proposed by Roeper (1988) for certain synthetic compounds. Roeper, too, proposes movement of the complement leftward with adjunction to X^0, although he assumes that the complement always originates under a maximal phrase as in (58) and (60). He must rule out the movement of complex structures such as that in (58) into X^0 by means of a semantic constraint, however: only elements denoting generic classes can be incorporated into X^0. We have seen that in the present framework the prohibition on movement of phrases as in (58) follows directly from X-bar theory and Case theory.

Roeper (1988) also points out that the **First Sister Principle** of Roeper and Siegel (1978), also discussed in Selkirk (1982) and Lieber (1983a), follows from the sort of movement analysis that he proposes. Since Theta-roles are assigned under adjacency in English (Stowell 1981), a Theta-assigner can only assign a Theta-role to an immediately contiguous X^0. Only this noun will move leftward. I will not go into detail here, but the First Sister Principle also follows from the movement analysis of synthetic compounds proposed above.

Synthetic compounds can thus be accommodated within the theory being developed here, and several positive consequences follow from the proposed analysis, including the ability to explain why phrasal synthetic compounds do not occur, and why children acquire synthetic compounds as they do. But it must also be asked at this point at what cost we assume this analysis. Doesn't a movement analysis of synthetic compounds seriously undermine the predictive nature of this theory? Why does this analysis not open the way for using movement in any case where the order of elements in words does not conform to the order of elements in phrases? I wish to argue here that there are in fact only three circumstances in which we should find the order of elements in words deviating from that in phrases. One circumstance is when words, or whole word formation patterns, are borrowed from another language which might set the Licensing Conditions differently from the language in question. A second is when surface word order in a language is variable (see section 2.5.2). The final circumstance is when the setting of one or more of the Licensing Conditions has changed during the history of a language. It is the third circumstance that I would say obtains in English.

What I wish to argue here is that English synthetic compounds can appear to violate the Licensing Condition for complements and can be derived via movement only because they are a word formation type that has maintained its productivity since an earlier period in the history of English when this Licensing Condition was in fact set differently.[31] Although it is beyond the scope of this work to do a thorough study of word order in Old English,[32] the following fact seems relevant. It is well known that Old English (OE) was an underlyingly SOV language. Suppose that OE differed from modern English in not being strictly head initial with respect to complements. Suppose, rather, that within the framework of Travis (1990), OE had the head initial setting only as a default setting, and set the subdomain parameter for Theta-role marking so that Theta-roles were assigned to the left. In other words, OE had the Licensing Condition in (61) rather than the one in (50a):

(61) Theta-roles are assigned to the left. Heads are otherwise initial with respect to complements.

The other Licensing Conditions of OE would have been the same as those for modern English. The effects of (61) would be the following. Since Theta-roles are normally assigned to the left, the internal arguments of a verb would normally appear to its left. A complement might appear to the right of its head if Theta-identification could take place through a preposition (see Travis 1990, 267), or if Move-Alpha otherwise modified underlying order. The former might be the case in NPs, where internal arguments occur to the right mediated by a preposition. See van Kemenade (1987) for detailed discussion of Move-Alpha in OE, and its effects on underlying order.

If Theta-roles were indeed assigned to the left in OE, synthetic compounds like *āþ swaring* 'oath swearing', *gōdspellbodung* 'gospel preaching', *gold-gifa* 'gold-giver', and *man-slaga* 'man-killer' which are attested from the OE period (examples from Marchand 1969), would originally have been generated without movement. Van Kemenade (1987), citing a study by Canale (1978), dates the change from SOV to SVO order at about 1200 A.D. In terms of the analysis sketched here, the special Theta-marking clause in (61) would have been lost at this point, leaving the default head initial parameter as the only parameter governing the arrangement of head and complements. What is remarkable in the history of English is that the synthetic compounding pattern was so productive that it did not change after the parameter settings for English changed. Following the parameter change, synthetic compounds would have to be derived in a marked way, via movement. We will see below when we discuss French word formation that English could have developed another sort of synthetic compounding more consistent with its new parameter setting, that is, the sort of compound exemplified by *pickpocket* and *drawbridge,* but that this sort of compounding never became productive in English. In any case, it seems possible to conclude that the movement analysis of synthetic compounds in English does not represent an unwarranted weakening of the theory, but rather is justified by the historical change in the parameter settings for English.

We are in a position now to draw some conclusions about English. We

saw above that the Licensing Conditions in (50) were independently necessary to determine the phrase structure of English. Remarkably, the very
same Licensing Conditions come very close to characterizing the range of
word formation that can be found in English. Even with respect to synthetic compounds, the analysis that we are forced to by the strict assignment of Theta-roles to the right is historically justified and has benefits that
are unavailable in less restrictive theories, namely the ability to explain
why there are no phrasal synthetic compounds in English. We can conclude
that for English, as for Tagalog, there seems to be an intimate connection
between the position of the head in words and its position in phrases.

2.5 Comparison: English, French, Dutch

In the previous two sections we have seen that the theory being developed
makes reasonably accurate predictions about the sorts of word formation
that are found in Tagalog and English. In this section, I will develop brief
analyses of French and Dutch, both of which differ from English in one
parameter setting. My purpose is to show that several significant differences between the types of word formation found in English and those
found in French and Dutch follow from the differences in parameter
settings.

2.5.1 French

We start as usual with setting the Licensing Conditions for French. As the
examples in (62) show, heads precede their complements in French (complements are in boldface):

(62) a. Les passions [tyrannisent **l'homme**].   VP
          'Passions tyrannize man.'
      b. la construction **d'un pont**   NP
          'the construction of a bridge'
      c. de **mon voisin**   PP
          'of my neighbor'
      d. fier **de sa fille**   AP
          'proud of his daughter'

Although certain adjectives may precede the noun they modify, restrictive
modifiers typically follow their heads (modifiers are in boldface):

(63) a. un mot **vrai**
          'a true word'
      b. une statue **de bronze**
          'a statue of bronze'

c. les hommes **qui sont mortels**
'the men that are mortal'

Finally, specifiers precede their heads. Example (62a) illustrates the position of the head of IP. The examples in (64) illustrate the position of the possessive pronoun and of other sorts of specifiers (specifiers are in boldface).

(64) a. **ma** tante   'my aunt'
 b. **deux** livres   'two books'
 c. **quelque** endroit   'some place'
 d. **aucunes** troupes   'no troops'
 e. **très** pauvre   'very poor'

The Licensing Conditions for French will therefore be the ones in (65):

(65) a. Heads are **initial** with respect to complements.
 b. Heads are **initial** with respect to modifiers.
 c. Heads are **final** with respect to specifiers.

French thus sets only one Licensing Condition differently than is done in English, the one for modifiers. What sort of differences should we then expect to find between word formation in French and English? First, we would expect differences in the order of elements in root compounds; where modifiers precede their heads in English root compounds, we might expect the opposite order in French. Second, we would expect that French should not have the sort of synthetic compounds that we find in English; since we claim that the order of elements in English synthetic compounds is a holdover from an earlier stage in English in which complements preceded their heads, we would expect that this pattern should not occur in French. In fact, we might expect that compounds with the order head-complement might occur. Otherwise we would expect to find substantial similarities between the sorts of word formation occurring in English and French. We will see that each of these predictions is in fact borne out.

  Root compounding in French is primarily left-headed, with the second element acting as a modifier of the first. Some examples are given in (66). See Rohrer (1977) and Surridge (1985) for further examples of this sort.

(66) timbre poste   'postage stamp'
  rose thé   'tea rose'
  wagon poste   'mail van'
  noeud papillion   'bowtie'
  pneu ballon   'balloon tire'
  bateau phare   'light ship'

Note that although DiSciullo and Williams (1987, 81–82) call items like these "listed phrases," the majority of linguists that have discussed them call them compounds, for example, Giurescu (1975), Rohrer (1977), Bauer (1978), Selkirk (1982), and Surridge (1985). Rohrer, Bauer, and Surridge all argue that they are formed productively and are not merely listed or lexicalized items. Bauer (1978, 33) quotes the French scholar Darmesteter (1875, 120) on the subject of productivity:

La terminologie des arts et métiers, celles des sciences naturelles, la langue du commerce, de l'industrie, de la presse, fourmillent de composés . . . crées spontanement suivant les nécessités du moment et disparaissent d'ordinaire avec la même facilité qui les a fait naître: preuve indéniable que cette composition est vraiment vivante et tout à fait dans le génie de la langue.

The terminology of the arts and crafts, those of the natural sciences, of trade, of industry, of the press abound with compounds . . . which are created spontaneously as the need arises and disappear ordinarily with the same ease with which they are born: [this constitutes] undeniable proof that compounding is truly alive and completely within the genius of the language.

Note further that these compounds inflect for plural on the first noun (e.g., *timbres poste*), and take their gender from this element as well (e.g., *timbre* (m.) *poste* (f.), *timbre poste* (m.)).[33] There are in French some compounds that are right-headed (e.g., *radio-activité*), but Surridge (1985, 251) calls these "learned" compounds (composés savants), and suggests that they are based on Greek and Latin. Since this type receives little or no discussion in the literature, I assume that it is unproductive and that the few right-headed root compounds that exist are listed in the lexicon and not derived in the syntax. The significant sort of N-N compounding, however, is left-headed, with modifiers following the head, as predicted by Licensing Condition (65b).

   The second prediction made by our theory is borne out as well. French has no synthetic compounds of the sort *truck driver* or *pasta-eating*. Instead it has a productive sort of nominal compound that consists of a verb followed by a noun which serves as the internal argument of the verb. Examples are given in (67):[34]

(67) essuie-glace   'windshield wiper' (lit. wipe-windshield)
     tire-bouchon   'corkscrew'
     coupe-cigare   'cigar cutter'
     pèse-lettre   'letter scale'

Semantically, such compounds form instrument nouns, and less frequently agent nouns. DiSciullo and Williams (1987) analyze these compounds as syntactic phrases (VPs) that become Ns through a process of category

change. Such an analysis is not possible within the present framework for
reasons I go into in detail in chapter 5. Rather, what seems to be called for
is an analysis along the lines suggested in Rohrer (1977). Rohrer suggests
that these compounds are formed with a zero-affix, which in our terms
would be head of the compound. Several facts point in this direction. First,
these compounds have a consistent interpretation as instrument/agent
nouns, much as do verbs affixed with *-er* in English; French in fact lacks a
productive overt instrumental affix. Second, with very few exceptions (see
Surridge 1985; Bauer 1978), noun compounds formed on this pattern are
masculine in gender. It is typical, of course, for derivational affixes to sup-
ply the gender of the words they form. This suggests that these compounds
bear a derivational affix as well. The structure I propose for these compounds is therefore (68a); the lexical entry for the zero-suffix is in (68b):

(68) a.

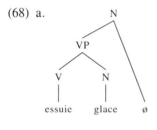

    b. -Ø   ]$_{VP}$ ——]$_N$
       LCS: x [LCS of input V] [35]

There is one detail in (68a) that is not crucial, namely whether the node
dominating the V and N is V^0 or VP. What is crucial for our purposes here
is that the relationship between the V and N inside the compound is a head
complement relationship, and that the verb precedes its complement as it
does in the phrasal syntax.[36]

    Our final prediction is that aside from differences expected in root and
synthetic compounds, word formation in French should be much the same
as in English. We find that derivational word formation in French is indeed
very similar to that in English. As in English, most category-changing derivation in French is suffixal. Some examples are given in (69):

(69) -iser   ]$_A$ ——]$_V$ américaniser   'Americanize'
      -ifier   ]$_{N,A}$ ——]$_V$ panifier   'turn into bread'
                           clarifier   'clarify'
      -eté   ]$_A$ ——]$_N$ pauvreté   'poverty'
      -ais   ]$_N$ ——]$_A$ japonais   'Japanese'
      -eux   ]$_N$ ——]$_A$ vaporeux   'vaporous'
      -eur   ]$_V$ ——]$_N$ voyeur   'voyeur'

Similarly, most prefixes do not change category, as the examples in (70)
show:

(70) contre- $_{N,V}[$——$_{N,V}[$ contrebalancer   'counterbalance'
                                        contrepoids   'counterweight'
      mé- (més-) $_{N,A}[$——$_{N,A}[$ mésaventure   'misadventure'
                                        mécontent   'discontent'
      re- $_V[$——$_V[$ refaire   'redo'
      par- $_V[$——$_V[$ parfaire   'complete'

Still, although Brousseau (1989) reports DiSciullo (1988) as saying that
French derivation is strictly right-headed, there do seem to be at least two
category-changing prefixes: *en-* and *dé-*.

(71) en- empocher   'to pocket'
          embouteiller   'to bottle'
          encaver   'to put in a cellar'
      dé- débarquer   'to disembark'
          décapuchonner   'to take a hood off'
          déculotter   'to take the pants off'

Although *en-* and *dé-* sometimes attach to verbs, in the case of the examples
in (71) there are no corresponding verbs *pocher, bouteiller, barquer,* etc.,
and it is therefore arguable that the prefixes have attached to noun bases
(nouns like *poche, bouteille,* etc., exist) to form verbs in cases such as
these. It is significant that the two category-changing prefixes in French
are, as in English, verb-forming. Furthermore, as we found in English with
the prefixes *en-* and *de-*, the French prefixes arguably assign a Theta-role
internally to their bases. As in English, *en-* in French appears to assign an
obligatory locative role to its base, and *dé-* the theme role to its base.[37]
    These facts are exactly what we would expect from our theory. Much of
French derivational morphology is right-headed, as it is in English. Left-
headed derivation occurs where a verbal affix assigns its Theta-role to the
right. Left-headed root compounds in which modifiers follow the head contrast with right-headed root compounds in English. And finally, the closest
counterpart in French to synthetic compounds in English have a complement following a verb, as would be expected from the setting of the head-
complement Licensing Condition.

2.5.2 Dutch

We will take Dutch as our second comparison with English, starting as before with setting the Licensing Conditions. Two of these are relatively
straightforward. First, specifiers uniformly precede the head in Dutch (examples are from Donaldson 1987, unless otherwise noted):

(72) a. **Annekes** boek   'Anneke's book'
      een fles bier   'a bottle of beer'
      duizenden mensen   'thousands of people'
  b. **De boom** is erg oud. 'The tree is very old.'
  c. (examples from van Riemsdijk 1978)
      diep onder het zand 'deep under the sand'
      pal boven de deur   'right above the door'

Modifiers, as in English, are a bit more complex. Bare adjectives and certain APs precede the head that they modify:

(73) a. het **cultureel** akkoord 'the cultural accord'
  b. de **in de jaren vijftig** 'the houses built in the fifties'
      gebouwde huizen
      een **mij bekend**   'a face familiar to me'
      gezicht
      (from Koopman 1984)

Other restrictive modifiers, including APs follow their heads, however:

(74) a. een kind **bang voor honden**   'a child afraid of dogs'
      (from Koopman 1984)
  b. de man **die ik gisteren zag**   'the man that I saw
                              yesterday'
      de persoon **aan wie ik de brief gaf** 'the person to whom I gave
                                    the letter'
  c. het schilderij **aan de muur**   'the picture on the wall'
      onze plicht **jegens onze ouders** 'our duty to our parents'

Example (74a) contains an AP modifier following the head, (74b) relative clauses, and (74c) prepositional phrases, which always follow the head.

I propose that Dutch is like English in terms of the Licensing Condition for modifiers. I suggest that modifiers always precede their heads in Dutch and that there is a rule which moves certain heavy modifiers to the right of the head. The movement rule will of course be somewhat different from its English counterpart. In English, all heavy modifiers, including those like (73b), move to the right of the head. In Dutch it seems that heavy modifiers can remain in prenominal position as long as the head of the modifier phrase is adjacent to the head noun that it modifies. Prepositional phrases (74c), relative clauses (74b), and APs in which the head is followed by a PP (74a) will therefore appear postnominally.

The most interesting and probably the most problematic issue in the phrase structure of Dutch concerns the position of complements with respect to their heads. The facts seem to be as follows.

First, complements precede verbs on the assumption that Dutch is an underlyingly SOV language (Koster, 1975; Evers 1975; van Riemsdijk 1978; Koopman 1984; among others):

(75) Je moet **je vader** helpen   'you must help your father'
      Ik heb **een auto** gekocht   'I have bought a car'
      (from van Kemenade 1987)
      omdat hij **het boek** kocht   'because he bought the book'

The complements of nouns, however, uniformly follow their heads:

(76) het koken van **groente**   'the cooking of vegetables'
      het schrijven van **romans**   'the writing of novels'

The facts for adjectives and prepositions are somewhat more complex. According to Hoekstra (1984), some adjectives only take a direct NP complement which precedes the adjective as in (77a). Other adjectives take a PP or clausal complement that follows the adjective as in (77b). Still others can have a PP complement which can either precede or follow the adjective as in (77c) (examples from Hoekstra 1984, 26):

(77) a.   **dat gezeur** moe   'that drivel weary-of'
           *moe **dat gezeur**
      b.   bang **om op te vallen**   'afraid to attract attention'
           *om op te vallen bang
           ?zeker **dat dat zal gebeuren**   'certain that that will happen'
           *dat dat zal gebeuren zeker
      c.   verliefd **op zijn moeder**   'in love with his mother'
           op zijn moeder verliefd   'with his mother in love'

Adpositions generally precede their complements (that is, they are prepositions), but sometimes, especially if they indicate motion, can follow them:

(78) aan **die muur**   'on the wall'
      de stad in   'into the city'

The data in (75)–(78) have generally been used to support the idea that the head-complement parameter is set differently for different categories in Dutch. Hoekstra (1984, 31), for example, proposes that [+V] categories (that is, A and V) follow their complements, and [−V] categories (N and P) precede their complements (see also van Kemenade 1987). The split setting is not, however, entirely satisfactory. It does not, for example, explain why PPs and clausal complements of adjectives can and sometimes must follow their complements, but bare NP complements must always precede their heads, nor does it explain why prepositions can sometimes follow their complements. I therefore suggest tentatively that the head-complement parameter in Dutch is set as in (79):

(79) Theta-roles are assigned to the left. Heads are otherwise initial with respect to their complements.

In other words, I am proposing that Dutch sets the head-complement parameter just as OE did, with Theta-roles being assigned leftwards, but with a default head initial setting. Note again what this means in the framework of Travis (1990): direct NP complements are expected to occur before their heads, but if complements follow their heads we would expect an intervening preposition to assign Theta-role via Theta-identification (Travis 1990, 267). This setting of the parameters comes quite close to accounting for the facts in the phrasal syntax. Direct NP complements occur in VPs and APs, and they indeed precede their heads. Where complements follow their heads—in NPs and APs—there indeed must be an intervening preposition to effect Theta-identification. The only fact that still requires explanation is why a bare NP complement can follow a preposition without the intervention of another preposition. The answer that I suggest tentatively is that a preposition like *in* can both assign a Theta-role directly to its left and effect Theta-identification to its right, so that both *in de stad* and *de stad in* are possible in Dutch. The parameter setting in (79) thus accounts somewhat better than a split setting for the facts, and fits as well into the schema envisioned by Travis (1990).

To summarize, then, we assume that the Licensing Conditions for Dutch are set as in (80):

(80) a. Theta-roles are assigned to the left. Heads are otherwise **initial** with respect to complements.
  b. Heads are **final** with respect to modifiers.
  c. Heads are **final** with respect to specifiers.

Dutch thus differs from modern English only with respect to the head-complement parameter, and even for that parameter, the default setting in Dutch is the setting in English.

We must now consider how the difference in this one parameter setting might be reflected in Dutch word formation. Note first that we should expect word formation in Dutch to be similar to word formation in English in many respects. Since heads are final with respect to both modifiers and specifiers, we would expect a substantial amount of right-headed morphology, including root compounds in which modifiers precede their heads. We would expect as well synthetic compounds in which complement precedes head. Where we might expect to find differences in word formation between English and Dutch would be in a relatively small area, namely the verb-forming prefixes. We saw in English that the prefixes *en-* and *de-* assign a Theta-role internally to the stem to which they attach. We should not expect to find exact counterparts of these prefixes in Dutch. We will discuss below to what extent the word formation actually found in Dutch fulfills our expectations.

We find first, as expected, that Dutch word-formation is heavily right-headed. Contained in (81) are examples of category-changing suffixes, and in (82) examples of non-category-changing prefixes:

(81) (examples from Trommelen and Zonneveld 1986; Booij 1977)

-ing	$]_V$ ——$]_N$	leiding	'pipe'
-sel	$]_V$ ——$]_N$	weefsel	'texture'
-te	$]_A$ ——$]_N$	hoogte	'height'
-isme	$]_{A,N}$ ——$]_N$	puurisme	'purism'
		magnetisme	'magnetism'
-isch	$]_N$ ——$]_A$	profetisch	'prophetic'
-ief	$]_N$ ——$]_A$	constructief	'constructive'
-lijk	$]_N$ ——$]_A$	vijandelijk	'enemylike'
-eer	$]_N$ ——$]_V$	signaleer	'to signal'
-iseer	$]_N$ ——$]_V$	periodiseer	'to periodize'

(82) (examples from Trommelen and Zonneveld 1986)

trans-	[—— $_{N,V,A}$[	transmissie	'transmission'
		transformeren	'to transform'
		transsexueel	'transsexual'
re-	[—— $_V$[	reorganizeren	'to reorganize'
voor-	[—— $_V$[	voorkomen	'to prevent'
door-	[—— $_V$[	doorlopen	'to run through'

Nominal root compounds are also right-headed, where the first element is always interpreted as a modifier of the right-hand head:

(83) (examples from Trommelen and Zonneveld 1986)

de diepzee	$[A-N]_N$	'deepsea'
de blauwdruk	$[A-N]_N$	'blueprint'
het naaiwerk	$[V-N]_N$	'sewing' (lit. sew-work)
het balspel	$[N-N]_N$	'ballgame'
het naamwoord	$[N-N]_N$	'noun' (lit. name-word)

Phrasal compounds in Dutch are also right-headed, with the first element acting as a modifier of the right-hand head:

(84) (examples from Hoeksema 1988)
 lach of ik schiet humor 'laugh or I shoot humor'
 blijf van mijn lijf huis 'stay off my body house'
         (shelter for abused women)

Root compounds and phrasal compounds are thus similar to those in English, as expected.

Dutch also has productively formed synthetic compounds of exactly the sort we expect to find, that is, with the complement directly preceding the nominal head:

(85) (examples from Booij 1988a)
 schoenmaker   'shoemaker'
 ijsverkoper   'ice seller'
 aardappeleter   'potato eater'
 jeneverdrinker   'gin drinker'
 aardappelgevreet 'excessive potato eating'

Note that unlike in English, synthetic compounds in Dutch are generated directly via the base component of the grammar; since bare NP complements can receive their Theta-role directly from a head to their right, synthetic compounds in Dutch need not be generated by movement rule. If a complement of a deverbal noun like *drinker* occurs to its right, it must have an intervening preposition to effect Theta-identification (hence phrases like *drinker van jenever* 'drinker of gin'), but if it occurs to the left, that is, in a compound, no preposition is needed. The structure of synthetic compounds in Dutch is illustrated in (86):

(86)

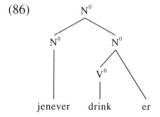

Thus, the theory at hand makes correct predictions with respect to this type of compound as well.

Where we would expect to find differences between Dutch and English is in the nature of category-changing prefixes. Specifically, we would expect that if Dutch has category-changing prefixes at all, they should not be the sort which assign a Theta-role to their stems, since prefixes in Dutch ought not to be able to assign a Theta-role rightwards. Dutch does indeed have several category-changing prefixes, which are listed in (87):

(87) (examples from De Vooys 1967 and Trommelen and Zonneveld 1986)

be-	$_V[$ ——— $_{N,A}$ [	bemantelen	'to cloak'
		benijden	'to envy'
		bekoelen	'to cool down'
		bekorten	'to shorten'
ont-	$_V[$ ——— $_{N,A}$ [	onthaaren	'to depilate'
		onthoofden	'to decapitate'
		ontheiligen	'to desecrate'
ver-	$_V[$ ——— $_{N,A}$ [	zich verslaaven	'to enslave'
		verkolen	'to carbonize'
		verdiepen	'to deepen'
		verarmen	'to make poor'

Of the prefixes in (87), *ver-* seems clearly to be the sort we would expect. If *zich verslaaven* is interpreted as 'to make oneself a slave', and *verkolen* as 'to make X carbon', the nominal bases are predicates rather than arguments of the verbal prefix. Similar predicate interpretations can be given to the adjectival bases to which *be-* and *ont-* attach: *bekorten* is 'to make X short' and *ontheiligen* 'to make X unholy'. However, *be-* and *ont-* with nominal bases seem to be interpreted much as *en-* and *de-* are in English: *bemantelen* is 'to put X in a cloak', *onthoofden* 'to take the head from X'. These two prefixes would therefore appear to run counter to our predictions, since they appear to assign Theta-roles rightwards to their stems.

It is not clear that these prefixes pose a serious threat to our theory, however. Baayen (1990 and p.c.)[38] reports that the productivity of *be-* and *ont-* is rather low, and perhaps even marginal: P for *be-* is 0.015 and for *ont-* is 0.097, versus 0.002 for simplex verbs in Dutch. Baayen cautions that these figures must be taken with a grain of salt for the following reasons. Neither prefix is represented by a large number of types in the CELEX corpus, which makes the significance of the P statistic somewhat uncertain. A fair number of the types represented have highly lexicalized meanings. Furthermore, Baayen notes (p.c.) that some of the *be-* and *ont-* forms which were analyzed as *be* + N and *ont* + N are arguably cases of *be* + V and *ont* + V. Removing such forms from the *be* + N and *ont* + N data would result in a lower productivity figure for these affixes. Baayen also notes that new coinages in *be-* and *ont-* do not have the sort of unintentional flavor that is the mark of new words resulting from fully productive means of word formation. Rather, they are words that would be noticed as new. For example, words like *ontoren* 'to take the ears away' or *ontpoten* 'to remove the legs (e.g., of an insect)' would very likely stand out for the hearer as new forms.

All of this suggests that *be-* and *ont-* are at best marginally productive and that word formation with these prefixes is a relatively marked phenomenon. Nevertheless, the question still remains why Dutch should allow even borderline productive affixes which violate the word order parameters of Dutch. One possibility which Baayen suggests is the following. Although it is typical of verbs in Dutch to assign their Theta-roles leftwards (that is, Dutch is underlyingly an SOV language), main clauses in Dutch frequently exhibit surface SVO order, where the NP receiving its Theta-role from the verb appears to the right of the verb. Prefixes like *be-* and *ont-* exhibit exactly the surface order of main clauses in Dutch. This raises the possibility that they should be derived via movement. Recall that in section 2.4 it was suggested that one of the circumstances that might motivate movement would occur in a language in which several surface word orders are possible. A plausible derivation for a form like *onthoofden* is sketched in (88):

(88) a.

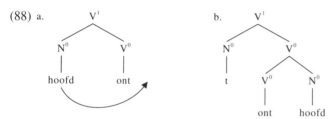

In (88a) the noun *hoofd* receives its Theta-role from *ont-* in the usual manner, since at D-structure it occurs to the left of *ont-*. *Hoofd* fails to receive Case, since it is an N^0 rather than an NP, and therefore Head Movement is forced. The noun adjoins to the prefixal verb, as shown in (88b).[39] The relative complexity of the derivation required for these verbs accords well with the intuitions of their marked status. We would assume as well that such forms would be acquired relatively late, as was the case for the English synthetic compounds which also required a movement analysis.

2.6 Conclusions

In this chapter I have tried to defend the position that the direction of headedness in morphology need not and should not be set separately from the direction of headedness in the syntax. I have argued that the parameters of X-bar theory and related modules of the grammar are neither purely syntactic nor purely morphological; they are general principles that determine structural configurations both above and below word level. Directional parameters are set just once for each language.

Given this theory, it is not accidental that Tagalog, a language which is consistently head initial in phrasal syntax, also exhibits a robustly left-headed morphology. Nor is it an accident that English, although predominantly right-headed in morphology and syntax (recall that heads follow modifiers and specifiers at both levels), displays left-headed **verbal** morphology; since complements occur to the right of their heads in English, a verbal prefix can precede a noun complement to which it assigns a Theta-role. In French the theory predicts, and we do in fact find, left-headed root compounds with modifiers following heads and substantially right-headed derivation with the exception again being verb-forming prefixes which assign a Theta-role to the right. It predicts the absence of synthetic compounds like *truckdriver* and *pasta-eating,* and indeed such compounds are absent. Even in Dutch, the predictions of the theory are substantially correct. It predicts right-headed root compounds with modifier preceding head, synthetic compounds with complement preceding head, and other predominantly right-headed derivational morphology. All of these do in fact occur in Dutch. A verbal prefix of the predicted sort (that is, *ver-*) also exists. And even *be-* and *ont-*, the verbal prefixes which seemed problematic at first glance, receive a reasonable explanation within this theory.

The theory proposed in this chapter has the virtue of being highly restrictive. If the direction of headedness can only be set once for all levels, we should not expect to find languages which are consistently head initial (left-headed) above word level, but consistently head final (right-headed) below word level, or vice versa. It remains to be seen whether this prediction can be maintained over a wide range of the world's languages. Nevertheless, from the cases we have seen in this chapter, it appears to be a promising theory. And it is a theory in which the phrasal compounds and derivations discussed in chapter 1 can be generated in a natural and unproblematic way, since morphology is not strictly segregated from the syntax.

So far, then, I have been able to defend the claim that grammar can do without a distinct morphological component containing rules and principles different from those of phrasal syntax. In this chapter, however, I have dealt only with basic principles of construction. Still to be discussed are the distribution of features within words, the anaphoric properties of sublexical items, and other areas in which general principles of grammar might be expected to extend below word level. We next turn to the distribution of features.

3   Feature Percolation and Inheritance

In chapter 2 I tried to show that the basic principles of word construction were in fact none other than the principles of the X-bar system that were independently necessary in the grammar. These principles along with the subcategorization information about individual morphemes determine the basic linear order and hierarchical structure found in words. But X-bar theory alone cannot account for everything that is relevant in the construction of complex words. X-bar theory determines the position of the head in words and sentences, but it says nothing about the actual mechanism that effects labeling of nodes within words,[1] that is, the process by which categorial information and other features are projected up from lexical entries to produce fully labeled word structures. This process has been called **feature percolation.** Some process of feature percolation has been assumed in most theories of generative morphology of the 1980s: Lieber (1980, 1983a), Williams (1981a), Selkirk (1982), DiSciullo and Williams (1987), among others. Here too we will need to propose a mechanism by which features are passed from node to node in lexical (and phrasal) structures.

Below I will first review three versions of feature percolation that have been proposed in the literature on morphology, and I will show that there are several areas in which these theories are insufficiently explicit. Little attention has been paid to precisely what features percolate, where features are allowed to percolate from, and how features percolate in languages in which a lexical item may have more than one marking for a single feature, such as person, number, or case. I will argue in the sections that follow that only morphosyntactic features percolate, but not features for diacritics or argument structures. In fact, I suggest that argument structures should not be encoded in binary-valued features at all. I propose that there are two simple principles of percolation and that the process of percolation is regulated by a frame called the **categorial signature.** These two principles, along with a simple assumption about the internal organization of the categorial signature, account for the distribution of features in languages which allow multiple markings for a feature on a single lexical item. We will see further that the theory of percolation that is developed here has interesting ramifications. It suggests a difference between inflectional and derivational affixes, which in turns leads to the conclusion that current syntactic analyses that make Infl the head of the inflected verb are problematic from the point of view of percolation. The final section of this chapter is devoted to a consideration of **inheritance,** the process by which Theta-grids, or argument structures, are passed from node to node in complex words. Since we rule out equating inheritance with percolation, we must determine what inheritance is, and how it is to be accounted for within our theory.[2]

3.1 Previous Treatments of Percolation

Contained in (1) are three of the early statements of feature percolation in the morphological literature, those of Lieber (1980), Williams (1981a), and Selkirk (1982):

(1) a. Lieber (1980, 49–54)

Convention I: All features of a stem morpheme including category features percolate to the first nonbranching node dominating that morpheme.

Convention II: All features of an affix morpheme including category features percolate to the first branching node dominating that morpheme.

Convention III: If a branching node fails to obtain features by Convention II, features from the next lowest labeled node are automatically percolated up to the branching node.

Convention IV (Compounds): In compound words in English, features from the right-hand stem are percolated up to the branching node dominating the stems.

b. Williams (1981a, 247)

If both X and the head of X are eligible members of category C, then $X \in C \equiv$ head of $X \in C$.[3]

c. Selkirk (1982, 76)

Percolation (revised)

i. If a head has a feature specification $[\alpha F_i]$, $\alpha \neq u$, its mother node must be specified $[\alpha F_i]$ and vice versa.

ii. If a nonhead has a feature specification $[\beta F_j]$, and the head has the feature specification $[u F_j]$, then the mother node must have the feature specification $[\beta F_j]$.

The three statements of feature percolation in (1) differ in minor ways, but basically give the same results. Lieber's conventions build the notion of head into the feature percolation conventions themselves; Selkirk's and Williams's define the head independently as the rightmost element in the word, as we saw in chapter 2. Lieber's and Selkirk's conventions allow for the percolation of features from a nonhead morpheme if the head lacks a specification for the relevant features; Williams's convention (1b) does not provide for feature percolation from the nonhead, although in his more recent work (DiSciullo and Williams 1987), provision for percolation of the nonhead is made. In any case it is clear, given some set of percolation conventions like these, how percolation is intended to proceed. Illustrated in (2) is a simple example of percolation from the head, and in (3) of percolation from a nonhead morpheme:

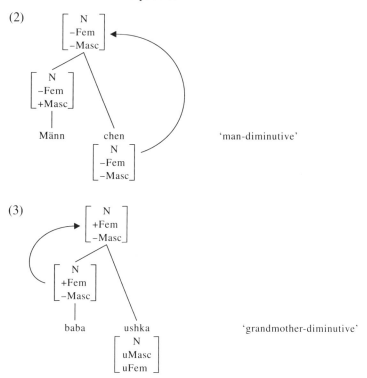

(2)   'man-diminutive'

(3)   'grandmother-diminutive'

Still, none of the three statements of feature percolation in (1) is sufficiently explicit about the mechanism of percolation. None gives specific directions about which features percolate. Williams (1981a) and DiSciullo and Williams (1987) are silent on this point. Lieber (1980) and Selkirk (1982) mention in passing that both morphosyntactic and diacritic features percolate, but neither defends this claim explicitly. Nor are the statements of feature percolation in (1) sufficiently explicit about how features percolate. All three assume that if a feature is available from both the head and a nonhead morpheme, that the head feature has absolute priority, and **over-**

rides the same feature on the nonhead, as was the case in (2). We will see below, however, that this simple "traffic rule" is sometimes inadequate. In section 3.2, we will begin to explore these issues, and to clear the way for a more precise theory of percolation.

3.2 What Features Percolate

The three statements of feature percolation in (1) allow any sort of feature whatever to percolate. In this section I will provide arguments which suggest that this view is not sufficiently restrictive. There is no reason to believe that diacritic features ever need to percolate. Nor is there any evidence that argument structures should be encoded in features and percolated as morphosyntactic features are. On the contrary, I will show that there is good evidence to suggest that argument structures or Theta-grids should not be factored into features and should not percolate.

3.2.1 Diacritics

There is very little in the published literature to date that deals directly with the question of whether diacritic features percolate; as mentioned above, although both Lieber (1980) and Selkirk (1982) note in passing that diacritics percolate, neither provides clear arguments in favor of this position. Here I will consider three examples which suggest that diacritics should not percolate.

Lieber (1980) in fact inadvertently provides an argument against percolation of diacritic features in her analysis of Latin verbal morphology. Lieber argues that Latin verbs may have more than one listed stem form and that various inflectional suffixes subcategorize for particular stem forms. In order for the morphological subcategorizations of inflectional suffixes to be able to refer to the particular stem forms they must attach to, stem forms are designated as bearing two binary valued diacritic features $[\pm T]$ and $[\pm D]$. Roots are designated $[-T,+D]$, theme vowel stems $[+T,+D]$, and perfect stems $[+T,-D]$. Since some inflectional affixes also must attach to other inflectional affixes, some inflectional affixes are also marked with the diacritic feature $[+T]$. Relevant stems and affixes, together with their subcategorizations are listed in (4) and (5) below:

(4) Stems   'love'   am $\begin{bmatrix} -T \\ +D \end{bmatrix}$

                   amā $\begin{bmatrix} +T \\ +D \end{bmatrix}$

                   amāv $\begin{bmatrix} +T \\ -D \end{bmatrix}$

(5) Affixes

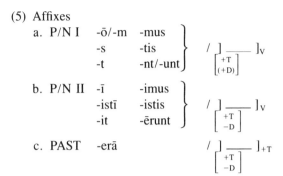

    a. P/N I   -ō/-m   -mus

The P/N I suffixes attach directly to theme vowel stems (e.g., *amās*, *amāmus*), or to other suffixes marked [+T]. P/N II suffixes attach to the perfect stem, that is, the stem marked [+T,−D] (e.g., *amavī*, *amāvistī*, etc.). The case that seems to suggest that diacritics do not percolate is the pluperfect paradigm, which starts out before percolation as illustrated in (6):

(6)

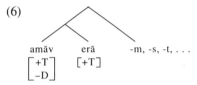

Note, first of all, that the correct P/N affixes can be attached in (6) without any percolation taking place, if each morpheme can see the features of the morpheme to its left. Morphemes in Latin in fact need look no further to meet their subcategorizations than the morpheme immediately to their left. Indeed, the correct P/N affixes can only be attached if no percolation has taken place. Consider what happens if percolation occurs:

(7)   *

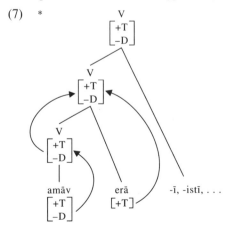

In (7) the features [+T, −D] percolate to the node immediately dominating *amāv*. [+T] then percolates from *erā* to the node dominating it. Since this node is unmarked for the feature [D], [D] then percolates from the lower node. But once this has happened, the correct P/N suffixes can no longer attach, since they must attach to [+T,(+D)] constituents, and the node immediately dominating *erā* is [+T, −D]. Only the incorrect P/N II suffixes can now attach. So Lieber's (1980) analysis of Latin verb paradigms suggests that diacritic features need not and indeed should not percolate.

Selkirk (1982) suggests that Dell and Selkirk (1978) provides some evidence for the percolation of diacritics. The latter work argues for a diacritic feature [±Learned] which governs the operation of a morphophonological alternation in French. Certain stems which have front vowels in underlying form appear with back vowels when followed by certain affixes. In (8) are several examples of this alternation, which Dell and Selkirk call **Learned Backing** (examples from Dell and Selkirk 1978, 9–11):

(8) [œ] ~ [ɔ]: fleur   'flower'   floral   'floral'
                 seul   'alone'   solitude   'solitude'
                 terreur   'terror'   terroriser 'terrorize'

     [ɛ] ~ [a]:   vain   'vain'   vanité   'vanity'
                   clair   'clear'   clarifier   'clarify'
                   mer   'sea'   marin   'sailor'

Dell and Selkirk also point out that not all roots with underlying vowels [œ] and [ɛ] undergo Learned Backing; roots such as *portrait, duel,* and *écrivain* maintain their underlying vowels, even when followed by suffixes which normally trigger Learning Backing (*portraitiste* 'portrait painter'; *duelliste* 'duelist'; *écrivainisme* 'dabbling in literary work'). In addition, suffixes with low vowels which themselves trigger Learned Backing in turn undergo Learned Backing if they are followed by another suffix which triggers Learned Backing (*africain* 'African' ~ *africaniste; immortel* ~ *immortalité* 'immortality'; *ovaire* 'ovary' ~ *ovarien* 'ovarian'). Dell and Selkirk argue on the basis of this data that morphemes which either trigger or undergo Learned Backing (or both) should be marked with the diacritic [+L] (L for Learned). All other morphemes are marked [−L]. The rule of Learned Backing is then stated as in (9):

(9) Learned Backing (Dell and Selkirk 1978, 16):

$$\begin{bmatrix} +\text{syl} \\ +\text{low} \end{bmatrix} \rightarrow [+\text{back}] \quad \backslash \quad \begin{bmatrix} \text{Y} \underline{\quad} \text{C}_0 \\ +\text{L} \end{bmatrix} \quad \begin{matrix} \text{X} \\ + \ +\text{L} \end{matrix}$$

In other words, low vowels in [+L] morphemes are backed only when followed by another [+L] morpheme.

Dell and Selkirk (1978, 40ff.) also point out that the operation of Learned Backing is strictly local: "A [+L] morpheme will not undergo LB if the [+L] element triggering LB is 'too far away' in the word." They note, for example, that in the example in (10), the suffix *-iste* cannot trigger Learned Backing on the root *clair* ([klɛr]):

(10) $_N[_N[_V[e _A[klɛr]]_V$ až $]_N$ ist $]_N$
$\quad$ +L $-$L $-$L $\quad$ +L $\qquad -$L $\qquad -$L $\qquad$ +L

Since all morphemes in French are designated as either [+L] or [$-$L], and since Learned Backing applies strictly locally (two [+L] morphemes must be adjacent for Learned Backing to apply), there is thus far no evidence for percolation of the diacritic [±L].

In fact, the only cases that provide an argument for percolation of the diacritic are those represented by the data in (11):

(11) sel $\qquad$ 'salt' $\qquad$ saler $\qquad$ 'to salt'
$\quad$ contraire 'opposite' $\quad$ contrarier 'to thwart'
$\quad$ pain $\qquad$ 'bread' $\qquad$ paner $\qquad$ 'to fry in bread crumbs'
$\quad$ majeur $\qquad$ 'major' $\qquad$ majorer $\qquad$ 'to increase'

Dell and Selkirk (1978, 33) point out that the verbs in these pairs appear to be zero-derived from the corresponding nouns or adjectives, and appear to have undergone Learned Backing, although there is no overt suffix involved in the derivation that could have triggered the rule. The infinitive suffix itself could not be a [+L] suffix, for example. There are other zero-derived denominal verbs whose underlying noun roots are otherwise known independently to undergo LB which do not however exhibit the effects of Learned Backing: e.g., *laine* 'wool' ~ *lainer* 'to teasel'; *peuple* 'people' ~ *peupler* 'to populate'. If the infinitive suffix were marked [+L], then we would expect forms like **laner* and **populer,* which in fact do not occur.

Dell and Selkirk (1978) suggest two possible solutions to this problem. One is to postulate a zero suffix which bears the diacritic [+L]; the verbs *saler* and *majorer* would then have the underlying representations in (12):

(12) $[[[sɛl]_{+L} \emptyset]_{+L}$ er$]_{-L}$ $\qquad [[[majœr]_{+L} \emptyset]_{+L}$ er$]_{-L}$

Rule (9) would then apply normally to such forms; under this analysis Learned Backing is still local and requires no percolation.

Dell and Selkirk (1978, 37) suggest an alternative analysis, however. The alternative postulates no zero affix, but instead simply assumes a category-changing rule which adds a set of V brackets marked [+L]; the verb *saler* therefore has the underlying representation in (13):

(13) $[[[sɛl]_N]_V$ er$]$
$\qquad$ +L +L

Learned Backing is then restated to apply to a [+L] morpheme immediately dominated by a [+L] diacritic:

(14) Dell and Selkirk (1978, 37)

$$\begin{bmatrix} +\text{syl} \\ +\text{low} \end{bmatrix} \rightarrow [+\text{back}] / _{+\text{L}}[X _{+\text{L}}[Y \underline{\hspace{1cm}} C_0]_{+\text{L}} Z]_{+\text{L}}$$

Once Learned Backing has been restated as in (14), percolation then appears to be necessary in the cases with overt [+L] suffixes; the verb *salifier*
would have to have the [+L] diacritic percolated up to the node dominating
the suffix -*ifi* as in (15) in order for Learned Backing (14) to apply correctly.

(15)

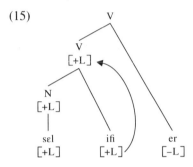

    The argument for percolation of diacritics in French thus hinges on the
analysis of so-called zero-derived verbs; it is indeed sound only if the
category-changing rule deriving verbs such as *saler* is correct. However,
there is good reason to believe that the category-changing rule is not the
optimal way to derive such forms.
    The category-changing analysis shares with the zero affixation analysis
a problem that was pointed out in Lieber (1980, 1982).[4] Lieber argues that
many proposed cases of zero affixation turn out not to be like affixation at
all. Proposed zero affixes frequently do not act like overt derivational
affixes in the sense that they do not add a consistent set of features to the
word as a whole. For example, zero affixes almost never place derived
nouns into a single declension class or gender, or derived verbs into a
single conjugation class, as overt derivational affixes do.[5] Indeed, if verbs
like *saler* and *lainer* are to be derived by zero affixes, we would have to
postulate **two** zero affixes, one which bears the feature [+L] to derive *saler*
from *sel,* and another which bears the feature [−L] to derive verbs like
lainer from *laine.* A zero affixation analysis thus requires the proliferation
of phonologically null affixes. And the same argument can be made against
the category-changing analysis that Dell and Selkirk propose; for that
analysis we would also need two category-changing rules for deriving

verbs from nouns—one which adds the diacritic [+L] along with the V brackets to form verbs like *saler,* and one which adds [−L] to form verbs like *lainer.* Again, the category-changing analysis can only be maintained at some cost to the grammar.

The alternative suggested in Lieber (1980, 1982) is simply to list stems such as *sel* and *sal* individually, *sel* as a [+L] noun root, and *sal* as a verb root. The two stems would be related by a redundancy rule. One reason to consider the listing analysis as plausible for this particular set of French data is that there are few stems which would have to be listed. Dell and Selkirk do not state explicitly whether their list of verbs like *saler* is exhaustive; still, earlier in the article (1978, 17), they do state clearly that there are a limited number of [+L] roots, and that new morphemes are invariably added as [−L] forms (1978, 20–21). It seems clear then that fairly few pairs of stems like *sel* and *sal* would have to be listed.

If verbs like *saler* are not derived by a category-changing rule, then Learned Backing may be stated as (9) rather than (14). And if Learned Backing is stated as (9), then the diacritic [±L] need never percolate. We can thus rule out the percolation of diacritics.

Another possible example of percolation of diacritics comes from prefixed verbs in German. Toman (1987, 9) suggests that certain verbs in German may need to bear the diacritic [+Strong] and that this diacritic may need to percolate. German, like English, has verbs whose past and participial stems are formed by vocalic ablaut, the so-called "strong" verbs—e.g., *schreiben* 'write' ~ *schrieb* 'wrote'. When other verbs are formed from these strong verbs by prefixation, the derived verbs are strong as well: *beschreiben* 'describe' ~ *beschrieb* 'described'. Toman suggests that in verbs like *beschreiben* a diacritic [+Strong] percolates as indicated in (16). However, he actually offers no motivation for percolating the diacritic. That is, the diacritic [+Strong] would only need to percolate if some affix attached after the prefix attaches only to [+Strong] or [−Strong] forms. For example, the diacritic [+Strong] would have to percolate if a special set of P/N suffixes were to attach to all Strong verbs:[6]

(16)

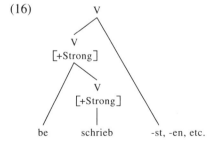

The argument here would be that the P/N endings would need to sub-categorize for [+Strong] verbs and that affixation of P/N suffixes must follow attachment of the prefixes, since derivation is usually thought to precede inflection.

Still, such an analysis appears not to be necessary. Both strong and weak verbs in German in fact appear to take the same set of P/N endings, if we assume as Wurzel (1970) does, that schwas (orthographic e) are inserted by rule in German. In fact, such an analysis is worked out in Lieber (1980, 192). In that analysis the P/N endings for both strong and weak verbs have lexical entries as in (17):

(17) Sg. 1   -e   /   ]$_V$ ——
                          [-Past]
        2   -st   /   ]$_V$ ——
        3   -t   /   ]$_V$ ——
                          [-Past]
   Pl. 1   -en ⎫
        2   -t   ⎬   /   ]$_V$ ——
        3   -en ⎭

Stems like *schrieb*, as well as the regular (weak) past tense morpheme *-te* bear the morphosyntactic feature [+Past]. Since [+Past] is a bona fide morphosyntactic feature, it will percolate to the top of the tree in *beschrieb*, and the P/N endings will then attach correctly. The diacritic [+Strong] in fact appears to play no role in German.

In the morphological analyses using diacritics that I know of, there seems to be no evidence then that diacritic features must be allowed to percolate. In other words, I know of no reason to reject the restriction forbidding percolation of diacritics.

3.2.2 Argument Structures

Another class of lexical information that has sometimes been assumed to be subject to percolation is the Theta-grid or argument structure of a morpheme. For example, in Lieber (1983a, 258) it is asserted that argument structures percolate: "Included in the properties which the compound as a whole adopts from the second stem is the argument structure of that stem, if it has one." It is clear that the argument structure of a compound like *handweave* (V) is in some way a function of the argument structure of its head, just as the category of *handweave* is dependent upon the category of its head. Others who have suggested that argument structures are suscep-tible to percolation are Roeper (1987), Hoekstra (1986), Haegeman and van Riemsdijk (1986), and Pollock (1989). Toman (1983) also assumes that argument structures percolate, although in a later work (Toman 1987) he begins to question whether what he calls inheritance of argument structure is really the same process as percolation of morphosyntactic features. As I will try to show below, Toman has good reason to want to distinguish the two phenomena.

There are several reasons to suspect that the passing of argument structures from one node to another (what I will henceforth, following Toman and others, call **inheritance**) is not the same as the passing of morphosyntactic features (**percolation**) from one node to another. First, it is not at all clear that argument structures, which are often represented as arrays of Theta-roles, as in (18) (following Williams 1981b) (or as predicate argument structures, as in the lexical entries in chapter 1), can be factored into binary features:

(18) argument structure for *put* (**agent,** theme, location)

  devour (**agent,** theme)

Toman (1987, 8) considers it possible to factor argument structures into features, without, however, suggesting a feature system. Marantz (1984) in fact begins to develop such a system, but his system is not without problems.

Marantz (1984) assumes at the outset the feature percolation conventions of Lieber (1980), although he proposes a more explicit treatment of argument structure within that framework. Specifically, he proposes that argument structure is encoded in features like [±Transitive] and [±Logical Subject], and that these features percolate just as any other features do. However, he also discusses a particular affixation process in Kinyarwanda (1984, 240–241) which suggests that argument structure features are **not** like other features. The particular affixation process in question adds one place to the argument structure of a verb, regardless of how many arguments the verb takes to begin with. Marantz argues on the basis of this data that the feature [Transitive] is not binary valued, but rather is multi-valued, so that an intransitive verb bears the feature [0 Transitive], a verb with one object [+1 Transitive], and so on. The abovementioned affixation process in Kinyarwanda then makes a [0 Transitive] verb [+1 Transitive], a [+1 Transitive] verb [+2 Transitive], etc. Immediately, then, it appears that argument structure features are different from morphosyntactic features in having the possibility of being multivalued rather than binary valued.[7]

The Kinyarwanda example also points to another difference between the inheritance of argument structures and the percolation of features. As the examples in (2) and (3) suggest, morphosyntactic features of the head typically have priority over morphosyntactic features of nonheads; nonhead features are in fact blocked from percolating unless the head is unmarked for the feature in question. Not so with inheritance of argument structures. As the Kinyarwanda example indicates, the head—that is, the suffix that is attached—adds a value to the features of the nonhead—that is, the verb stem. These nonhead features are not blocked, but rather are acted upon (i.e., added to or subtracted from). Indeed it seems from recent research (Roeper 1987, Toman 1987, among others) that the argument structure of the head often acts as an operator on the argument structure of the nonhead. The adjective-forming suffix *-able* in English, for example, makes an internal argument of the nonhead into the external argument (*she washed the socks* ~ *the socks are washable*). We will return to this subject in section 3.7.

Similarly, although morphosyntactic features, as we will see in the next section, cannot be permitted to percolate cross-categorially, (that is, there is no reason to believe that nouns derived from verbs, for example, are marked for verbal features like tense and aspect), argument structure typically **does** cross categorial lines. For example, since the argument structure of a nominalization like *destruction* is clearly related to the argument structure of the verb *destroy* from which it is derived, we have every reason to believe that the argument structure of *destroy* is inherited and subsequently acted upon by the nominalizing suffix *-tion*. Again, where morphosyntactic features are blocked from percolating, argument structures are freely inherited. I therefore assume that the mechanisms of feature percolation are not the mechanisms of inheritance. In section 3.7 we will return to a consideration of what inheritance is.

3.2.3 The Categorial Signature

What we are left with once we eliminate diacritic features and argument structures from the domain of percolation are morphosyntactic features, that is, those features that mark agreement across categories, possible sequences of clauses, and the like. Clearly, morphosyntactic features must be allowed to percolate. In this section, I argue that morphosyntactic features do not percolate in a random fashion. Rather percolation takes place within a frame that I call the **categorial signature.**[8] I will develop the notion of a categorial signature below, and then argue that the idea of a categorial signature has been implicit in treatments of feature percolation all along.

The categorial signature is a frame of morphosyntactic features headed by the category features $[\pm N]$, $[\pm V]$ that are of syntactic relevance for a particular category in a particular language. Categorial signatures for a given category may differ from one language to the next, depending upon which morphosyntactic features are active in that language. For example, the categorial signature for N in English will contain the features [+Plural], [±I], [±II], as illustrated in (19), where the latter two are person features (i.e., [+I,−II] = first person, [−I,+II] = second person, [−I,−II] = third person). The same category in German will contain in addition gender and case features. Gender may be encoded in two features [±Fem] and [±Masc] ([+Fem,−Masc] = feminine, [−Fem,+Masc] = masuline, [−Fem,−Masc] = neuter), as shown in (20). How to represent the four cases in German in terms of features is somewhat less clear. For present purposes it is enough to suppose that some set of two or more binary features can be found to represent the four cases. Here I will schematically represent them as [±Case$_i$], [±Case$_j$]. Nothing in what follows hinges on the exact names of these features. In a language like Mandarin Chinese which has no agreement between nouns and verbs or adjectives for person, number, or gender, the categorial signature for N will perhaps contain only the category features, as in (21):

(19) Categorial signature for nouns in English

$$\begin{bmatrix} \text{N} \\ \pm\text{Plural} \\ \pm\text{I} \\ \pm\text{II} \end{bmatrix}$$

(20) Categorial signature for nouns in German

$$\begin{bmatrix} \text{N} \\ \pm\text{Plural} \\ \pm\text{Case}_i \\ \pm\text{Case}_j \\ \pm\text{Fem} \\ \pm\text{Masc} \\ \pm\text{I} \\ \pm\text{II} \end{bmatrix}$$

(21) Categorial signature for nouns in Chinese
[N]

The categorial signatures for several particular nouns in these three languages are illustrated in (22):

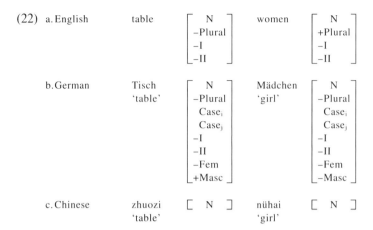

(22) a. English   table

$$\begin{bmatrix} N \\ -\text{Plural} \\ -\text{I} \\ -\text{II} \end{bmatrix}$$

women

$$\begin{bmatrix} N \\ +\text{Plural} \\ -\text{I} \\ -\text{II} \end{bmatrix}$$

   b. German   Tisch 'table'

$$\begin{bmatrix} N \\ -\text{Plural} \\ \text{Case}_i \\ \text{Case}_j \\ -\text{I} \\ -\text{II} \\ -\text{Fem} \\ +\text{Masc} \end{bmatrix}$$

Mädchen 'girl'

$$\begin{bmatrix} N \\ -\text{Plural} \\ \text{Case}_i \\ \text{Case}_j \\ -\text{I} \\ -\text{II} \\ -\text{Fem} \\ -\text{Masc} \end{bmatrix}$$

   c. Chinese   zhuozi 'table' $\begin{bmatrix} N \end{bmatrix}$ nühai 'girl' $\begin{bmatrix} N \end{bmatrix}$

I am proposing then that the categorial signature contains only **morphosyntactic** features. Presumably individual lexical nouns, verbs, adjectives, etc., also have semantic representations, and semantic representations in turn contain semantic features such as [±Animate], [±Concrete], and so on, that is, features that are relevant for selectional restrictions and the like.[9] The feature [±Fem] might therefore be part of the semantic representation or Lexical Conceptual Structure of nouns like *women* in English or *nühai* 'girl' in Chinese, but it will not be part of the categorial signature in those languages.

Although none of the works cited in (1) explicitly claims the existence of the categorial signature, it appears that the notion of categorial signature has been implicit in most treatments of feature percolation to date. Consider the word schematized in (23):

(23) a.

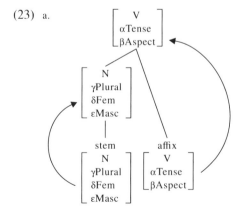

b.

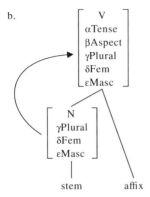

The structure in (23a) illustrates percolation from the head. If the affix in this schematic word is the head, then the word as a whole will adopt the category and other morphosyntactic features of the head. Now if we assume that each category in each language is characterized by a categorial signature, and that the categorial signature for N in this hypothetical language contains the features [γPlural, δFem, εMasc], the categorial signature for V the features [αTense, βAspect], then percolation will cease in the example in (23a). But if we do not assume categorial signatures to be a real part of the representation of categories, and if we allow percolation from the nonhead in case the head is unmarked for some features, as is assumed in Lieber (1980), Selkirk (1982), and DiSciullo and Williams (1987), then nothing will prevent the percolation of features that has occurred in (23b). We will produce a verb marked for the number and gender of its nominal base. Since denominal verbs do not ever in fact seem to be marked for the number and gender of their base (although they may be marked to agree with the number and gender of their subject and/or object in some languages), (23b) represents what must be an inadmissible sort of percolation. That is, in a theory without the notion of categorial signature, either explicit or implicit, nothing will prevent the percolation of morphosyntactic features marking one category to another category. Since in practice no theory of percolation that I am aware of has claimed the cross-categorial percolation of morphosyntactic features, I will assume that the notion of a categorial signature has been implicit all along. Here I merely propose to make this notion explicit.

3.3 Head and Backup Percolation

Each category in each language will possess a frame listing the morphosyntactic features which are relevant to that category in that language. Items

belonging to a particular category may be unmarked for certain features
(e.g., the Russian diminutive morpheme *-ushka* for gender); those items
will lack a value for those features in their lexical representations, but they
will not lack the feature itself. The categorial signature will regulate the
operation of percolation, preventing features of one category from passing
across categorial lines. Only two feature percolation conventions will now
be necessary in our theory: [10]

(24) a. Head Percolation
    Morphosyntactic features are passed from a head morpheme to
    the node dominating the head. Head Percolation propagates
    the categorial signature. [11]

   b. Backup Percolation
    If the node dominating the head remains unmarked for a given
    feature after Head Percolation, then a value for that feature is
    percolated from an immediately dominated nonhead branch
    marked for that feature. Backup Percolation propagates only
    values for unmarked features and is strictly local.

Head Percolation actually causes the transfer of a categorial signature from
a head morpheme to the node dominating it. Backup Percolation fills in
values of features that are left unmarked after Head Percolation. The Russian diminutive noun *babushka* 'grandmother-DIMIN.' will, for example,
be derived as in (25):

(25) a. Head Percolation

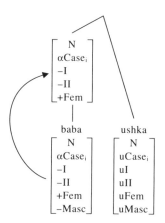

b. Head Percolation   c. Backup Percolation

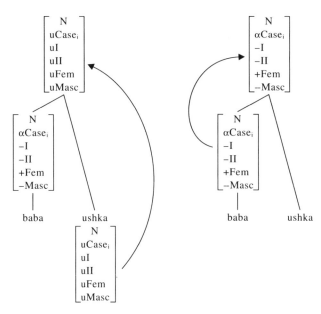

It can be seen from the percolation in (25a) and (25b) that Head Percolation will pass the categorial signature from the diminutive morpheme to the dominating node. Then, since all of these features are unmarked, the values for these features are passed up from the nonhead morpheme by Backup Percolation.

It is relatively clear how percolation will work in languages like English, German, French, and Russian, languages whose categories manifest a fairly straightforward array of morphosyntactic features for number, gender, person, tense, and so on. As I will try to show below, however, significant questions still arise in trying to work out the mechanics of feature percolation in languages with highly complex morphology.

3.4 Multiply Marked Features

It is typical in languages for complex words to allow only one marking for each feature. For example, each noun in German can have only one gender, so that in the word below the gender marking of the diminutive suffix (which is head) overrides the gender marking on the noun stem:

(26)

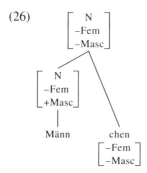

Still, it is not always true that only a single marking for each feature is possible. There are languages in which a single noun may bear more than one case-marking affix, and therefore more than one set of case features, or in which a verb may be marked more than once for person and number. In this section we will consider the operation of feature percolation in languages which allow such multiple markings.[12]

Consider first the case of Kayardild, an Australian language spoken in the south Wellesley Islands, as reported in Evans (1985) and Dench and Evans (1988). Kayardild allows nouns to be marked with as many as four distinct case markers. According to Evans (1985, 61–62), case markers may have one of five different functions:

> The **Adnominal** function, typified by the GENitive of possession, relates one NP to another. The **Relational** function either relates core arguments to the verb (e.g., nominative on subjects) or peripheral arguments like location, destination, etc., to the clause as a whole. **Modal** case indicates the tense/mood of the clause. **Associating** case links NPs with nominalized verbs. **Complementizing** case applies to whole clauses, and indicates either that they are an argument of the matrix clause, or that certain marked coreference relationships exist between matrix and subordinate clause.

A particular noun like *dangka* in (27) may be marked for its own function within an NP (Adnominal case, GEN), for the function of the larger NP of which it is a part (Relational case, INSTR), for the predicate in which it occurs (Modal case, MABL), and for the evidentiality of the entire clause that it belongs to (Complementizer case, COBL—used here to indicate that the entire clause in (27) is an inference):[13]

(27) (from Evans 1985, 74):

maku-ntha   yalawu-jarra-ntha yakuri-naa-ntha
woman-COBL catch-PAST-COBL fish-MABL-COBL

dangka-karra-nguni-naa-ntha mijil-nguni-naa-nth
man-GEN-INSTR-MABL-COBL net-INSTR-MABL-COBL
'The woman must have caught the fish with the man's net.'

As (27) indicates, case markers are ordered with those having the smallest scope preceding those whose scope is a larger constituent.

Evans (1985) takes some pains to show that although these case markings may have rather divergent functions, they are indeed still the same case markers. According to Evans (1985, 75), case marking suffixes, "have the same form, and range of allomorphy, regardless of their function, except for variations resulting from exposed vs. internal position, which are clearly derivative." He argues that the only other alternative—postulating five distinct sets of homophonous case affixes—is implausible. Under this view it would be purely accidental that each case should show the same forms with the same allomorphy across all five functions. However, if all five functions make use of the same case morphemes, with a single noun being capable of bearing up to four separate markings, we must make provision in our theory for case features to be marked up to four times without overriding each other.

The same conclusion can be reached by a consideration of a language which allows multiple markings for person on verbs.[14] Such a language is Yavapai, a Yuman language spoken in central Arizona. Yavapai verbs are marked for person of both subject and object, as the data in (28), taken from Kendall (1976) illustrate. In (29) are rough glosses for each morpheme.

(28) ʔ-ta:v-km   'I hit him.'
     m-ta:v-km   'You hit him.' *or* 'He hit you'
     ʔñ-m-ta:v-km   'You hit me.'
     ñ-ta:v-km   'I hit you.' *or* 'He hit me'

(29) ʔ-   first person subject, except when object is second person
     m-   second person subject or object, except when subject is first person
     ʔñ-   first person object with second person subject
     ñ-   first person subject with second person object, or first person object with third person subject
     ta:v   hit
     -km   incompletive
     (note that third person is unmarked in Yavapai)

How should person features be represented for Yavapai, and how should they be distributed among the prefixes in (28)? One possibility, of course, would be to assign entirely different morphosyntactic features for subject and object person, as in (30):

$$
\begin{array}{lll}
(30) \;\; \text{1st person subject} & \begin{bmatrix} +\text{ISubject} \\ -\text{IISubject} \end{bmatrix} & \text{1st person object} \;\; \begin{bmatrix} +\text{IObject} \\ -\text{IIObject} \end{bmatrix} \\[3ex]
 \;\; \text{2nd person subject} & \begin{bmatrix} -\text{ISubject} \\ +\text{IISubject} \end{bmatrix} & \text{2nd person object} \;\; \begin{bmatrix} -\text{IObject} \\ +\text{IIObject} \end{bmatrix} \\[3ex]
 \;\; \text{3rd person subject} & \begin{bmatrix} -\text{ISubject} \\ -\text{IISubject} \end{bmatrix} & \text{3rd person object} \;\; \begin{bmatrix} -\text{IObject} \\ -\text{IIObject} \end{bmatrix}
\end{array}
$$

But there is good reason to believe that (30) is not the right way to represent subject and object person features. Two of the person morphemes, specifically *m-* and *ñ-,* appear to carry the same features for subject and object. With the system of features in (30), there is no way to express the generalization that first or second person is often marked in the same way, whether it is the subject or the object that is of concern. Again, it appears to be an accidental fact for a theory which uses the features in (30), that a single form like *m-* or *ñ-* should bear the same person marking for either subject or object. Moreover, as Anderson (1982, 597) pointed out, this situation is not unusual in languages which mark the person and number of both subject and object; there are other languages, like Potawatomi, in which a single form can carry the same features for either subject or object. The generalization can be captured only if the P/N features are the same features for subject and object.

Anderson (1982) suggests that rather than proliferating features as we did in (30), P/N features for subject and object be the same features; subject features will be distinguished from object features only by their position within a layered structure. Anderson (1982, 598, quoting from Anderson 1977, 21 f.) states the layering convention within his own framework as follows:

When a rule of grammar assigns features to [a morphosyntactic representation], and that [representation] already carries specifications for those features, then (unless, of course, the rule is explicitly stated so as to **change** the features involved, rather than simply to add to them), the result is not that the new features and the old merge within the same complex, but rather that a new layer of structure is created, taking the old feature complex as its base.

The framework that I am developing here differs from Anderson's in that it does not have rules to create layered structures. Rather I propose that the layered structure must be part of the categorial signature, and that it will be filled in by percolation. Each language will have to set the number of layers possible for each morphosyntactic feature, depending on how many times a particular feature can be marked on a lexical item in that language.[15] For Yavapai, there will be two layers to the P/N complex.[16] We will see below that the inner layer will contain subject features and the outer layer object features.[17]

(31) $\begin{bmatrix} \pm\text{I} & \begin{bmatrix} \pm\text{I} \\ \pm\text{II} \\ \pm\text{Pl} \end{bmatrix} \\ \pm\text{II} \\ \pm\text{Pl} \end{bmatrix}$

Nouns in Kayardild will have as part of their categorial signatures a structure with four layers for case features. Again, I use a schematic representation here, since nothing hinges on the particular choice of features.[18]

(32) $\begin{bmatrix} \pm\text{Case}_i & \begin{bmatrix} \pm\text{Case}_i & \begin{bmatrix} \pm\text{Case}_i & \begin{bmatrix} \pm\text{Case}_i \\ \pm\text{Case}_j \\ \pm\text{Case}_k \\ \pm\text{Case}_l \end{bmatrix} \end{bmatrix} \end{bmatrix} \\ \pm\text{Case}_j \\ \pm\text{Case}_k \\ \pm\text{Case}_l \end{bmatrix}$

We must now consider how feature percolation fills in the layers in these nested structures. We will use the derivation of the Yavapai verb form *ʔñ-m-taːv-km* 'You hit me' to illustrate the mechanics of percolation in layered structures. The first question that arises is what features each of the individual morphemes carries. The stem *taːv* will contain a complete categorial signature, including category features and all of the other morphosyntactic features for which verbs in Yavapai can be inflected. (Here we will list only the features I, II, Plural, and Compl (completive) that figure in the derivation of this form. See Lieber 1989 for a discussion of the other features.)

(33) taːv

$$\begin{bmatrix} & \text{V} & \\ \begin{bmatrix} \text{I} & \begin{bmatrix} \text{I} \\ \text{II} \\ \text{Pl} \end{bmatrix} \\ \text{II} \\ \text{Pl} \end{bmatrix} \\ & \text{Compl} & \end{bmatrix}$$

The categorial signature of this verb stem will contain the nested structure, but since verb stems are inherently unspecified for person or number, the layers will not contain values for these features. The representation of the prefix *m-* is somewhat less straightforward, however. Suppose the inflectional prefix *m-* were listed in its lexical entry with the entire categorial signature for verbs. Clearly, *m-* must bear the feature [+II] somewhere, since it signals second person. But if *m-* has a complete categorial signature, the [+II] value must be located in either one layer or the other:

(34) a.
$$\begin{bmatrix} V \\ \begin{bmatrix} I \\ II \\ Pl \end{bmatrix} \begin{bmatrix} I \\ +II \\ Pl \end{bmatrix} \\ Compl \end{bmatrix}$$
b.
$$\begin{bmatrix} V \\ \begin{bmatrix} I \\ +II \\ Pl \end{bmatrix} \begin{bmatrix} I \\ II \\ Pl \end{bmatrix} \\ Compl \end{bmatrix}$$

The problem with the representations in (34) is that neither one alone is sufficient. As we saw before, *m-* carries the second person feature sometimes for subject and sometimes for object. Representation (34a), however, says that *m-* carries the [+II] feature only in its (inner) subject layer, and (34b) that *m-* carries [+II] only in its (outer) object layer. In other words, if *m-* carries the whole categorial signature it is still not possible to state the generalization that needs to be stated—that *m-* is second person regardless of whether it marks subject or object. The alternative to investing the lexical entry of *m-* with the full categorial signature is to say that it is simply marked in the lexicon with the feature [+II], but that it does not itself possess a categorial signature. The affix *ʔñ-* will similarly bear only the feature [+I], and *-km* the feature [−Compl].[19] We can now begin to see how feature percolation must work:[20]

(35) a.

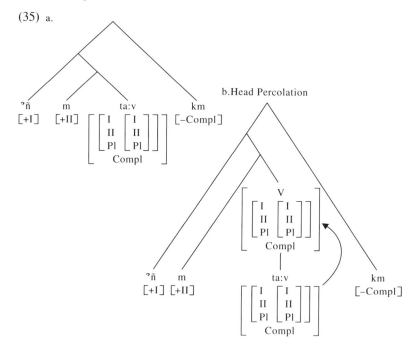

c. Head Percolation
   Backup Percolation

d. Head Percolation
   Backup Percolation

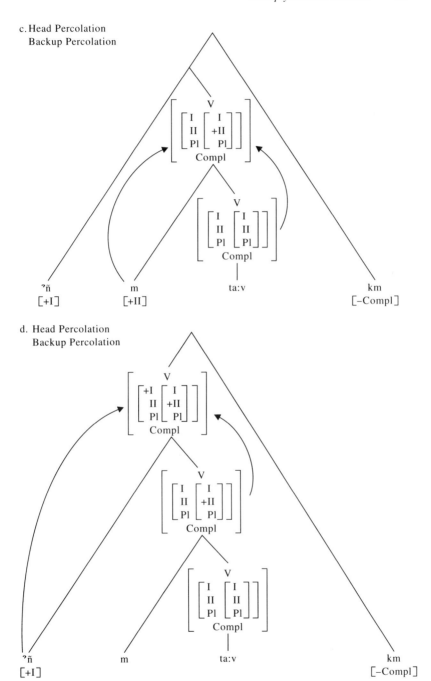

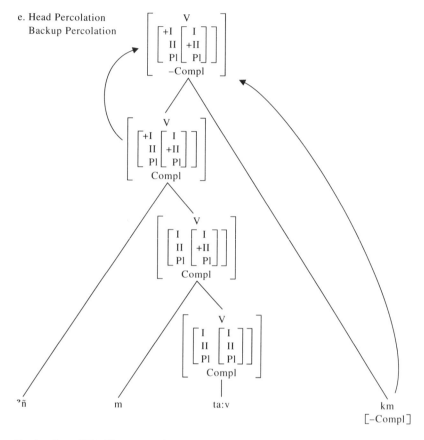

Derivation (35) illustrates the operation of percolation. The underlying representation before percolation is shown in (35a). In (35b,c) the categorial signature of *ta:v* has been percolated first to the node immediately dominating *ta:v,* and then to the node dominating that, since *m-* has no categorial signature of its own to contribute. Backup Percolation then fills in the inner layer of the nested structure with the [+II] value of *m-* (also in (35c)). Head Percolation again raises the categorial signature to the node dominating *ʔñ-,* and Backup Percolation passes the [+I] feature from *ʔñ-* to the outer P/N layer (35d). Note that Backup Percolation could not place the [+I] feature from *ʔñ-* into the inner layer; since this layer already contains the feature [+II], adding [+I] would result in a combination of features [+I, +II] that is inadmissible in Yavapai. Finally, Head Percolation once again raises the categorial signature to the node dominating the suffix *-km,* and Backup Percolation fills in the [−Compl] feature from the suffix

(35e). At this point I will assume that default (negative) values of the remaining unspecified features are filled in, giving the final representation in (36):

(36)

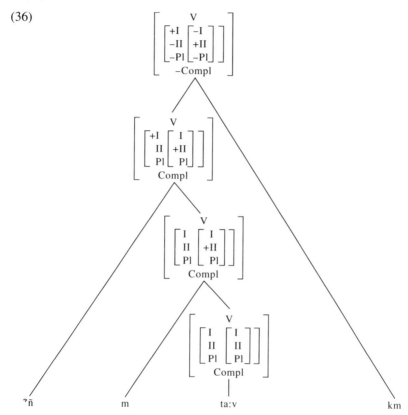

Layered structures are filled in then from inside to outside. Additional values for a multiply marked feature are not overridden as long as there are unmarked slots in the nested structure to be filled in.

3.5 A Case Study: P/N Marking in Vogul

We have thus far reached several conclusions about feature percolation: (i) only morphosyntactic features, not diacritics or argument structures, percolate; (ii) all percolation is regulated by the categorial signature; (iii) features are percolated by two conventions, Head and Backup Percolation; (iv) categorial signatures may contain layered structures which allow multiple marking for certain morphosyntactic features; and (v) one feature does not override another as long as there are slots left unspecified in the layered structure for that feature. There are a number of ramifications that follow from the proposals that I have made above, but before I attempt to draw them out, I will pause for a moment to show how the systems of feature percolation developed here can lead to a simple and elegant analysis of a rather complex body of data. I will examine here the verbal paradigms of Vogul, a Uralic language which marks the number of both subject and object on the verb. My sources for Vogul are Kálmán (1965, 1984), Collinder (1957), and Liimola (1968).[21]

Kálmán (1965) discusses the northern dialects of Vogul which, according to Liimola (1968), preserve the greatest number of paradigm distinctions. In (37) are given the Vogul paradigms for the verb *tot-* 'to bring' (Kálmán 1965, 49–52; division into morphemes my own):

(37) Indefinite (Subjective) Conjugation

Active, Indicative

		Singular	Dual	Plural
Present	1.	tot-ēγ-^{u}m	tot-i-men	tot-ew
	2.	tot-ēγ-ən	tot-ēγ-ən	tot-ēγ-ən
	3.	tot-i	tot-ēγ	tot-ēγ-ət
Preterite	1.	tot-s-^{u}m	tot-s-^{u}men	tot-s-uw
	2.	tot-s-ən	tot-s-ən	tot-s-ən
	3.	tot-(ə)s	tot-s-iγ	tot-s-ət
Conditional	1.	tot-nuw-^{u}m	tot-nuw-amen	tot-nuw-uw
	2.	tot-nuw-ən	tot-nuw-ən	tot-nuw-ən
	3.	tot-nuw	tot-nuw-iγ	tot-nuw-ət

Definite (Subjective) Conjugation

Present

		Singular Object	Dual Object	Plural Object
Subject				
Singular	1.	tot-i-l-^{u}m	tot-ij-aγ-^{u}m	tot-ij-an-^{u}m
	2.	tot-i-l-ən	tot-ij-aγ-ən	tot-ij-an-ən
	3.	tot-i-t-e	tot-ij-aγ-e	tot-ij-an-e
Dual	1.	tot-i-l-^{u}men	tot-ij-aγ-men	tot-ij-an-amen
	2.	tot-i-l-ən	tot-ij-aγ-ən	tot-ij-an-ən
	3.	tot-i-t-en	tot-ij-aγ-en	tot-ij-an-en

Plural	1. tot-i-l-uw	tot-ij-aɣ-uw	tot-ij-an-uw
	2. tot-i-l-ən	tot-ij-aɣ-ən	tot-ij-an-ən
	3. tot-ij- -anəl	tot-ij-aɣ-anəl	tot-ij- -anəl

Preterite

	Singular Object	Dual Object	Plural Object
Subject			
Singular	1. tot-əs-l-^{u}m	tot-s-aɣ-^{u}m	tot-s-an-^{u}m
	2. tot-əs-l-ən	tot-s-aɣ-ən	tot-s-an-ən
	3. tot-əs-t-e	tot-s-aɣ-e	tot-s-an-e
Dual	1. tot-əs-l-amen	tot-s-aɣ-men	tot-s-an-amen
	2. tot-əs-l-ən	tot-s-aɣ-ən	tot-s-an-ən
	3. tot-əs-t-en	tot-s-aɣ-en	tot-s-an-en
Plural	1. tot-əs-l-uw	tot-s-aɣ-uw	tot-s-an-uw
	2. tot-əs-l-ən	tot-s-aɣ-ən	tot-s-an-ən
	3. tot-s- -anəl	tot-s-aɣ-anəl	tot-s- -anəl

Conditional

	Singular Object	Dual Object	Plural Object
Subject			
Singular	1. tot-nuw-l-^{u}m	tot-nuw-aɣ-^{u}m	tot-nuw-an-^{u}m
	2. tot-nuw-l-ən	tot-nuw-aɣ-ən	tot-nuw-an-ən
	3. tot-nuw-t-e	tot-nuw-aɣ-e	tot-nuw-an-e
Dual	1. tot-nuw-l-amen	tot-nuw-aɣ-men	tot-nuw-an-men
	2. tot-nuw-l-ən	tot-nuw-aɣ-ən	tot-nuw-an-ən
	3. tot-nuw-t-en	tot-nuw-aɣ-en	tot-nuw-an-en
Plural	1. tot-nuw-l-uw	tot-nuw-aɣ-uw	tot-nuw-an-uw
	2. tot-nuw-l-ən	tot-nuw-aɣ-ən	tot-nuw-an-ən
	3. tot-nuw- -anəl	tot-nuw-aɣ-anəl	tot-nuw- -anəl

Vogul verbs can occur in two different sorts of conjugations: the Indefinite (subjective) conjugation, and the Definite (objective) conjugation. The latter is used when the object is "defined," which is, "1. when it is preceded by a demonstrative pronoun . . . 2. when it has a possessive suffix . . . 3. when the object is a personal pronoun . . . 4. when it is already known or has been previously mentioned . . . 5. when the object is in a subordinate clause" (Kálmán 1965, 53). The Indefinite conjugation is used elsewhere.[22]

Vogul verb stems will carry the categorial signature in (38), with two layers available for number marking. The outermost marked layer will always be the subject layer in Vogul.

$$(38) \quad \begin{bmatrix} \pm I \\ \pm II \\ \begin{bmatrix} \pm Pl \\ \pm Du \end{bmatrix} \begin{bmatrix} \pm Pl \\ \pm Du \end{bmatrix} \\ \pm Def \\ \pm Pres \\ \pm Pret \end{bmatrix}$$

The features will be interpreted as follows. Singular arguments will be $[-Pl, -Du]$, dual will be $[+Pl, +Du]$, and plural $[+Pl, -Du]$. All verbs in the Definite conjugations will receive the feature $[+Def]$. I assume that this is a morphosyntactic feature which signals that in the syntax one of the five conditions mentioned above must be met. Present tense verbs will bear the features $[+Pres, -Pret]$, preterite verbs will be $[-Pres, +Pret]$, and conditional verbs $[-Pres, -Pret]$.

I will assume that some features which are predictable need not be specified underlyingly, but may be filled in by redundancy rules. For example, if a morpheme is $[+Du]$, it is predictably $[+Pl]$ as well. If it is $[-Pl]$, it is predictably $[-Du]$. Values not filled in at the end of a derivation will be supplied by a redundancy rule, or if no redundancy rule applies, by default. Generally the default value of a feature is the negative value. This is not to say, however, that negative values for morphosyntactic features are never present underlyingly. As can be seen below, the conditional suffix *-nuw* and several other morphemes must have negative values specified in their lexical entries.

The suffixes that make up the verbal paradigms of Vogul will have the lexical entries in (39):

(39) a. Tense/Aspect

-i	$[+Pres]$	/	$]_V \underline{\qquad}]$
-s	$[+Pret]$	/	$]_V \underline{\qquad}]$
-nuw	$\begin{bmatrix} -Pres \\ -Pret \end{bmatrix}$	/	$]_V \underline{\qquad}]$

b. Object Number

-l	$\begin{bmatrix} -Pl \\ +Def \end{bmatrix}$	/	$\begin{bmatrix} \alpha Pres \\ \beta Pret \end{bmatrix}]_V \underline{\qquad}]$

-aɣ $\begin{bmatrix} +\text{Du} \\ +\text{Def} \end{bmatrix}$ / $\begin{bmatrix} \alpha\text{Pres} \\ \beta\text{Pret} \end{bmatrix} \Big]_V \underline{\quad}\Big]$

-an $\begin{bmatrix} +\text{Pl} \\ -\text{Du} \\ +\text{Def} \end{bmatrix}$ / $\begin{bmatrix} \alpha\text{Pres} \\ \beta\text{Pret} \end{bmatrix} \Big]_V \underline{\quad}\Big]$

c. Subject P/N

-m $\begin{bmatrix} +\text{I} \\ -\text{Pl} \end{bmatrix}$ / $\begin{bmatrix} \alpha\text{Pres} \\ \beta\text{Pret} \end{bmatrix} \Big]_V \underline{\quad}\Big]$ #

-men $\begin{bmatrix} +\text{I} \\ +\text{Du} \end{bmatrix}$ / $\begin{bmatrix} \alpha\text{Pres} \\ \beta\text{Pret} \end{bmatrix} \Big]_V \underline{\quad}\Big]$ #

-uw $\left.\begin{array}{l} \begin{bmatrix} +\text{I} \\ +\text{Pl} \\ -\text{Du} \end{bmatrix} \\ \begin{bmatrix} +\text{II} \\ -\text{Pl} \end{bmatrix} \\ \begin{bmatrix} +\text{II} \\ +\text{Du} \end{bmatrix} \end{array}\right\}$ / $\begin{bmatrix} \alpha\text{Pres} \\ \beta\text{Pret} \end{bmatrix} \Big]_V \underline{\quad}\Big]$ #

-n $\begin{bmatrix} +\text{II} \\ +\text{Pl} \\ -\text{Du} \end{bmatrix}$ / $\begin{bmatrix} \alpha\text{Pres} \\ \beta\text{Pret} \end{bmatrix} \Big]_V \underline{\quad}\Big]$ #

-įɣ $\begin{bmatrix} +\text{Du} \\ -\text{Def} \end{bmatrix}$ / $\begin{bmatrix} \alpha\text{Pres} \\ \beta\text{Pret} \end{bmatrix} \Big]_V \underline{\quad}\Big]$ #

-t $\begin{bmatrix} +\text{Pl} \\ -\text{Du} \\ -\text{Def} \end{bmatrix}$ / $\begin{bmatrix} \alpha\text{Pres} \\ \beta\text{Pret} \end{bmatrix} \Big]_V \underline{\quad}\Big]$ #

-te [23] $\begin{bmatrix} -\text{Pl} \\ +\text{Poss} \end{bmatrix}$ / [+Def]]$_V$ \underline{\quad}] #

-ten $\begin{bmatrix} +\text{Du} \\ +\text{Poss} \end{bmatrix}$ / [+Def]]$_V$ \underline{\quad}] #

-anəl $\begin{bmatrix} +\text{Pl} \\ -\text{Du} \\ +\text{Poss} \end{bmatrix}$ / [+Def]]$_V$ \underline{\quad}] #

Note that none of the inflectional affixes in (39) bears a complete categorial signature. I will return to a justification of this point in section 3.6. Since they do not have their own categorial signatures, however, the categorial signature from a verb stem like *tot-* will be percolated from node to node by Head Percolation. Features from affixes then percolate via Backup Percolation to fill in empty slots in the categorial signature.

The Tense/Aspect (T/A) markers must attach first to the verb stem, since all other morphemes are marked to attach to forms already bearing values for the features [Pres] and [Pret], or [Def]. The values for [Pres] and [Pret] will percolate to the categorial signature as shown in (40a). Note that a second T/A morpheme is blocked from attaching now, since there is no longer any room in the categorial signature for its T/A values to percolate to. This is illustrated in (40b).[24]

(40) a.

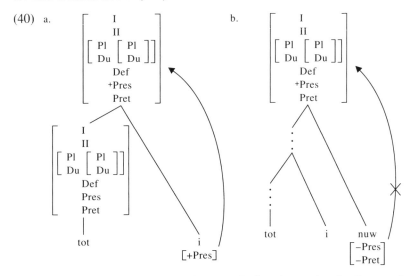

The subject P/N markers can then attach directly to give the forms of the Indefinite conjugation. Their values for the features [Du] and [Pl] will percolate to the inner layer. Default values for the feature [Def] and redundant values for the remaining P/N and tense features may be filled in at this point (these values are circled in (41)):

(41)

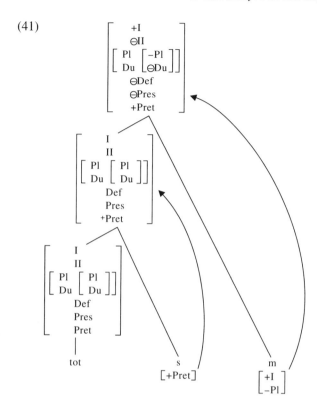

(Phonological rules later operate to insert the *u*—a labialized *ə* according to Kálmán—between the *-s* and the *-m*.) Other forms in the Indefinite paradigms are derived in a similar fashion. Note that nothing can attach outside of the Subject P/N markers, since they are marked to occur word finally. Note as well that the values of [Pl] and [Du] are interpreted as being subject number values; although they are in the inner P/N layer, this is the *outermost marked* layer, that is, the outermost layer which receives values for features, and therefore the subject layer.

One detail that must be addressed at this point is the allomorphy of the present tense morpheme. In the Indefinite conjugations the present tense marker is sometimes *-i* and sometimes *-ēγ*. In the Definite conjugations it also appears as *-ij*. The allomorphy appears to be phonologically conditioned. I assume that the present morpheme is underlyingly *-i*. The *-i* lengthens before *ə* (remember that the raised *u* is a labialized *ə*). Kálmán notes that the long counterpart to [i] is [ē], that is, a vowel which is lowered

as well as long. The present tense morpheme then spreads to form an onset
to the following syllable if it does not already have one. That will happen
everywhere that the present tense morpheme is followed by a vowel initial
suffix. The orthographic reflex of the onset formation rule is *j* (a high
glide) following *i*, and γ (which is nonhigh) following *ē*. Two derivations
are illustrated in (42):

(42) tot + i + n
        ən
      ē
      ēγ
    totēγən
    (INDEF-PRES-2.SG)

    tot + i + aγ + m
                      ^{u}m   Schwa Insertion
                      —   Lowering
              ij   Onset Formation
    totijaγ^{u}m
    (DEF-DU.OBJ-PRES-1.SG.SUBJ)

Two forms in the Indefinite present conjugation still require special attention. In the third person dual present form we find *totēγ*. I assume that
what we have underlyingly is *[tot+i+iγ]* (the *i* in the P/N suffix is underlyingly *i*, according to Kálmán). This sequence *i* + *i* is interpreted phonologically as a long vowel, with the consequent lowering that accompanies
length in vowels. In addition, the first person present indefinite form appears as *totew* rather than as the expected *totijuw;* here I assume that the
underlying representation is *[tot+i+uw]*, and that the sequence *i* + *u* becomes *ē* before Onset Formation operates.

   The forms of the Definite conjugation are generated by affixing the object number suffixes of (39b) to the T/A marked verb stem, and then
adding the subject P/N markers. Structure (43) illustrates the derivation of
the form *totijaγmen* (first person dual subject, dual object). As before, default and redundant values of features are circled.

(43)

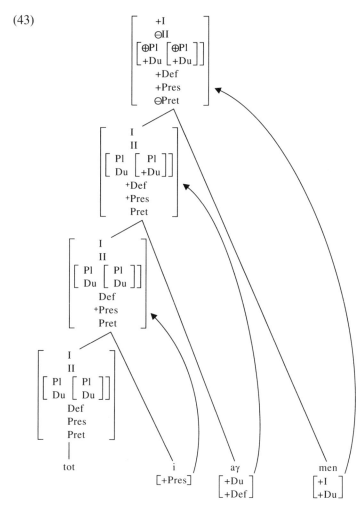

As usual, the categorial signature is propagated from node to node by Head Percolation and Backup Percolation fills in the features from each successive morpheme. Default and redundant values are added at the very end. The derivation of the first and second person forms in the Definite conjugations is therefore entirely straightforward.

Deriving the third person forms in the Definite conjugations is somewhat less straightforward, however. Note first that although the subject P/N affixes for the Indefinite and Definite conjugations are the same in the first and second person forms, there are different subject forms for third person in the two conjugations. The third person suffixes for the indefinite conjugations are *-iγ* (dual) and *-t* (plural). Third person singular is un-marked. These two suffixes will attach only to the T/A marked verb stem; since they have the feature [−Def], they are blocked from attaching by the inability to percolate this feature to a verb which is already marked [+Def]. This is illustrated schematically in (44):

(44)

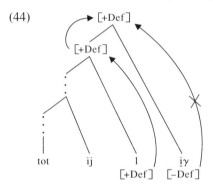

The other third person suffixes, however, are subcategorized to attach to forms which are already marked [+Def].

Probably the most thorny problem in analyzing the Vogul verb conjuga-tions is how to treat the third person subject suffixes in the Definite conju-gations. When the object number is singular we find a *t* preceding the third person singular *-e* and third person dual *-en*, rather than the expected *-l*. Before the third person plural *-anəl*, we find no overt object marker at all. Both Kálmán (1965) and Collinder (1957) suggest that the *-t* is an al-lomorph of the singular object suffix *-l*, although neither has an explana-tion for the absence of any overt singular object affix at all before *-anəl*. Liimola (1968), however, gives a clue as to what might really be going on.

Citing work by József Budenz (no year of citation given), Liimola points out that the third person subject affixes in the Definite conjugations appear to be identical to the third person possessive affixes *-te, -ten*, and *-anəl*. He argues that the *-l* suffix was originally a nominal suffix that was transferred to the verbal paradigms. The *t* preceding the third person sin-gular and dual morphemes is therefore probably *not* an allomorph of *-l* at all. Following Liimola, I will postulate here that the third person mor-phemes are in fact the possessive morphemes *-te, -ten*, and *-anəl*, and that they still bear a feature [+Poss].[25] I will speculate then that the underly-ing forms in the third person definite conjugation are *tot + i + l + te, tot + i + l + ten, tot + i + l + anəl*, and the like.[26] A minor rule will delete the singular object suffix *-l* when it precedes a [+Poss] morpheme. Note that the [+Poss] feature cannot percolate in the verb forms, since the categorial signature for verbs has no slot for this feature. I will assume that the [+Poss] feature has become purely diacritic in the verbal paradigms of Vogul, and that nothing but the minor rule mentioned above makes reference to it.

There are still two problems with the analysis of the third person definite forms offered here. First, if the underlying forms of the third singular and third dual subject suffixes are respectively *-te* and *-ten*, then we should expect to find forms like *totijaɣte* (3.SG.SUBJ-DU.OBJ) and *totijanten* (3.DU.SUBJ-PL.OBJ), rather than the forms *totijaɣe* and *totijanen* that do occur. I propose here that *totijaɣte* and *totijanten* are indeed the correct underlying representations of these forms, and that the phonological rule in (45) deletes the *t* when it is preceded by a nonstrident consonant:

(45) $\text{t} \rightarrow \emptyset \quad / \quad \begin{bmatrix} -\text{Strid} \\ +\text{Cons} \end{bmatrix}$____

The second problem that we find occurs with the third person plural subject, plural object forms. Rather than the expected *totijananəl, totsananəl,* and *totnuwananəl,* we find *totijanəl, totsanəl,* and *totnuwanəl.* I can only speculate here that Vogul avoids a repetition of syllables such as occurs in these forms, and that some sort of phonological rule truncates the repeated syllable *an.*

We can see then that the forms of both Indefinite and Definite verbs in Vogul can be accounted for relatively simply, assuming subcategorization frames of the sort in (39), two layers of number features, and the feature percolation conventions developed in this chapter. The analysis of the Vogul paradigms presented here also illustrates another characteristic of the mechanism of feature percolation: derivations may be blocked if a morpheme has a feature that cannot percolate because the categorial signature already has a value specified for that feature. This will happen only when the mechanism of percolation is Backup Percolation, that is, when the morpheme in question does not itself have a categorial signature to be propagated by Head Percolation (if the morpheme had its own categorial signature with values specified, these would automatically be percolated by Head Percolation). We will see in the next section that this leads to an interesting observation about the distinction between inflectional and derivational affixes, long one of the most controversial issues in the theory of morphology.

3.6 Ramifications

3.6.1 Inflection vs. Derivation

There is still one assumption about the operation of feature percolation in the analyses above that I have not yet clearly unpacked. The lexical entries for the Yavapai prefixes *m-*, *ñ-*, and *ʔñ-*, and also those for the Vogul suffixes in (39) contain only the features positively specified for each morpheme. These features are *not* contained within a full (although otherwise unspecified) categorial signature, and they are moved by Backup Percolation. On the other hand, a morpheme such as the Russian diminutive *-ushka* in (25) is invested with a complete categorial signature, which, although unspecified for everything but the category features themselves, percolates via Head Percolation. The choice between one sort of representation and the other is not a random or arbitrary one, made individually for each morpheme, but rather is systematic; the former affixes are inflectional ones and the latter are derivational. In this section I will clarify the distinction I am making between inflection and derivation, and give several arguments to support it.

The proposal I am making is the following. Only stems, bound bases, and derivational affixes will have full categorial signatures. Inflectional affixes will be marked only with individual features for which they contain specified values. In derivational word formation the value for a feature of a head morpheme will supercede or override that of an inner morpheme. Features from inflectional morphemes can never override features from their bases, but can only fill in values unspecified in the categorial signatures of their bases. Inflectional word formation is therefore **additive** in a way that derivational word formation and compounding are not. A corollary of this is that while derivational affixes may or may not be heads of their words, inflectional affixes will never be heads.[27] The categorial signatures of derivational affixes (or stems) will be percolated by Head Percolation if these morphemes are heads. The features of inflectional morphemes will only be affected by Backup Percolation.

Let me first try to justify the claim that inflectional morphemes do not carry complete categorial signatures. We have already encountered one sort of argument for this position. In section 3.4 I argued that morphemes like *m-* and *ñ-* in Yavapai could not have categorial signatures. In order to capture the generalization that the former always carries the feature [+II] and the latter [+I], regardless of whether the feature is for the subject or the object, we needed to assume that these morphemes had no categorial signature. If they did possess the categorial signature for verbs in Yavapai, the features [+I] and [+II] would have to be located in one or the other layer for P/N features, and would therefore be designated rigidly as either a subject or an object feature. The same sort of argument can be made even more powerfully for the case affixes of Kayardild. Remember that a noun in Kayardild can be marked with up to four different case affixes. The categorial signature for N in Kayardild might therefore be something like that in (46):

(46)
$$
\begin{bmatrix}
& & \text{N} & & \\
\begin{matrix} \pm\text{Case}_i \\ \pm\text{Case}_j \\ \pm\text{Case}_k \\ \pm\text{Case}_l \end{matrix} &
\begin{bmatrix} \pm\text{Case}_i \\ \pm\text{Case}_j \\ \pm\text{Case}_k \\ \pm\text{Case}_l \end{bmatrix} &
\begin{bmatrix} \pm\text{Case}_i \\ \pm\text{Case}_j \\ \pm\text{Case}_k \\ \pm\text{Case}_l \end{bmatrix} &
\begin{bmatrix} \pm\text{Case}_i \\ \pm\text{Case}_j \\ \pm\text{Case}_k \\ \pm\text{Case}_l \end{bmatrix}
\end{bmatrix}
$$

Suppose that the values of the case features for the Oblique suffix *-nja, -ntha* were $[+C_i, -C_j, +C_k, -C_l]$. What would the lexical entry for *-nja, -ntha* be if it had a complete categorial signature like that in (46)? The dilemma is that the values for the case features must be placed in some layer of the nested structure, but we do not know which one until we know the way the Oblique suffix is functioning (i.e., as a Relational, Modal, Associating, or Complementizing case)[28] in a given word in a sentential context, and what other cases the noun is marked for. That is, the layer for which the case features for the Oblique morpheme are specified is not part of the inherent lexical information of this suffix. Only the values of the features themselves belong to this affix. The conclusion that can be drawn is that at least some inflectional affixes cannot have categorial signatures. And since some inflectional affixes cannot have categorial signatures, it seems likely that none of them should have them.

A second sort of argument supports this conclusion as well. Remember that in section 3.5 I solved the problem of the *t* in the third person subject, singular object forms in Vogul by postulating that the *t* was not an allomorph of the singular object *-l* suffix, but rather that it was part of the third person singular and third personal dual subject morphemes themselves. The third person subject affixes in the Definite conjugations were in fact possessive suffixes borrowed from the nominal paradigms. Let us consider here what historical change would have to have taken place for suffixes from the nominal paradigms to have been borrowed into the verbal paradigms.

Suppose first that all inflectional morphemes do have categorial signatures. The possessive suffixes in the noun paradigms might then have a lexical entry like that in (47), with slots for case, person, number and possessive features.[29]

(47) -te (3.SG.POSSESSIVE)
$$
\begin{bmatrix}
\text{N} \\
\text{Case}_i \\
\text{Case}_j \\
\text{Case}_k \\
\text{Case}_l \\
-\text{Pl} \\
+\text{Poss}
\end{bmatrix}
\quad / \;]_\text{N}\underline{\quad}]
$$

For the possessive morpheme to be borrowed into the verbal paradigm, it would have to lose much of its categorial signature, specifically the category and case features (although not the features [−Pl] or [+Poss] for which it actually has values), and acquire the categorial signature of a verb (the one in (38)). In addition, its subcategorization would have to change, so that it could attach to verbs. Suppose, on the contrary, that inflectional affixes have no categorial signature, but rather carry only the morphosyntactic features for which they are actually specified (as I represented them in sections 3.4 and 3.5). The possessive suffix *-te* in Vogul would then have the lexical entry in (48):

(48) -te $\begin{bmatrix} -\text{Pl} \\ +\text{Poss} \end{bmatrix}$ / $]_N$ ——]

The transfer to the verbal paradigm would then entail only a single, simple change, that is, the addition of V to the left bracket of the subcategorization frame. Since *-te* would not have the category and other morphosyntactic features of nouns, it would not have to lose them, and it would not have to acquire the category and other features of verbs. Transfer of an inflectional affix from one category to another is thus much simpler under the assumption that inflectional affixes do not possess categorial signatures.

The argument that derivational affixes must have categorial signatures is relatively simple. Since derivational affixes can be category-changing, they must be able to contribute to the word that they form all of the features of that category of item which they form. For example, the suffixes *-heit* and *-ung* in German form nouns, the former from nouns or adjectives (*die Menschheit* 'humanity', *die Schönheit* 'beauty') and the latter from verbs (*die Hoffnung* 'hope', *die Mitteilung* 'communication'). Both contribute to the word as a whole not only the category features, but also gender features (both form feminine nouns), person features ([−I, −II]), and number features ([−Pl]), that is, all the features in the categorial signatures of nouns in German. It seems relatively uncontroversial, then, to assume that derivational morphemes have full categorial signatures, whereas inflectional morphemes do not.

One small ramification of the distinction between derivation and inflection that I have made here is that it permits a simple analysis of the English possessive morpheme *-s*, discussed briefly in chapter 1. There I suggested that *-s* is a phrasal affix, but did not actually provide an analysis. Here we are in a position to do so. Suppose then that the possessive morpheme in English has the lexical entry in (49):

(49) -s [+Poss] / $]_{NP}$ ——]

The possessive affix, like other inflectional affixes, lacks a full categorial signature. It is specified only for the feature that it actually contributes to the phrase as a whole (I have represented that feature here as [+Poss], although again, nothing hinges on the choice of case features). When it attaches to an NP, as illustrated in (50), the category and other features will percolate up from the head, and the resulting complex will have the same (phrasal) bar level as the item to which the possessive has attached:

(50)

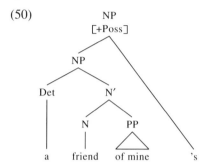

Thus, the possessive affix in English has a lexical entry like other inflectional affixes, except that it attaches to a phrasal category.[30] Otherwise, it is exactly like other inflectional affixes that we have seen in this chapter.

3.6.2 V Movement to Infl Analyses

The arguments in the preceding section also suggest another conclusion. It has been proposed in several recent works on syntax in the Government-Binding framework (e.g., Chomsky 1986a; Baker 1988a; Pollock 1989) and on morphology (Toman 1987) that inflection of verbs involves Head Movement of a V to a governing Infl node, with something like the structure in (51) as the result:[31]

(51)

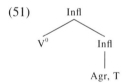

Since Infl is the locus of tense and agreement features in Government-Binding theory, presumably affixation of tense and agreement markers occurs after Head Movement has taken place. Tense and agreement affixes are thus in some sense category-changing.

That tense and agreement affixes are category-changing is of course incompatible with the conclusion reached in the preceding section that inflectional affixes do not possess categorial signatures. If Infl were a categorial node distinct from V, and if overt tense and agreement affixes were daugh-

ters of Infl, then at least one inflectional morpheme would have to be provided with a categorial signature for Infl. We saw above, however, that
several sorts of problems develop if agreement morphemes (e.g., P/N
affixes in Yavapai) were to have complete categorial signatures. The mechanics of percolation become difficult, if not impossible to work out if
inflections have complete categorial signatures.

However, one possible way of reconciling the analysis of percolation
developed here with the "V Movement to Infl" analysis might be to say
that Infl is a defective category in the sense that it lacks category features of
its own. If this were the case, the category features of the verb, and in fact
its whole categorial signature would have to percolate to the top of the Infl
node. Infl would then add features straightforwardly by Backup Percolation. It is beyond the scope of this chapter to work out the ramifications of
this proposal. Nevertheless, at first glance at least it appears compatible
with the percolation mechanisms developed here.[32]

3.7 Inheritance

There is still one issue that I have raised in this chapter, but which I have
not yet adequately discussed, namely, the subject of **inheritance.** In section 3.2.2 I argued that inheritance is not the same process as feature percolation. Argument structures or Theta-grids appear to be passed across
categorial lines, where ordinary morphosyntactic features are not. They
cannot be reasonably decomposed into binary valued features. And the argument structure of a nonhead may be acted upon by the argument structure of
the head morpheme, whereas in percolation the features of a nonhead are
entirely obliterated by the features of the head. It seems reasonable then to
draw the conclusion that inheritance is not the same as percolation. What
inheritance is is a harder question to answer, however. It is beyond the
scope of this work to treat this subject in any great detail. Here I will
merely review some suggestions that have been made in the recent literature on morphology and suggest what I believe to be the most promising
direction for future research.

Although a minority of investigators believe that inheritance of argument structures is erratic, unsystematic, and not to be explained by linguistic theory (e.g., Hoekstra and Van der Putten 1988), most researchers
agree that inheritance of argument structures does occur under certain circumstances, and that inheritance is in fact concerned with the passing on of
Theta-grids or argument structures, rather than syntactic subcategorization
frames (Hoekstra 1986; Booij and van Haaften 1988). Most agree that
there are a number of things that can happen to argument structures within

words (e.g., DiSciullo and Williams 1987; Roeper 1987; Randall 1988; Booij 1988a; Booij and van Haaften 1988; among others). Some affixes such as English process *-ing* have no argument structures of their own; the argument structure of their bases is therefore inherited entirely:

(52) a. the putting of books on shelves
     b. the handing of bottles to babies

Other affixes absorb or "bind" an argument of their base:

(53) a. -er   a baker of cakes
                     the driver of the truck
     b. -sel (Dutch) baksel 'baking (i.e., what has been baked)'
                     schraapsel 'scraping'

The English suffix *-er*, which creates agent and instrument nouns, binds the external argument of its base verb. According to Booij and van Haaften (1988, 33), the Dutch suffix *-sel*, which creates result nouns, binds an internal argument.

Some affixes add arguments to their bases; for example, the causative suffix *-ize* in English adds an agent role:

(54) a. Gambling is legal.
     b. They legalized gambling.

Other affixes act as operators on the argument structure of their bases. Williams (1981b), for example, suggests that the English adjective-forming suffix *-able* eliminates or blocks the external argument of its base, and externalizes its internal argument:

(55) a. They washed the socks.
     b. The socks are washable.

(See Randall 1988 and Roeper 1987 for slightly different analyses of this suffix. Also, Levin and Rappaport 1986 note that much of the change that an adjective-forming suffix like *-able* effects is not idiosyncratic to the affix, but rather follows directly from the change of category; roughly speaking, all adjectives require an external argument to be predicated of.) Finally, Roeper (1987) notes that yet another affix, English *-ful,* blocks the assignment of all internal arguments:

(56) a.   They hoped for rain.
     b.   *They are hopeful for rain.
     c.   They helped their parents.
     d.   *They are helpful of their parents.

There are therefore a range of operations that can occur to the argument structure of a base when an affix is attached to it, from full inheritance to full blocking. These operations are most often stated in the literature as operations on Theta-grids, that is, on lists of thematic roles belonging to lexical items.

Indications are, however, that work in the theory of inheritance could go beyond a mere cataloguing of what affixes can do to the argument structures of their bases. Recent, very promising work in the theory of lexical semantics raises the fundamental question of what Theta-roles, Theta-grids, and argument structures really are. Levin and Rappaport (1986), Jackendoff (1987, 1990), Rappaport and Levin (1988), Booij and van Haaften (1988), and Carrier and Randall (1989) all suggest that it is incorrect to represent Theta-grids or argument structures as lists of Theta-roles such as agent, theme, goal, that can be blocked, inherited, or operated on. They argue that Theta-roles are not primitives of linguistic theory. Rather, Theta-roles are no more than convenient labels for argument positions in what Rappaport and Levin call **Lexical Conceptual Structure** (LCS) (also called "conceptual" structure in Jackendoff 1987). LCS is a decomposition of the meaning of a word into such semantic primitives as CAUSE, GO, COME TO BE IN STATE, and so on; (57) gives an example of the LCS for the verb *put* (Carrier and Randall 1989, 9):

(57) PUT: $[_{Event}$CAUSE $([_{Thing}$ $], [_{Event}$GO $([_{Thing}$ $], [_{Place}$AT $[_{Place}]])])]$ [33]

The lexical entry for a word like *put* will contain its LCS. From this can be constructed what Rappaport and Levin (1988, 9) call a **Predicate-Argument Structure** (PAS),[34] which is "an explicit representation of hierarchical relations between the verb and its arguments." A possible representation of the PAS for *put* will be (58):

(58) PUT: $x < \underline{y}, P_{loc} \; z >$

This representation indicates that *put* has three arguments, x, y, z, corresponding to the three open slots in the LCS. The argument represented by the variable outside the angle brackets is external, the underlined variable y is the direct internal argument, and z is an indirect internal argument which is assigned its role by a locative preposition. PAS is a projection from LCS, but it does not represent a list of Theta-roles. Syntactic rules may refer to positions in PAS, but not to particular Theta-roles like agent or theme, since these do not in fact exist at any level of representation.

The theory of lexical structure developed by Levin, Rappaport, Jackendoff, and Carrier and Randall does not concern itself explicitly with the effects of affixation on argument structure, but it is fairly clear what the implications of these theories are for the theory of inheritance (this is also noted by Booij and van Haaften 1988, 34, and somewhat less directly by Fanselow 1988). To the extent that individual affixes add semantic material to their bases, they change the LCS of those bases. Some changes in LCS may in turn give rise to changes in PAS, what we have been calling throughout this chapter Theta-grids or argument structures. That is, changes in argument structures are a consequence of semantic changes at the level of LCS. For example, the suffix *-ize* in English will add a layer containing the semantic primitive CAUSE to the LCS of whatever adjective or noun it attaches to. The primitive CAUSE carries with it an open slot which in turn is mapped onto the external argument in the PAS of any verb with *-ize*. That is, *-ize* "creates" a new external argument as a consequence of the semantic change it effects. A possible representation of the LCS of *-ize* is given in (59a). The prefix *en-*, discussed in section 2.4, created verbs from nouns, where the base noun was assigned an obligatory locative Theta-role by the prefix. Within the present theory of lexical structure, the LCS of *en-* might be that in (59b).

(59)   a. -ize   LCS: [$_{Event}$CAUSE ([$_{Thing}$], [$_{Event}$ BE (**LCS of base**)])]
      b. en-   LCS: [$_{Event}$CAUSE ([$_{Thing}$], [$_{Event}$GO ([$_{Thing}$], [$_{Place}$AT [$_{Place}$ (**LCS of base**)]])])]

In each of these LCSs, the LCS of the base fits into and merges with the LCS of the affix to give the overall lexical conceptual structure of the resulting word. Presumably, the effects of other affixes can be analyzed in this way, although it is beyond the scope of the present work to do so.

Thus, it seems that the argument made in section 3.2.2 is confirmed from another direction as well. If changes in argument structure in general arise from changes in Lexical Conceptual Structure, we would not expect such changes to be effected within words by percolation. Rather we would expect that they would arise from whatever operations can be performed on Lexical Conceptual Structure—addition or deletion of semantic primitives and the like. It remains for future research to determine what the possible operations on LCS are, and what concomitant effects accrue to PAS.

3.8 Conclusions

In this chapter I have argued that the theory of percolation should be restricted in the following ways. Percolation must affect only bona fide morphosyntactic features. Neither diacritics nor argument structures are subject to percolation. Percolation is regulated by the categorial signature, that is, the frame of morphosyntactic features that are syntactically active in a particular category in a particular language. Two conventions, Head Percolation and Backup Percolation, actually effect the movement of features from one node to another. Head Percolation propagates an entire categorial signature. Backup Percolation moves values of features to slots in the categorial signature that are unspecified. Categorial signatures may contain layered structures which allow a feature to be multiply marked in languages in which Person/Number or case of more than one constituent can be marked on a single lexical item. In addition, we found that this theory reveals a difference in structure between derivational and inflectional morphemes; whereas the former have full categorial signatures, the latter are specified for only the features for which they carry values. Finally, inheritance finds its roots in the changes to Lexical Conceptual Structure effected by particular affixes.

It is important to repeat at this point that the theory of percolation I have outlined in this chapter is not a specifically **morphological** theory. Although I have talked primarily about percolation of features below the X^0 level, I assume that percolation of features also takes place above word level, accounting for processes of agreement and labeling of syntactic nodes in general. The theory of percolation then is intended to be a module of the grammar that is at work at all levels.

With this chapter we have worked through many of the mechanical aspects of word formation. Morphemes are put together following the principles of X-bar theory, subject to their subcategorizations. Feature percolation labels nodes with morphosyntactic features. So far we have been able to maintain the claim made at the outset that the principles of word formation are none other than the general principles of grammar. In the next chapter we will push this idea further, and begin to explore whether principles of grammar other than X-bar theory and feature percolation can be said to operate inside words.

4   Binding, Barriers, and X^0

The program of research initiated in chapter 2 is based on two related ideas: first, that there is no separate morphological component, and that no specifically morphological principles exist; and second, that the basic principles of word structure are the principles made available by X-bar theory and the theory of percolation. We have seen as well that the principles of Theta theory also act both above and below word level. We must now begin to consider whether any of the other modules of Government-Binding theory have any significance below the word level. Since morphology and syntax are no longer strictly separated by the Strong Lexicalist Hypothesis, we would expect to find evidence that syntactic principles other than those of X-bar theory apply below X^0. Alternatively, we would need to seek some reason, ideally following independently from other parts of the theory, for why those principles cannot apply.

In section 4.1 I consider the sort of sentences traditionally referred to as **Anaphoric Islands** (Postal 1969):

(1) a.   Reagan$_i$ites no longer believe in him$_{i,j}$.
     b.   *He$_i$ no longer believes in Reagan$_i$ites.

I will try to show that the pattern of coreference and disjoint reference allowed for these sentences in some English dialects can be explained by the Binding theory of Chomsky (1986b), assuming that morphemes of certain sorts inside words can receive indices, and that those sublexical indices are visible to the Binding theory. Other less permissive English dialects will be explained by a restriction on indexing below X^0. In this section I also consider two further questions, first the relationship between productivity and anaphoric islands sentences such as those in (1), and second the issue of whether a sublexical anaphor exists in English.

Section 4.2 is concerned with the operation of Move-Alpha inside words. I first consider the sort of movement discussed in Baker (1988a), Pollock (1989), and in chapter 2, noting why it is possible within the present theory. I argue that the theory of barriers developed in Chomsky (1986a) automatically excludes most other sorts of conceivable movements of morphemes into and out of words; many such conceivable movements turn out to violate the Empty Category Principle (ECP) under the assumptions developed here. This section will conclude with a discussion of the ramifications of our proposals for the treatment of so-called Bracketing Paradoxes; the sort of approach developed in Pesetsky (1985) is ruled out, but an alternative is possible within the present theory.

In section 4.3 I reconsider the motivation for the Strong Lexicalist Hypothesis. Although I have explicitly abandoned the Strong Lexicalist Hypothesis here, we will see that certain aspects of lexical integrity still remain in our theory. In the final part of this chapter we consider the extent to which words are still entities of a sort distinct from sentences.

4.1 Binding below Word Level[1]

Sentences such as those in (1) and in (2) below were to my knowledge first discussed in Postal (1969):

(2) a. Reagan$_i$ites think that he$_{i,j}$ should have faith.
    b. *He$_i$ thinks that Reagan$_i$ites should have faith.
    c. Reagan$_i$ites respect his$_{i,j}$ mother.
    d. His$_{i,j}$ mother respects Reagan$_i$ites.

The judgments in (1) and (2) are my own. Postal (1969) in fact claimed that coreference into words was never possible. Hence he dubbed these sentences Anaphoric Islands. Subsequent work, however, revealed some differences in judgments; Ross (1971), Lakoff and Ross (1972), Corum (1973), and Browne (1974) all argued that coreference was possible in sentences such as these, and suggested that they were "anaphoric peninsulas" or "anaphoric reefs", rather than anaphoric islands. Sproat (1985, 1988a) also discusses anaphoric islands, and he shares with Postal the judgment that no coreference in these sentences is possible.[2]

I can only assume from observing the split in judgments that (at least) two dialects of English exist, which I will henceforth call the permissive and nonpermissive dialects, permissive dialects being ones in which the pattern of judgments in (1) and (2) hold. I will primarily be concerned with accounting for the judgments in the permissive dialect (i.e., my own), and I will continue to call such sentences anaphoric islands, even though, strictly speaking, they are not islands in the dialect concerned. I will return to the other dialect below, where I offer some suggestions for dealing with the judgments of speakers such as Postal and Sproat.

The anaphoric islands literature raises some issues that I will not be concerned with here, however. Couched in the tradition of Generative Semantics, the early literature considered (3) to be an example of the same phenomenon illustrated in (1) and (2):

(3) *Orphans still love them.

That is, in the framework of Generative Semantics, the word *orphan* would be decomposed into smaller semantic units, the unit *parents* being part of that semantic representation. The D-structure of (3) would contain this semantic representation, so that *them* in (3) might potentially refer to *parents*. (In fact, Postal points out that *them* cannot refer to *parents;* my judgment accords with Postal's, in this case, as might be expected.) In any case, since it is not assumed within Government-Binding theory that elements of semantic representation comprise units at the level of D-structure (or S-structure, or any level of syntactic structure), a sentence like (3) is not to be accounted for in the same way as (1) or (2), and I therefore assume that the data to be accounted for are only those in which an overt sublexical morpheme (an X^0 within an X^0, that is) is available for indexing.

Also outside the scope of the discussion here will be sentences like (4), discussed in Postal (1969) and Sproat (1985, 1988a):

(4) *Bill was a McCarthy$_i$ite and Fred was a him$_i$ite too.

The unacceptability of (4) has nothing to do with the theory of co- and disjoint reference; rather it has to do with the word *himite*. Pronouns are closed class items. One of the consequences of this fact is that they are not available for further word formation.[3] Moreover, there is some evidence that the categorial signature of pronouns is somewhat different from that of nouns; pronouns must have case features in addition to number and gender. If the latter is true, then the morphological subcategorization of a suffix like *-ite* might be such that it could not attach to pronouns in any case.

Another issue raised in the early anaphoric islands literature is that some sentences with the form of (1) and (2) are more easily understood to allow coreferent readings than others; for example, although (5) appears to have exactly the same structure as (1a), a coreferent reading seems impossible:

(5) *Mission$_i$aries rarely go to it$_i$.

We will put aside the issue raised by (5) for the time being, returning to it in section 4.1.3.

Having put aside the issues that will not be of immediate concern here, let us clarify the central issue that the data in (1) and (2) do force us to consider. That is, if indeed it is possible within the permissive dialects for a pronoun to corefer to a sublexical antecedent, then within the theory I have been sketching here it ought to be possible to extend the subtheory dealing with co- and disjoint reference to account for cases like (1) and (2) as well. Since within the theory of Chomsky (1986a,b) it is the Binding theory which accounts for patterns of co- and disjoint reference within sentences, we would expect Binding theory to be able to predict when disjoint reference must be obligatory between a pronoun and a sublexical antecedent. I will argue in this section that the Binding theory does in fact predict the exact pattern displayed in (1), (2), and similar examples.[4]

Since the Binding theory makes use of indices in calculating whether pronouns, anaphors, or r-expressions are free or bound in a given domain, if the Binding theory were to apply to sentences such as those in (1) and (2), we would need first to assume that at least some sorts of morphemes within words can receive indices. I argue in section 4.1.1 that there is independent evidence that certain morphemes within words must be indexed. In section 4.1.2 I then show that the Binding theory indeed makes correct predictions about the pattern of co- and disjoint reference in the anaphoric islands data. As mentioned above, in section 4.1.3 I consider some of the variation in the anaphoric islands data in the light of productivity. I examine the possibility of sublexical anaphors in 4.1.4, and in 4.1.5 I return to the question of the nonpermissive dialect.

4.1.1 Sublexical Indexing

Perhaps the clearest independent argument for sublexical indexing comes from Finer (1985). Finer (1985) discusses the phenomenon of Switch Reference, a process by which a suffix on the verb of a subordinate clause marks whether the subject of the subordinate clause is the same as (SS) or different from (DS) the subject of the matrix clause. Switch reference systems of this sort occur in a number of Yuman and Hokan languages, in the Australian language Diyari, and others. Finer (1985, 37) cites the following Yavapai example from Kendall (1976):

(6) a. tokatoka-c   savakyuva   u-t-k/   cikwar-kiñ
      Tokatoka-SUBJ   Savakyuva   see-TEMPORAL-SS/   laugh-COMPL
      'When Tokatoka$_i$ looked at Savakyuva$_j$, he$_i$ laughed.'

    b. tokatoka-c   savakyuva   u-t-m/   cikwar-kiñ
      Tokatoka-SUBJ   Savakyuva   see-TEMPORAL-DS/   laugh-COMPL
      'When Tokatoka$_i$ looked at Savakyuva$_j$, he$_j$ laughed.'

In Yavapai, the morpheme -*k* affixed to a subordinate verb indicates that the subject of the subordinate clause and the subject of the main clause are obligatorily coreferent. An -*m* affixed to the subordinate clause verb indicates that the subjects are obligatorily disjoint. Finer (1985, 44) assumes the structure in (7) for sentences such as those in (6): [5]

(7)

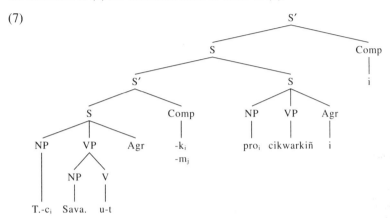

Finer's analysis is based on the generalized Binding theory of Aoun (1981, 1982). Finer proposes that the -*k* and -*m* morphemes are respectively an A-bar anaphor and an A-bar pronominal (the Agr position in (7) is of course an A-bar position). The Binding theory (see below for details) requires the former to be (A-bar) bound in its governing category, which is the main clause S', and the latter (A-bar) free in its governing category, also the main clause S'. [6] Finer argues that in order for the -*k* morpheme to be bound in its governing category, it must be coindexed with a c-commanding governor in this category, which in (7) above is the main clause Comp. Matrix Comp and Agr, on Finer's assumptions, [7] share the same index. And since the main clause Agr and the main clause subject must be coindexed by agreement, by transitivity, the -*k* and the main clause subject must bear the same index, and must therefore be coreferent. Similarly, for -*m* to be free in its governing category (again the matrix S'), -*m* must bear an index different from the main clause Comp. Since this Comp again must be co-indexed with Agr, and Agr coindexed with its subject by agreement, the -*m* is again required by transitivity to bear an index different from that of the matrix subject, and therefore to be obligatorily disjoint in reference from that subject.

Finer's analysis of Switch Reference is both elegant and convincing. For our purposes, it also provides some support for the idea that morphemes within words can be indexed; the indices that -*k* and -*m* receive in Finer's analysis must be the same indices as those used to indicate co- or disjoint reference of nouns in order for this argument to work.[8] Here we will assume for English at least that N^0s within X^0 can be freely indexed.[9] Other languages may require other sublexical elements, for example verbal inflections of certain sorts, to bear indices.

4.1.2 Binding Theory and Anaphoric Islands

I will start here by setting out the version of the Binding theory I will be assuming, roughly that of Chomsky (1986b), although I will differ in minor detail from Chomsky's version. Specifically, for our purposes it is sufficient to use the notion of **Minimal Governing Category** (1986b, 169) as the domain in which Conditions A and B apply, rather than the more exact but far less perspicuous final definitions set out by Chomsky (1986b, 171). The Binding theory that we will assume, then, is the following:

(8) a. α binds β if α c-commands β and is coindexed with β.

    b. Binding Principles
       A. An anaphor is bound in its minimal governing category.
       B. A pronominal is free in its minimal governing category.
       C. An r-expression is free (in the domain of the head of its chain).

    c. Minimal Governing Category/CFC (Chomsky 1986b, 169)
       . . . a governing category is a maximal projection containing both a subject and a lexical category governing α (hence containing α). A governing category is a 'complete functional complex' (CFC) in the sense that all grammatical functions compatible with its head are realized in it—the complements necessarily, by the projection principle, and the subject, which is optional unless required to license a predicate, by definition.

Let us see what this version of the Binding theory has to say about the data in (1) and (2). We begin with (1a), repeated here as (9a), to see if the Binding theory above accounts for the difference between it and (9b), its counterpart without the anaphoric island:

(9) a. Reagan$_i$ites no longer believe in him$_{i,j}$.
    b. Reagan$_i$ no longer believes in him$_{*i,j}$.

Example (9a) will have the structure in (10a), (9b) that in (10b):

(10) a.

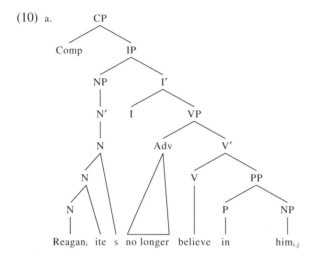

b.

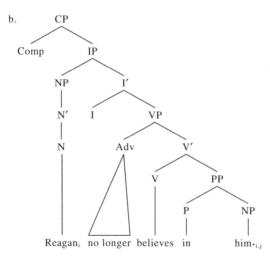

Condition B of the Binding theory requires that a pronoun be free in its minimal governing category. That will be true in (10a); *Reagan*ᵢ cannot bind *him* because it does not c-command *him*. (Note that the relevant notion for Binding theory must be c-command rather than m-command.) In (10b), however, *Reagan* does c-command *him*, and therefore binds *him* if they have the same index; since *him* must be free in its minimal governing category, which is IP, the coreferent reading in (10b) is ruled out. *Reagan* and *him* are obligatorily disjoint in reference in (10b).

Consider next (11a), where a reflexive is impossible, and (11b) where the reflexive is required.

(11) a. *Reagan$_i$ites puzzle himself$_i$.
   b. Reagan$_i$ puzzles himself$_i$.

The sentences in (11) have the structures in (12):

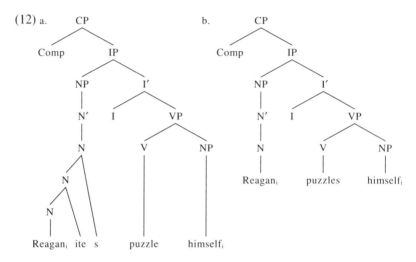

The form (11a,12a) is impossible; since *Reagan* does not c-command the reflexive, it cannot bind it. *Himself* is free in its minimal governing category, violating Condition A. In (11b,12b), however, *Reagan* does c-command the reflexive; *himself* is bound in its minimal governing category, satisfying Condition A.

The Binding theory also makes correct predictions with respect to sentence (1b), repeated here as (13), and its nonanaphoric island counterpart (13b):

(13) a. *He$_i$ no longer believes in Reagan$_i$ites.
   b. *He$_i$ no longer believes in Reagan$_i$.

Both (13a) and (13b) are violations of Condition C. In both an r-expression is bound by a c-commanding element, but r-expressions must be free.

Finally, Binding theory makes correct predictions with respect to the data in (2), repeated here as (14):

(14) a. Reagan$_i$ites think that he$_{i,j}$ should have faith.
   b. *He$_i$ thinks that Reagan$_i$ites should have faith.

    c.   Reagan$_i$ites respect his$_{i,j}$ mother.

    d.   His$_{i,j}$ mother respects Reagan$_i$ites.

In (14a), the pronoun *he* is free in its minimal governing category, the lower IP, in accordance with Condition B. *Reagan* in (14b) is bound by *he* in the main clause, a Condition C violation. Examples (14c) and (14d) are both consistent with the Binding Principles; since the c-command relation does not hold between *his* and *Reagan* in either case, neither *his* in (14c) nor *Reagan* in (14d) is bound. Binding theory thus predicts quite accurately the conditions under which reference into a word is possible and the conditions under which it is ruled out.

4.1.3 Binding below X⁰: A Closer Look at the Data

In the permissive dialect under discussion here, reference to sublexical morphemes cannot always occur; as we saw above, there are configurations in which, according to the Binding theory, disjoint reference is obligatory. Even in configurations in which coreference is not ruled out, however, coreference with a sublexical element may not be successful. Whether coreference is possible or not seems to depend on a number of factors including the nature of the sublexical elements (basically whether it is a name or not), its structural position in a word (whether it is head or not), and, most important, whether or not it occurs in a word that is derived productively (using the notion of productivity developed in the Prologue).[10]

    The most successful anaphoric islands sentences (that is, those in which coreference with a sublexical N is easiest to get) are those in which the word formation process in question is productive, and the sublexical element is both a name and structurally a nonhead. In the sentences below (P) indicates sentences taken from Postal (1969) (judgments mine, however); unlabeled sentences are my own creations:

(15) a. (P) Iroquoian<u>ists</u> are convinced it is related to Caddoan.

      b. (P) Harry is a New York<u>er</u>, but I wouldn't want to open a store there.

      c. Anti-Reagan <u>forces</u> believe him to be a threat.

      d. Pre-Reagan <u>activists</u> feel that he has little influence on them.

      e. Their unReagan<u>like</u> behavior caused him some embarrassment.

      f. Their Reagan<u>ish</u> behavior embarrassed him.

      g. Bush<u>ians</u> admire him greatly.

In sentences with generic nouns in the nonhead position the coreferent reading is a bit harder to get, but still clearly possible in the permissive dialect:

(16) a. (P) The long-legged girl wanted to insure them.
   b. (P) Harry was looking for a bookrack, but he only found racks for very small ones.
   c. (P) Max's argument was pointless, but Pete's did have one.
   d. Their jam has a fruity flavor, because they use so much of it.
   e. Abortionists don't like having to perform one.
   f. The girl's grandfatherish behavior made him laugh.

Presumably the coreferent reading is easiest to get in sentences like (15) because names are the quintessential referring expressions; as Sproat (1988a, 295) points out, a name like *Reagan* refers to a particular individual. In contrast, the sentences in (16) contain common nouns. Since common nouns within words lack specifiers, they are best interpreted as generic. Reference to a generic is somewhat less felicitous than reference to a name. Nevertheless it is possible.

Another factor which influences the ability to get a coreferent reading in sentences like these is what I would call the transparency or the syntactic integrity of the nonhead. Compare, for example, (15b) to the sentences in (17):

(17) a. ?*Harry is British, but I wouldn't want to live there.
   b. *Harry is Dutch, but I wouldn't want to live there.

That is, coreference is best when the nonhead is identical to the intended coreferent. It is impossible if the intended referent (e.g., *Holland* in (17b)) is entirely different from the nonhead. And it is at best extremely marginal if the intended referent is only partially similar to the nonhead (in (17a) the referent is *Britain* and the nonhead *Brit*).

The sentences in (15)–(17) have in common that the sublexical noun is structurally in a nonhead position. In (15) the underlined suffixes in (a), (b), (e), (f), and (g) are heads; the second stem in the compounds in (c) and (d) are heads. Heads are similarly underlined in (16). If a sublexical noun is in the head position, however, it cannot be referred to independently of the word in which it occurs:

(18) a. The neoNazi thought that he could get away with it.
   b. The subconstable believed that he was honest.
   c. The exgovernor believes that he is doing a good job.

That is, in the examples in (18), the pronoun *he* cannot be interpreted as referring to respectively an old Nazi, a regular constable, or the present governor. They may only be understood as referring to the whole nouns of which *Nazi, constable,* and *governor* are heads. These facts can be explained if we make a single, simple assumption about indexing, namely **that the head of a word may not bear an index distinct from that of the word as a whole.**[11] Put slightly differently, the index of the head is the index of the whole. We will assume that this is the case all the way up a projection to the maximal projection, i.e., XP. If this is true, then the head could not have a reference in (18) distinct from that of the word that it heads. We will see shortly that this indexing convention has interesting consequences.

The final and most important factor determining whether reference to a sublexical noun is possible is the productivity of the head affix. The affixes (and compounding process) used in (15)–(17) are of high productivity, witness the ability to coin words in (15) based on names like *Reagan* and *Bush*. The suffix *-ish* has a P value of 0.0050, according to Baayen and Lieber (1991), as opposed to 0.0001 for simplex nouns. With less productive and fully unproductive affixes two things may be noted: first that it is impossible to use these affixes to create new words based on a name like *Reagan* (the results have at best the jocular or cute flavor that is the mark of creative, i.e., nonproductive coinage), and second, that it is much more difficult to refer to the sublexical noun.[12]

(19) a.   -ary forming Ns
           *Missionaries don't often go there/visit it.
           *Fred is a visionary, but he doesn't have one/them very often.
           *a Reaganary
      b.   -ship
           *The Duchy is governed by a dictatorship, but he's not so bad.
           *a Reaganship (i.e., a government ruled by Reagan)
      c.   -age
           *The town subsidizes the orphanage, but he still doesn't like it
               there.
           *a Reaganage (i.e., a place for housing Reagan)

This pattern of facts receives a straightforward explanation within the present theory. If we assume that many familiar words bearing nonproductive or marginally productive affixes are listed in the lexicon, these words will have no internal structure; they are unanalyzable wholes with respect to syntactic rules and principles.[13] If we assume that the indexing device can only assign an index to an item that is inserted independently into a tree (either a word or a phrase structure tree), then nouns like *mission, dictator,* or *orphan* in (19) could not receive an independent index. They are not separate nouns in words like *missionary, dictatorship,* and *orphanage.* In contrast, productively derived words such as those in (15) and (16) will be assembled in the syntax; nouns like *Reagan* in (15c–f) or *book* in (16b) will be inserted into trees (presumably at D-structure, although nothing hinges on this point) and may receive an independent index. Only those internal elements which bear an independent index can be referred to by the Binding theory. Reference to sublexical elements is impossible in (19) because the indexing device encounters no sublexical elements.

4.1.4 Sublexical Anaphors

We have seen above that the Binding theory makes accurate predictions about the pattern of co- and disjoint reference possible in the so-called anaphoric islands sentences. I have also suggested that there are independent reasons why sublexical pronominals do not exist; words like *himites* are morphologically ill-formed because pronouns are closed class items. We have not yet considered the possibility of sublexical anaphors, however. English does indeed have a likely candidate for a sublexical anaphor, the noun *self,* and I will argue in this section that the Binding theory predicts accurately the pattern of interpretation exhibited by *self* compounds.[14]

Self is a morpheme which forms right-headed compounds with adjectives and nouns:

(20) Ns   self-love   As   self-evident
         self-contempt   self-destructive
         self-control   self-explanatory

Sproat (1985) claims that *self* also attaches to verbs, although he gives no convincing examples of this; verbs like **self-wash,* **self-admire,* and *self-explain seem clearly impossible.[15] I will assume that *self* has the lexical entry in (21) (omitting phonological representation):

(21) self   [____]ₙ
         LCS: reflexive anaphor

Note that *self* is not the head of the words in (20), a fact which will assume some importance below.

    Consider now the pattern of coreference that occurs in sentences containing *self* words (I will confine discussion below to cases in which *self* is compounded with nouns, although as far as I can tell, nothing hinges on this):

(22) a. Fenster$_i$ often talks about [John's$_j$ self$_{*i,j}$-contempt].
      b. [John's$_j$ self$_{*i,j}$-contempt] disturbs Fenster$_i$.
      c. Fenster$_i$ is afraid of [self$_{i,arb}$-contempt].
      d. [Self$_{arb}$-contempt] is an unhealthy attitude.

In (22a) and (22b), *self* is obligatorily coindexed with *John*, the specifier of its NP. In (22c), *self* may be coindexed with *Fenster*, the subject of IP, or it may have an arbitrary reading. In (22d), *self* has only the arbitrary reading. The latter two sentences where *self* has an arbitrary interpretation may at first glance suggest problems for the Binding theory—after all, if reflexives must be bound in their minimal governing categories under Condition A, how can an arbitrary interpretation arise? We will see below, however, that Binding Theory does indeed explain these facts.

According to Condition A of the Binding theory, a reflexive must be bound in its minimal governing category (henceforth MGC), the maximal projection which contains *self*, a lexical category governing *self*, and a subject. In (22a) and (22b), the relevant MGC is the NP containing *self-contempt*, shown below in (23):

(23)

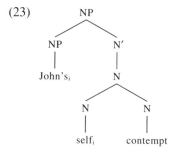

As (22a) and (22b) show, *self* must be coindexed with *John's*, the only NP in its MGC to which it can be bound. *Self* cannot be coindexed to *Fenster* in either (22a) or (22b), since it would then not be bound in its MGC.

The two possibilities exhibited by (22c) are also easily explained by the Binding theory. Recall that specifier/subject of NP is optional. I show in (24a) a possible structure for (22c) in which the specifier of the *self* noun is absent. In (24b) is the alternative structure in which the NP has a specifier, namely PRO with arbitrary reference (arb):[16]

(24) a.

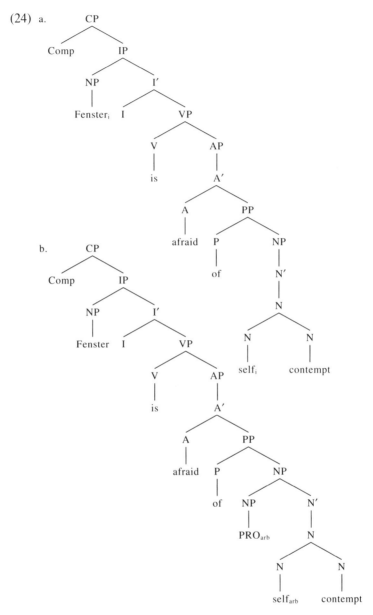

In (24a) *self-contempt* is an NP which has no subject. Its MGC is therefore IP, and it must be bound within that IP to Fenster. In (24b) the NP containing *self-contempt* has a subject, a PRO with arbitrary interpretation, so the

NP is the MGC for *self*. *Self* is bound to PRO and receives its arbitrary interpretation from it.

Example (22d) can be explained in a similar fashion. If the NP *self-contempt* has PRO$_{arb}$ as its subject, *self* must be bound in NP, its MGC; it therefore is bound to PRO$_{arb}$ and receives its arbitrary interpretation. If the NP containing *self-contempt* lacks a subject, the MGC for *self* is its IP, but since there is no c-commanding NP in that IP for *self* to be bound to, this representation is ruled out. The sentence in (22d) therefore has only the arbitrary interpretation.

The pattern of facts illustrated in (22) can therefore be explained easily by Binding theory if we assume that the subject of NP can sometimes be PRO with arbitrary reference. The examples in (22) represent relatively simple cases, however, since the nouns to which *self* is compounded are underived. When *self* is compounded with a derived noun, the pattern of facts is more complicated. Both Sproat (1985) and Farmer (1987) have pointed out that coindexing in (25a) is impossible, although neither note the contrast between the derived (deverbal) base and the underived base in (25b):

(25) a. his$_{*i,j}$ self$_i$-admirer [17]
       b. his$_i$ self$_i$-contempt

The contrast in (25) might lead one to suspect that derived nouns in general behave differently than underived nouns with respect to Binding theory, but the examples in (26) suggest that this is not correct. If the noun to which *self* attaches is a deverbal noun formed with an affix other than *-er,* then the derived noun behaves exactly as the noun with the underived base does:

(26) a. his$_i$ self$_i$-admiration
       b. his$_i$ self$_i$-denial

Farmer (1987) notes this fact, and bases her analysis on the argument structure of *-er.*[18] We will see below that the argument structure of *-er* has something to do with the pattern of facts in (25) and (26), although only in conjunction with Binding theory. Sproat (1985) recognizes the role of Binding theory in explaining the facts in (25) and (26), but admits (1985, 296) that his analysis cannot explain the obligatory disjoint reference of *his* and *self* in examples like (25a). We will make use of some of Sproat's assumptions below, however.

The data in (25) and (26) raise two questions. First, why can't *his* and *self* bear the same index in (25a), although they *must* bear the same index in (25b) and (26)? And second, if *self* bears an index different from *his* in (25a), why is this not a violation of Condition A, since *self* appears to be unbound in its MGC? We will see that these questions receive a natural explanation within the framework developed here, but first we must explore the effects on argument structure of the *-er* suffix in English, and examine the derivation of *self-[[V]er]* nouns within this framework.

As argued in section 3.7, we assume that affixes may add to or change the Lexical Conceptual Structure (LCS) of the base to which they attach and that this in turn may give rise to changes in Predicate Argument Structure (PAS). The lexical entries for the verb *admire* and for the *-er* affix are shown in (27) (the form of the representation is adopted from Booij 1989, 6). The LCS and the PAS of the resulting complex noun *admirer* are shown in (28):

(27) a. admire   V
                    LCS: [x ADMIRE y]$_{\text{ACTION}}$
                    PAS: x $<\underline{y}>$

     b. -er   ]$_{\text{V}}$——]$_{\text{N}}$
                    LCS: x [LCS of input V]

(28)   admirer   LCS: x [x ADMIRE y]
                        PAS: $<\underline{y}>$

In other words, *-er* in some sense "links" the first argument of *admire*,[19] which maps at PAS to the external argument; the PAS of *admirer* therefore contains only the direct internal argument.

Note next that the noun *self* in compounds like *self-admirer* is interpreted as being the direct internal argument of the noun *admirer;* that is, *self* is assigned a Theta-role (theme) by *admirer.* Since, as argued in chapter 2, Theta-roles may only be assigned rightwards in English (since complements obligatorily follow heads), we must assume that the noun *self-admirer* is derived as shown in (29), exactly as synthetic compounds like *truckdriver* were derived in 2.4:

(29) a.   b.

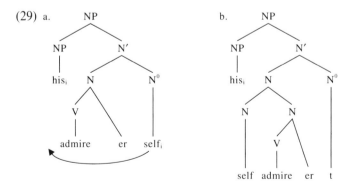

Admirer assigns its Theta-role rightwards to *self. Self* is then forced to move. As we saw in section 2.4, N^0 cannot receive Case because it is not a maximal projection. Note that the derivation in (29) accounts for the observation made by Farmer that *his* cannot be interpreted as an internal argument of *admirer.* Since this Theta-role/argument is assigned to *self*, it cannot also be assigned to *his; his* therefore can only be interpreted as possessive.

We are now at a point where we can begin to see why the coindexing in (25a), repeated in (29), is impossible. Remember that a MGC is defined as the maximal projection which contains a subject and a governor. Suppose, following a suggestion of Sproat's (1985, 296), that we relax the definition of MGC in (8a) to (30):

(30) Minimal Governing Category (revised)
      The MGC of α is a projection β containing both a subject and a
      lexical category governing α.

That is, we require that the MGC be a projection, but not necessarily a maximal projection. Let us also suppose that the affix *-er* which "links" the external argument of the verb to which it attaches actually is the external argument. That is, let us suppose that *-er* is actually the subject of *admire,* and that it can receive its own index, as shown in (31). If so, then the MGC of *self* in (30) will be N', rather than NP:

(31)

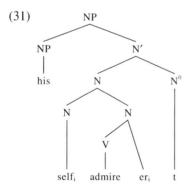

It might be wondered at this point what can bind *self* within N'. The obvious candidate is *-er,* but *-er* does not c-command *self* in (31). We have already assumed however (section 4.1.3), that the index of the head of a word is the index of the whole head projection. If so, then the indexing should be as in (32):

(32)

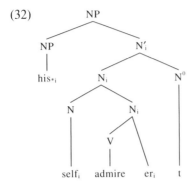

If *admirer* bears the index of its head, then *admirer* c-commands *self* and can bind *self*. Thus, assuming the convention on indexing that we independently needed in 4.1.3, *self* is bound in N', its MGC, satisfying Condition A.

Why now can't *his* in (32) have the same index as *self*? Condition B of the Binding theory requires that a pronominal be free in its MGC. Chomsky (1986b, 170) argues that the MGC for a pronominal specifier of NP is the NP itself. The MGC of *his* in (32) is therefore the NP of which it is the specifier. If the index of the head passes up the head projection in (32), then *his* will be bound in its MGC, violating Condition B. So *his* may not have the same index as *self*.[20]

This then raises the question of why *his* may (indeed must) have the same index as *self* in (25b). Example (25b) has the structure shown in (33):

(33)

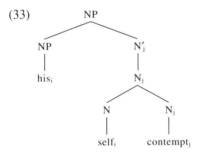

Remember that *self* is not the head in a *self* compound. The head in (33), rather, is *contempt*. If we assume, as seems reasonable, that *contempt* cannot receive the same index as *self* (for one thing, it bears selectional features that are different from *self*), the index of *contempt* will be passed up the head projection. *His* will not bear the same index as anything which c-commands it, and will therefore be free in its MGC. Since *self* does not c-command *his*, it cannot bind *his*. *His* does, however, bind *self*, whose MGC in this case is the NP rather than the N′ (since the N′ contains no subject); *self* therefore satisfies Condition A.[21] Thus, the Binding theory, together with otherwise reasonable assumptions about indexing and the argument structure of *-er* nouns, explains a large range of facts concerning the interpretation of words with the sublexical anaphor *self*.

4.1.5 Permissive vs. Nonpermissive Dialects

We return, finally, to the observation made at the outset, that some speakers do not accept coreferent readings in anaphoric islands sentences like (1a) or (2a,c,d), while others, myself included, do. How can we account for this difference in judgments? Note that one option that is not open to us is to say that speakers of the nonpermissive dialect simply do not allow sublexical indexing. As far as I know, all English speakers, whether they belong to the permissive or nonpermissive anaphoric islands dialect, get the same judgments for the sentences containing the sublexical anaphor *self* discussed in section 4.1.4. Sproat (1985), for example, disallows sentences like (1a), (2a,c,d), but assumes the relevance of the Binding theory in explaining the interpretation of *self* forms. Presumably, then, we would need to assume sublexical indexing at least for *self* for all speakers.

Another possibility for accounting for the dialect split for the anaphoric islands sentences is this. Let us assume that there is a gradation in the referentiality of nominal morphemes[22] from the most referential to the least. Clearly the most referential of nominal morphemes are the reflexives, since they are obligatorily coreferential. Pronominals, perhaps, come next, then, as suggested in section 4.1.3, names and common nouns without specifiers. We saw above that pronominals don't take part in productive word formation, so we will set them aside here. Permissive dialect speakers allow sublexical indexing of all nominal elements, although sentences deteriorate somewhat with generic nouns rather than names. Nonpermissive dialect speakers appear to have a restriction on sublexical indexing for all but the most referential of nominals, the reflexives. Perhaps there are "dialects" in between that permit sublexical indexing for reflexives and names, but not for common, generic nouns. What exactly constrains the indexing device in the nonpermissive dialect—whether it is a matter of grammar or pragmatic factors—must remain unexplored here. I will merely stress the point that the Binding theory must be allowed to look below word level in all dialects; wherever there is sublexical indexing, the Binding Conditions will apply in the same way.

4.2 Move-Alpha, Barriers, and X^0

We have seen that it is reasonable to suppose that the principles of X-bar theory and Binding theory apply in the same way both above and below X^0. And if these modules of the grammar do not take X^0 as the lower limit of their domain, we would expect the same to be true of other modules. In this section we will consider the operation of Move-Alpha below X^0. The operation of Move-Alpha below X^0 has been argued for in several recent works, most prominently Baker 1988a and Pollock 1989, and I argued in chapter 2 that Move-Alpha was involved in the generation of synthetic compounds. In this section I attempt to answer the following question: if Move-Alpha is allowed to move morphemes into and out of words, is it already sufficiently constrained by existing locality principles such as subjacency and the ECP, or do we need to add something to the present theory to constrain the movement of sublexical elements? The need for some sort of auxiliary locality principle would obviously be undesirable—I have claimed that no such specifically morphological principles exist. I will therefore try to show that no auxiliary principle is needed: in fact, the ECP already rules out all impossible movements of sublexical elements. These movements break down into three types. In section 4.2.1 I consider the movement of morphemes into words, in 4.2.2 the movement of morphemes out of words, and in 4.2.3 the movement of morphemes from one position to another within words. In section 4.2.4 I consider the subject of Bracketing Paradoxes in light of the previous discussion.

4.2.1 Movement into Words

Movement of morphemes into words has been proposed to account for such phenomena as Incorporation, which according to Baker (1988a) takes an input like the Mohawk sentence in (34a) and yields an output like (34b), and also to account for such phenomena as verb raising and what has traditionally been called "Affix Hopping" (Chomsky 1986a; Pollock 1989).

(34) Baker (1988a, 20)
  a. Ka-rakv ne sawatis hrao-nuhs-aʔ.
     3N-be.white DET John 3M-house-SUF
     'John's house is white.'

  b. Hrao-nuhs-rakv ne sawatis.
     3M-house-be.white DET John
     'John's house is white.'

Baker (1988a) contains an extensive discussion of the constraints on a movement analysis of Incorporation within Government-Binding theory. I will review his arguments briefly here, and use them as the starting point for a discussion of other sorts of conceivable operations of Move-Alpha below X^0.

Baker (1988a) shows that the sort of movement of a morpheme into a word required by his analysis of Incorporation is constrained by the Head Movement Constraint (HMC) of Travis (1984), and that the HMC is itself derivable from the Empty Category Principle (ECP). Relevant definitions are given in (35)–(41) ((35)–(40) are taken from Chomsky (1986a), (41) from Baker (1988a, 53)):

(35) Government
   A governs B iff A c-commands B and there is no category C such that C is a barrier between A and B.

(36) ECP
   A trace must be properly governed. A properly governs B if A Theta-governs or antecedent-governs B.

(37) Theta-Governs
   A Theta-governs B iff A is a zero-level category that Theta-marks B, and A,B are sisters.

(38) Blocking Category (BC)
   G is a blocking category for B iff G is not L-marked and G dominates B.

(39) Barrier
   G is a barrier for B iff (a) or (b):
   (a) G immediately dominates D, D a BC for B.
   (b) G is a BC for B, and G is not IP.

(40) L-Marking
   X^0 L-marks a YP to which it assigns a Theta-role or Case.

(41) Head Movement Constraint (HMC)
   An X^0 may only move into the Y^0 which properly governs it.

I will not reiterate Baker's arguments in any detail here, because they are lengthy and technical (see Baker 1988a, 51–63), but will merely summarize his explanation for why the structure in (42), which is the structure that results from Incorporation, (his (46)) can satisfy the ECP.

(42)

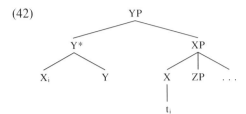

For X_i to properly govern its trace t_i, it must either Theta-govern or antecedent-govern t_i. Baker assumes that an X^0 category dominated by XP (like X in (42)) can never be Theta-marked. Rather the XP that dominates X would be Theta-marked. Theta-marking does not percolate downwards. Therefore in (42), t_i can never be properly governed via Theta-government.

That means that if t_i is to be properly governed, it must be antecedent-governed by X_i. And if X_i is to antecedent-govern t_i, X_i must govern t_i, and must therefore c-command t_i. Baker (1988a, 55) assumes that a node formed by adjunction like Y* does not count for c-command. Discounting Y*, then, X_i c-commands t_i. To show that X_i governs t_i, we must next show that no barriers intervene between X_i and t_i. Is XP a barrier? If YP=VP, Y,Y*=V, and XP=NP, then XP typically will be L-marked, will not be a BC, and hence will not be a barrier between X_i and t_i.[23] Antecedent-government will hold, and t_i will therefore be properly governed.

If, however, XP is not L-marked (say XP is an adjunct), it will be a barrier and t_i will not be properly governed. And if X_i in (42) had been moved somewhere within its own XP (rather than into YP), it would not c-command its trace; for example, if X landed inside ZP or some other maximal projection within XP, the first branching node dominating X_i would be ZP or the other maximal projection, and X_i would not be in a position to c-command its trace. Thus, according to Baker, the ECP effectively limits the positions from which and into which Incorporation can occur.

The same can be said about the operation of Move-Alpha in forming synthetic compounds (chapter 2) and *self* nouns (4.1.4), as proposed here, although we will need to propose a minor (and as far as I can tell innocuous) modification to the ECP. First, I show that the movement analysis of synthetic compounds and *self* nouns satisfies the ECP. I then show that other conceivable sorts of movement are ruled out. Consider first the structure in (43):

(43)

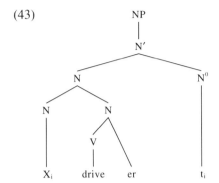

Is t_i in (43) properly governed? According to the definitions in Chomsky (1986a), t_i will be properly governed if it is Theta-governed or antecedent-governed. We have assumed above that X_i is assigned a Theta-role prior to movement, so it appears that t_i is Theta-governed. This is probably not correct, however: if t_i is Theta-governed by *driver* it would be properly governed no matter where it moved to, a result that we do not want. Here I must propose a small change to the definition of the ECP in (36). Let us suppose that an X^0 can be Theta-marked (and hence Theta-governed) if it is a sister to a Theta-role assigner (as is the case in (43)), but that it cannot be L-marked. According to the definition in (40), only **maximal projections** can be L-marked. Let us suppose further that the ECP requires either antecedent government or both Theta-government and L-marking. The revised ECP is stated in (44):

(44) ECP (revised)
A properly governs B iff A Theta-governs and L-marks B, or antecedent-governs B.

Note that this modification will have no consequences for the theory except in cases like (43). Normally *only* maximal phrases are Theta-marked and Theta-governed, and such maximal phrases will also be L-marked. Only when an X^0 is generated as a complement of an X^0—that is, in a case like (43)—will the two sorts of marking not coincide.

With the modification in (44), we find then that t_i in (43) is not L-marked. To be properly governed, it must therefore be antecedent-governed. Assuming, again, that an X^0 formed by adjunction does not count for c-command, X_i does c-command t_i. There are no potential barriers between X_i and t_i. Remember that the N^0 immediately dominating t_i cannot count in the calculation of barriers, as noted in n. 23. Antecedent-government succeeds in (43); the movement involved in forming synthetic compounds satisfies the ECP.

Suppose that we try to move X_i outside its own NP. Structure (45) contains two possible scenarios:

(45)

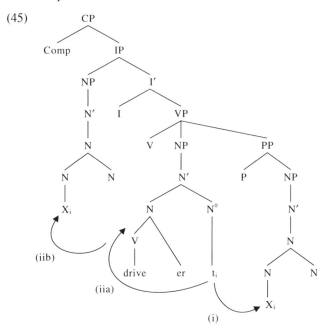

Consider first scenario (i), where X_i moves from its own NP into the NP object of the preposition. X_i does not c-command t_i, and therefore the ECP is violated. The movement in (i) is therefore ruled out.

Scenario (ii) is a movement that must take place in two steps. According to Chomsky (1986a), movement of X_i out of VP must proceed in two steps for the following reason. Since VP is not L-marked, it would always be a barrier to movement. Chomsky therefore proposes that elements moving out of VP adjoin first to VP before moving on. Movement (iia) satisfies the ECP; the NP out of which X_i moves is L-marked by the V and therefore not a barrier, and VP does not count as a barrier since X_i crosses only one segment of VP. What about movement (iib) then? In other words, does X_i properly govern t'_i in (46)?

(46) $_{IP}[[[[X_i \ N]_N]_{N'}]_{NP} \ _{I'}[_{VP}[t'_i \ _{VP}[\ldots \ t_i \ ]]]]$

VP is not a barrier to movement here for the same reason as above. The NP into which X_i moves, however, is a barrier. According to Chomsky the subject NP is not L-marked (1986a, 13) by an X^0. NP dominates X_i and therefore stands as a barrier between X_i and t'_i. Movement (iib) is ruled out since t'_i is not properly governed. The reader may verify that other conceivable movements of X_i are ruled out for similar reasons.

4.2.2 Movement Out of Words

I have demonstrated in 4.2.1 that movement of morphemes into words is strictly limited; if the trace of such movements is subject to the ECP, then a morpheme can only move to the position of a head that governs that morpheme or the phrase of which it is the head (this is more or less the version of the Head Movement Constraint stated in Chomsky (1986a, 71)). We must now consider what limits the movement of morphemes **out of** words. There are two cases to consider: (i) what prohibits the movement of an affix out of a word,[24] and (ii) what prohibits the movement of a free morpheme out of a word. We will start first with affixes; what, for example, is to prohibit the sort of movement illustrated in (47)?

(47)

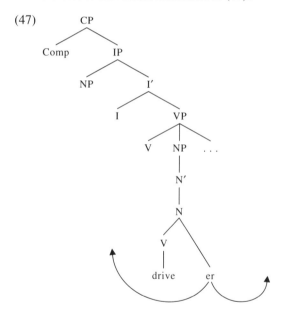

Baker (1988b) suggests that there is a morphology-specific principle, the "No Stray Affix" principle, that prevents an affix from remaining unattached in the syntax. The No Stray Affix principle would rule out most cases in which Move-Alpha dislodges an affix out of a word.[25] However, there is good reason to believe that the No Stray Affix principle is not a separate principle of grammar, much less a principle specific to mor-

phology. In fact, it seems clear that the effects of the No Stray Affix principle follow independently from an assumption we must make about the
lexicon in any case, namely, that affixes are items listed in the lexicon with
subcategorization frames, and that they must fulfill their subcategorizations in the syntax. If Move-Alpha dislodges *-er* in (47) and deposits it
somewhere else, the subcategorization of *-er* will invariably be violated.[26]
This is transparently true if *-er* attaches to nothing after movement. But it
is also true if *-er* is attached to something. Specifically, *-er* cannot attach to
Ns or categories other than V. If *-er* is moved to V in (47), one of two
things will happen. If *-er* adjoins to V, it will form a V, violating its own
subcategorization (*-er* forms nouns). If *-er* attaches to V forming an N,
this will result in an illicit projection, a VP headed by an N. So either way
-er cannot be moved to V in (47), and if it cannot be moved to V, it cannot
be moved anywhere.

What now is to prevent the movement of a free morpheme out of a
word? Consider the sort of hypothetical movement out of a compound illustrated in (48):

(48)

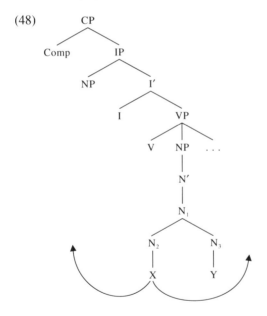

If X moves out of N_1 into some other maximal phrase in VP, it will not
c-command its trace, and the ECP will be violated. If X moves out of VP,
the ECP will still be violated. N_1, not being a maximal projection, is not
L-marked. Although the NP in the VP may be both Theta-marked and

L-marked, these characteristics of course do not percolate downwards. In fact **any** movement out of N_1 will violate the ECP. If N_1 is not L-marked, it is a BC, and therefore a barrier to government of a trace inside the compound. Hence movement of free morphemes out of words is prohibited.[27]

4.2.3 Movement of Morphemes within Words

We have only one other logical possibility to consider, movement from one position to another within a word. Consider, for example, the hypothetical movement in (49):

(49)

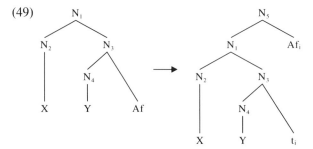

Suppose, in other words, that we raise a suffix from the position in which it is originally attached, and adjoin it to the word as a whole. We must assume that the position of the t_i is not L-marked, since this is not the position of a maximal projection. If t_i is to be properly governed, it must therefore be antecedent-governed. Af_i c-commands t_i. However, N_1 is again a node which is not L-marked, and as such it is a BC, hence a barrier between Af_i and t_i. Since t_i is not properly governed, the movement in (49) is ruled out by the ECP. Again, the ECP appears to place adequate constraints on the operation of Move-Alpha below X^0.

4.2.4 ECP and Bracketing Paradoxes

If the movement of morphemes in words should be constrained by the ECP, as seems to be the case, this will have consequences for at least some possible analyses of Bracketing Paradoxes. Specifically forbidden will be movement analyses of the sort advocated by Pesetsky (1985).[28] Pesetsky (1985) argues that Bracketing Paradoxes such as those illustrated by the words *unhappier* and *transformational grammarian* can be handled by a movement rule operating between S-structure and LF. In this section, I will first briefly review Pesetsky's analysis. Then I will show why it is ruled out within the present theory, and finally discuss several possible alternative analyses of Bracketing Paradoxes.

Words such as *unhappier* and *transformational grammarian* are considered Bracketing Paradoxes for the following reason. On phonological grounds the structures of these words seem to be those in (50):

(50) a.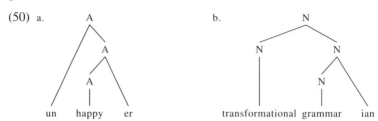

It is well known that the English comparative suffix *-er* can attach only to one-syllable adjectives (*redder, purer*) and to two-syllable words with light second syllables (*happier, tawdrier, *directer, *obtuser*). The suffix *-er* does not attach to three-syllable adjectives (*eloquenter, *fidgetier*). So to fulfill its phonological restrictions, *-er* must attach to *happy* in (50a) before the negative prefix *un-* attaches. The suffix *-ian* in (50b) seems clearly to form a phonological word with *grammar;* hence it must be attached to *grammar* before the compound is formed.

But semantically the words in (50) have another structure:

(51) a.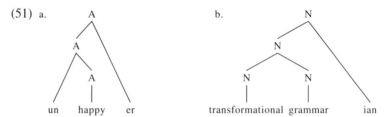

We understand the word *unhappier* to mean "more unhappy" rather than "not more happy" as the phonological bracketing in (50a) suggests. Similarly, a *transformational grammarian* is "someone who does transformational grammar," rather than "a grammarian who is transformational" as the phonological bracketing in (50b) suggests. Words such as *unhappier* and *transformational grammarian* are called Bracketing Paradoxes because the structure that is called for on semantic grounds is at odds with the structure that is necessary for the phonology.

Pesetsky (1985) suggests that Bracketing Paradoxes such as these can be accounted for if we assume that words like *unhappier*, etc., have different structures at different levels of representation. At S-structure *unhappier* has the structure in (50a). This structure serves as the input to PF. Between S-structure and LF, however, a movement rule which Pesetsky (1985) equates with the Quantifier Rule (QR) (May, 1977) raises the suffix -*er,* resulting in the structure in (52):

(52)

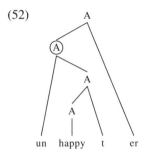

The word *transformational grammarian* has an analogous derivation.

A comparison of structures (50a) and (52) with the hypothetical derivation in (49) will show that they represent the same case. As we saw above, the trace in a structure like (49) or (52) is not properly governed; although the affix c-commands its trace, the circled A node in (52), like the N_1 node in (49), is not L-marked, and hence is a barrier to government. Assuming that the trace of movement at LF is subject to the ECP, as the trace of Move-Alpha at S-structure is, Pesetsky's analysis of Bracketing Paradoxes cannot be permitted within the present framework.

What then to do about Bracketing Paradoxes? There has developed over the last decade or so a copious literature dealing with Bracketing Paradoxes, including Williams (1981a), Strauss (1982), Selkirk (1982), and Fabb (1984), among others. And there are of course several proposed analyses of Bracketing Paradoxes compatible with the sort of framework developed here, including the mapping analyses proposed in Marantz (1988) and Sproat (1985, 1988b). Here I will merely sketch one analysis which is compatible with the framework I have been developing in this book, and which will figure as well in the treatment of reduplication in chapter 5. This analysis should perhaps be seen as a further development of ideas first proposed in Booij and Rubach (1984), and in Sproat (1985), specifically as an attempt to make precise the nature of both the syntactic and phonological representations of words that constitute Bracketing Paradoxes and the relationship between them.

Booij and Lieber (1989) argue that many of the commonly discussed Bracketing Paradoxes are not paradoxical at all within a theory which allows simultaneous reference to both morphological and prosodic structure. It should be clear by now what I mean by "morphological structure." By "prosodic structure" I mean the hierarchy of prosodic categories—syllable, foot, phonological word, and so on—into which phonological segments are arranged. The theory of prosodic structure is discussed extensively in Nespor and Vogel (1986), Selkirk (1984), McCarthy and Prince (1986), Cohn (1989), and Booij and Lieber (1989), among others. The latter work argues specifically that morphological structure and prosodic structure must be built in tandem and be present simultaneously (Cohn 1989 argues for a similar position). If this is the case, then a simple account is available for some of the classic Bracketing Paradoxes.

Booij and Lieber (1989), following an idea of Booij and Rubach (1984), suggest that the comparative suffix *-er* is subcategorized to attach to adjectives, but that it also has a prosodic condition on its attachment:

(53) (Booij and Lieber 1989, 33)

$$-er \qquad]_A \text{——}]_A$$
$$\wedge$$
$$\sigma \ (\sigma_c) \ ] \ \text{——}$$

The lexical entry in (53) states that *-er* attaches to adjectives that have a core syllable σ_c (that is, a syllable containing no more than a CV) as the second syllable of the prosodic word. Booij and Lieber (1989) argue that a morphological word like *unhappy* in fact consists of two prosodic words: $(un)_{Wd} \ (happy)_{Wd}$. The structure of *unhappier* under this analysis is that given in (54), with prosodic structure represented above and morphological structure below the segments:

(54)

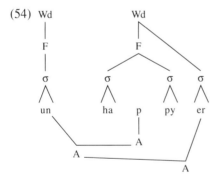

The suffix *-er* is absorbed into the prosodic word *happy*, but syntactically it is attached to the constituent *unhappy*. No movement of affixes is necessary. Both prosodic structure and morphological structure are necessary within the present theory, and given these two coexisting hierarchies, there is nothing paradoxical about the word *unhappier*. Booij and Lieber (1989) show that other so-called paradoxes—for example, words like *ungram-*

maticality, underestimation, and *extrametricality* can be accommodated within this framework as well.

4.3 The Lexicalist Hypothesis and the Notion of Lexical Integrity

We have now come to a point where it might be useful to take another look at the Lexicalist Hypothesis and to consider whether any notion of lexical integrity remains within the theory developed here. Consider once again Lapointe's version of the Lexicalist Hypothesis (1980, 8):

(55) Generalized Lexicalist Hypothesis
  No syntactic rule can refer to elements of morphological structure.

How exactly the Lexicalist Hypothesis is construed depends of course on what sorts of syntactic rules are admitted within a given theory.

It is relatively clear how the Lexicalist Hypothesis was construed in the morphological literature of the late seventies and early eighties (e.g., Aronoff 1976; Lieber 1980; Williams 1981a, 1981b; Selkirk 1982). "Syntactic rules" referred to transformations, particularly to the detailed, construction-specific transformations that were characteristic of *Aspects*-style generative syntax. Analyses such as that of Lees (1963) in which transformations changed sentences into words were of course ruled out. Also ruled out were the sort of analyses sanctioned within Generative Semantics in which transformations turned semantic representations into words. But in addition to ruling out the operation of transformations in the creation of words, the Lexicalist Hypothesis stood as a general manifesto proclaiming that words and the lexicon were worth studying in their own right and on their own terms.

Lexical Phonology (Pesetsky 1979; Kiparsky 1982; Mohanan 1982) perhaps took the Lexicalist Hypothesis the most seriously in the sense that the Lexicalist Hypothesis was translated into a technical device within this theory: Bracketing Erasure was a mechanism that applied to obliterate internal structure at certain points in the derivation, for example, at the end of a level in the morphology/phonology. Syntactic rules could not refer to elements of morphological structure because words quite literally had no internal structure when they emerged from the lexicon.[29]

Of course, our assumptions about the construction and organization of the grammar have changed a great deal since the mid-seventies, and thus it is necessary to raise the lexicalist question in a somewhat different fashion now: is it still desirable to say that the rules and principles of current syntactic theory should be prevented from applying to structure below X^0?[30]

Note that the rules and principles of Government-Binding theory—X-bar theory, Theta theory, Move-Alpha, Binding theory, the ECP, the principles of barriers—do not specifically say anything about **not** applying below X^0, so the Lexicalist Hypothesis would have to be an extra stipulation added to the theory if we wanted to rule out application of rules and principles of syntax below X^0.

In this chapter, and in the two preceding it, I have tried to show that such a lexicalist stipulation would be undesirable. If general rules and principles of grammar do not apply to structure below X^0, then we would not be able to explain the correlations between the position of the head in phrases and words in languages like English and Tagalog. We would not be able to explain why phrases like *the driver of the truck* and compounds like *truckdriver* display the same Theta-relations, at least not without creating some analog to Theta theory within the lexicon. Similarly, we would not be able to explain the patterns of obligatory disjoint reference in anaphoric islands sentences or of obligatory coreference in sentences with *self* compounds. And here it seems that the option of creating an analog to Binding theory to operate below X^0 would not be open to us; by their very nature the anaphoric islands and *self* data require simultaneous reference to items above and below X^0. And finally, if we do not allow Move-Alpha to apply to X^0s then we must find alternative analyses for phenomena like Incorporation.[31] It seems that there is now something to be lost by adhering to the Lexicalist Hypothesis.

This is not to say, however, that the rules and principles of grammar apply indiscriminately below X^0. We would hardly expect them to within Government-Binding theory, since rules and principles of grammar do not apply indiscriminately above X^0 either. The rule of Move-Alpha is perhaps the best example here. Move-Alpha is restricted from indiscriminately moving phrases out of other phrases by such principles as the ECP, and the system of barriers. Similarly we have seen that Move-Alpha cannot indiscriminately move morphemes into and out of words; again ECP and the system of barriers prevent unwanted movements. A notion of lexical integrity remains within the present theory—there are certain things that cannot happen to words—but our notion of lexical integrity has now moved closer to our notion of phrasal integrity.

I do not believe that the term "phrasal integrity" has ever been used in the vast literature on phrasal syntax, but surely some such notion exists, and has existed ever since Ross's (1967) ground-breaking work on island phenomena. The very notion of an island is that there are certain syntactic operations that cannot "see into" phrases of certain sorts, that is, that cannot violate "phrasal integrity." The exact characterization of those constraints has changed radically through the last twenty years of syntactic research from the particularistic "Island Constraints" of Ross (1967), to the broader constraints of the late seventies (subjacency, The Tensed S Condition, the Specified Subject Condition, the Nominative Island Constraint), to their present incarnations in the ECP and barriers. Nevertheless, behind all of these constraints lies the notion of locality: rules cannot create relationships between phrases or items within phrases that are too far apart. To do so violates "phrasal integrity."

Characterizing the notion of lexical integrity thus becomes within the present theory part of the general task of specifying conditions on locality within syntax, where I now intend a conception of syntax including structural relations both above and below X^0. Characterizing the notion of lexical integrity can no longer be done by fiat or by stipulation. It becomes part of a much larger enterprise, and one which is of course on-going. We should therefore expect that our notion of lexical and phrasal integrity will not remain static, but we should also expect that if they change, they will change together.

Beyond Affixation and Compounding

Up to this point the theory of morphology/syntax that I have been developing has dealt almost exclusively with conventional concatenative word formation, that is, affixation and compounding. Of course, if I am to maintain the claim that there are no separate principles of morphology and that there is no distinct morphological component of the grammar, I must venture beyond the safe confines of conventional affixation and compounding, and show that other sorts of morphology can be accommodated in this theory as well. In this chapter I will therefore survey a range of word formation types that (at least at first glance) present some challenge to the theory developed here. Almost all of these word formation types are ones which have been treated traditionally as processes or operations on strings. Nevertheless I argue in what follows that all of these types of word formation are amenable to treatment within the theory developed in chapters 1–4. No specifically morphological operations, processes, rules or principles will be necessary.

I begin in section 5.1 with circumfixation, and show how discontinuous affixes can be represented in this theory. Section 5.2 is concerned with what is often called conversion. Here I suggest that two types of analysis are consistent with the present theory, a zero-affixation analysis or a relisting analysis, and that each possibility is suitable for a different sort of data. Sections 5.3–5.5 are concerned with so-called nonconcatenative morphology, types of word formation such as consonant mutation and umlaut, reduplication, and root and pattern morphology, precisely the word formation types that seem least amenable to treatment in the present theory. In these sections I survey recent work which suggests that these are not "processes" at all, but rather that nonconcatenative word formation is largely reducible to concatenative word formation. I concentrate in these sections on several proposals within the theory of nonconcatenative morphology which might pose problems for the claim made here that there are no specifically morphological principles. In section 5.4 I discuss Clements's so-called "Parafixation" analysis of reduplication (1985) and Aronoff's (1988) notion of "Head Operations," both of which are incompatible with the present theory. In section 5.5 the Morphemic Plane Hypothesis (McCarthy

1979, 1981, 1986) is considered, and my conclusions from these analyses are presented in section 5.6.

5.1 Circumfixation

Bauer (1988) rightly points out that generative theories of morphology have devoted little or no attention to circumfixes, that is, affixes which appear to consist of two discontinuous parts. He gives examples of circumfixes such as those in (1):[1]

(1) Bauer (1988, 20)
    a. German
        ge. . .t   forming past participles of weak verbs
        gemacht 'made'   machen (inf.) 'to make'

    b. Tondano
        pəM. . .an   forming "an attenuative marker to adjectival roots
                          denoting a physical affliction"
        pəluntəŋan 'hard of hearing'   luntəŋ 'deaf'

    c. Dutch
        ge. . .t   forming collective nouns
        het gebeente 'the skeleton'   het been 'the bone'
        het gebergte 'the mountains'   de berg 'the mountain'

To Bauer's examples we can add the following ones from Tagalog:

(2) Tagalog (from Schachter and Otanes 1972)[2]
    a. ka. . .an   the class or group of X
        kabukiran 'fields'   bukid 'field'
        kabundukan 'mountains'   bundok 'mountain'
        katagalugan 'the Tagalogs'   Tagalog 'a Tagalog'

    b. ma. . .in   requiring the quality designated by X or
                   characterized by a mutual manifestation
                   of the quality designated by X
        mabilisan 'requiring speed'   bilis 'speed'
        madalian 'requiring speed'   dali 'speed'
        mahigpitan 'characterized by   higpit 'closeness (of
                 mutual closeness   competition)'
                 (of competition)'
        mahirapan 'characterized by   hirap 'difficulty'
                 mutual difficulty'

We are led to call these formatives circumfixes rather than a separate prefix and suffix for the following reason. In each case there are no words in the language in question which consist of a base plus the prefix or the suffix alone. For example, in Dutch there are no words with the structure [ge[N]] or [[N]te] to support an analysis like [[ge N]te] or [ge[N te]]; rather, the correct structure seems to be [ge[N]te], with the discontinuous affix sandwiched around the base. Circumfixes are admittedly rather rare creatures, yet our theory must provide for them when they occur.

It seems, indeed, that nothing new need be added to our theory to allow for the generation of words with circumfixes. We will assume that circumfixes, like all bound morphemes, have lexical entries indicating their category, subcategorization, semantic representation, and so on. The Dutch circumfix *ge. . .te* and the Tagalog circumfixes *ka. . .an* and *ma. . .in* will have the lexical entries in (3):

(3) a. Dutch
    ge. . .te $[_N$——$[_N$]——$]$
                 LCS: collective nouns
                 [+neuter]
                 etc.

   b. Tagalog
    ka. . .an $[$——$[_N$]——$]$
                 LCS: the class or group designated by the base
    ma. . .in $[_A$——$[_N$]——$]$
                 LCS: characterized by or requiring X

Since the X-bar theory elaborated in chapter 2 does not restrict us to binary-branching structure (a constraint proposed by Kayne 1984, but not adopted here), there is nothing to rule out the ternary-branching structures that will project from the lexical entries in (3).

A somewhat more vexing question is raised by the existence of circumfixes like those in (1) and (2), however. If circumfixes are discontinuous affixes, which part of the circumfix (if either) is the head, and from which part (if either) do morphosyntactic features percolate? It might seem that we would be forced to choose arbitrarily for each circumfix whether the beginning or ending part of the circumfix is the head. However, this arbitrary choice is in fact not necessary for three of the circumfixes in (1) and (2). Notice that in all but one of the examples in (1) and (2), the category of the base is also the category of the derived word. *Ge. . .te* in Dutch derives nouns from nouns, as does Tagalog *ka. . .an*. Tondano *pəM. . .an* derives adjectives from adjectives, and German *ge. . .t* forms past tense verbs

from verb stems. Only one of these circumfixes, Tagalog *ma. . .in* is transparently the head of the word it attaches to. Of the remaining examples
listed in (1) and (2), there is only one other, the Dutch example, that shows
any evidence of the status of the circumfix as a head. In the case of the
Dutch circumfix, the second example in (1c) shows that the circumfix provides the gender of the word as a whole, a sure sign that it is head. Let us
set these two examples aside for a moment.

For the German, Tondano, and Tagalog *ka. . .an* circumfixes, we can
simply say that they are not heads, which is to say that we need not choose
which part of the circumfix bears category and other morphosyntactic features. If these circumfixes have any morphosyntactic features to add to the
word as a whole, they will be percolated via Backup Percolation. As far as
I can tell, it does not matter whether such features percolate from the initial
part of the circumfix or the final part.

As for the two circumfixes which seem to be heads, we might say this.
The parameter settings for Dutch and Tagalog will automatically designate
one part of the circumfix as the head. That is, it was suggested in section 2.3
that Tagalog word formation is largely left-headed and in section 2.5.2 that
in Dutch morphology heads follow modifiers and specifiers. The concrete
effect of this for Dutch was that much derivational morphology in Dutch
turned out to be right-headed. Assuming that the circumfixes in question
here are in line with the rest of the morphology in these languages, the
former part of the circumfix in Tagalog and the latter part of the circumfix
in Dutch will be designated as the heads, and the categorial signature will
percolate up the head side.[3] Note that we need not add anything to the theory to obtain this result. Since the X-bar parameters are set once and for
all, the side of the circumfix which accords with those parameter settings
will be the locus of the categorial signature and therefore the source of features for Head Percolation.

5.2 Conversion

We turn next to conversion, the morphological process that relates forms
such as *paint*$_N$ and *paint*$_V$ in English and *Ruf*$_N$ 'call' and *rufen*$_V$ 'to call' in
German. Several different analyses have been proposed in traditional treatments of word formation and in generative morphology for conversion
phenomena: category-changing rules, derivation by zero affixes, and relisting. In this section I will first show that the category-changing analyses are
ruled out automatically within the present theory on the grounds that they
add a new, specifically morphological rule to the theory. I will try to show
that each of the two sorts of analysis that remain open to us is appropriate

in different sets of circumstances; the zero affixation analysis is appropriate to cases of conversion that show the characteristics of true affixes, the re-listing analysis to those that do not show these characteristics. My argu-ments are largely the same as those in Lieber (1980, 1981); to these I add several new arguments in favor of a relisting analysis for conversion in En-glish and German.

There are two sorts of conceivable category-changing analyses of con-version which are illustrated in (4):

(4) a. $_X[$ $] \rightarrow {}_Y[$ $]$,   where X,Y are categories, e.g.,
$$paint_N \rightarrow paint_V$$

b. $_X[$ $] \rightarrow {}_Y[_X[$ $]]$,   where X,Y are categories, e.g.,
$$paint_N \rightarrow {}_V[paint_N]$$

In the first sort of analysis only category labels are changed; for example, *paint* is changed from a noun to a verb, or *throw* from a verb to a noun. The second sort of analysis (which is essentially the one proposed by Dell and Selkirk (1978) for French—cf. section 3.2.1) adds a second set of labeled brackets around its base. The two analyses differ only in whether or not they add a new layer of structure to their base. Category-changing analyses have an intuitive sort of appeal. They give formal status to the feeling that native speakers of a language have that one item in a pair of words related by conversion is the basic form and that the other item is derived, for example that somehow the noun *chair* in English is more basic than the verb. And such analyses do so with a minimum of "machinery"; no invisible affixes need to be postulated.

Both sorts of category-changing analysis, however, are ruled out within the present theory for a simple reason. Category-changing rules of this sort cannot be reduced to independently needed rules or principles of the Gov-ernment-Binding framework. They do not follow from X-bar theory (X-bar theory is category-neutral in any case), and they certainly bear no resem-blance to Move-Alpha or to principles of any other subtheory. That is, if we were forced to analyze conversion as the result of a category-changing rule, we would have to admit within our theory a rule that is purely mor-phological. And I have claimed that no such purely morphological rules or principles are necessary. However, since there are other analyses of con-version available within our theory, we are not forced to adopt a category-changing analysis.

Our two alternatives, as mentioned above, are a traditional zero affixa-tion analysis and what I will call here a "relisting" analysis. These analy-ses are sketched in (5):

(5) a. Zero Affixation
     i. Conversion results from the affixation of a zero morpheme to a base.
    ii. Zero morphemes have lexical entries that are like the entries of other affixes, except that a phonological representation is lacking.

   b. Relisting
     i. The lexicon allows for the addition of new entries.
    ii. Conversion occurs when an item already listed in the lexicon is re-entered as an item of a different category.

Note that neither of the analyses in (5) would force us to add anything new to the theory developed in chapters 1–4. The zero affixation analysis requires only the addition to the lexicons of languages with conversion the lexical entries for one or more phonologically null affixes.[4] Nor does the relisting analysis require the addition of anything new. Because speakers of a language are always adding new words to their lexicons, we must assume in any theory that there is a mechanism for creating new entries in the lexicon. Whatever this mechanism is, it will also allow for the relisting of items already in the lexicon under new entries.

The two analyses sketched in (5) make rather different predictions about the sorts of conversion data we ought to find in languages. The zero affixation analysis predicts that items derived via conversion should be like other items formed through derivational affixation. Specifically, derivational affixes typically determine the category of words to which they attach, as well as their morphosyntactic features (for example, gender) and diacritic features (for example, membership in a particular conjugation or declension class) (see Lieber 1980 for illustrations). Derivational affixes also typically have some sort of uniform effect on the Lexical Conceptual Structure (LCS) and Predicate Argument Structure (PAS) of their base (see section 3.7 and references cited there). We would expect that zero affixes should show the characteristics of overt derivational affixes as well; the results of zero affixation should display the same sort of uniformity of feature composition, LCS, and PAS that other words formed by derivation do.

On the other hand, the relisting analysis sketched in (5b) predicts no such uniformity of outcome. Rather, since relisting of items takes place piecemeal, one at a time, we should expect that the outcomes of conversion will show a certain degree of randomness: membership in different genders, conjugations, or declensions, differences in PAS, and the like. The relisting analysis also predicts that native speakers of a language should have no intuitions about the lexical characteristics of a newly converted item; for example, speakers of English should have no intuitions as to the LCS and PAS of a newly converted verb "to knob."[5]

In fact, both sorts of analysis seem to be needed. In chapter 2, we saw a set of data for which a zero affixation analysis seemed truly justified. Instrument/agent compounds of the sort *essuie glace* 'windshield wiper' and *coupe cigare* 'cigar cutter' in French display the sort of uniformity of gender and interpretation that usually results from affixation. They are (with only a couple of exceptions) masculine in gender, and have very much the same sort of interpretation, and therefore of LCS, that the agentive/instrumental affix *-er* has in English. I therefore proposed in section 2.5.1 that they be derived via zero affixation, so that the internal structure of the form *essuie glace* would be: $_N[_{VP}[_V[essuie]_N[glace]]\emptyset]$.

On the other hand, much of Lieber (1980, chapter 3) and (1981) are devoted to showing that the outcomes of conversion in German and English do not show the sort of uniformity predicted by the zero affixation analysis. I will briefly repeat those arguments here. The first argument can be made on the basis of nouns derived from verbs in German. In Lieber (1980, 1981) it is argued, following Wurzel (1970), that all German nouns take the case endings in (6):

(6)   sg.   pl.
N   -e
A   -e
G   -s (MASC, NEUT)   -e
D   -n

Nouns may exhibit a number of allomorphs. Since these allomorphs are not predictable on any grounds—phonological, semantic, or otherwise—they must be listed in the lexical entry for each noun stem (see Lieber 1980, 1982) for arguments supporting the listing analysis of allomorphy). Some representative German nouns are listed in (7) with their stem allomorphs.

(7) a. Bach   Bäch   'brook'
       Vater   Väter   'father'
    b. Streik   Streiks   'strike'
       Auto   Autos   'auto'
    c. Geist   Geister   'spirit'
       Mann   Männer   'man'
    d. Bär   Bären   'bear'
       Staat   Staaten   'city'

The inflectional affixes in (6) are subcategorized in their lexical entries to attach to one or another of the listed allomorphs.[6] Noun-forming affixes generally have more than one allomorph as well, and thus fall consistently into one of the classes listed in (7). The noun-forming suffixes *-heit* and *-ung* have the allomorphs *-heiten* and *-ungen,* respectively, which is to say that every form derived by affixation of *-heit* or *-ung* falls into exactly the same class with respect to allomorphy (also with respect to gender—all nouns in *-heit* and *-ung* are feminine).

Noun stems may also be formed by conversion from verb stems in German. If conversion is a process of zero affixation, we should expect the zero affix to behave in the same way that the noun-forming suffixes *-heit* and *-ung* do; all the outcomes of zero affixation should be uniform with respect to allomorphy class and gender. This turns out not to be the case, however, as the data in (8) indicate:

(8) a. der Ruf   (MASC) 'call'   no allomorphs
       (from *rufen*)
     der Find   (MASC) 'find'   no allomorphs
       (from *finden,* past participle stem *fund*)
     der Band (MASC) 'tie, bond'   no allomorphs
       (from *binden,* perfect stem *band*)

    b. der Klang (MASC) 'sound'   allomorph: Kläng
       (from *klingen,* perfect stem allomorph *klang*)
     der Band (MASC) 'volume, binding' allomorph: Bänd
       (from *binden,* perfect stem *band*)

    c. das Grab (NEUT) 'grave'   allomorph: Gräber
       (from *graben*)
     das Band (NEUT) 'ribbon'   allomorph: Bänder
       (from *binden,* perfect stem *band*)

As (8) shows, the outcomes of zero affixation are sometimes masculine and sometimes neuter. Some, like *der Ruf* and *der Fund* have no plural stem allomorphs, which is to say that the inflectional affixes in (6) always attach to the same stem. Other zero-derived nouns do have stem allomorphs, and significantly, not always the same ones, as the examples in (8b,c) show. So the zero affix forming nouns from verbs in German would not have the "uniform outcome" property of derivational affixes.

A similar argument can be made on the basis of noun to verb conversion in English and German. It seems to be the case that when verbs are formed from other categories by overt derivational affixation, the affix in question imposes a uniform argument structure on the outcome. So, for example, the English verb-forming suffix *-ize* (as mentioned in 3.7) will add a layer to the Lexical Conceptual Structure (LCS) of the nouns and adjectives it attaches to, and when LCS is projected to PAS this will result in the addition of an argument to the PAS of the derived verb. Put simply, all verbs formed by affixation of *-ize* will be transitive. As mentioned in Lieber (1981, 178), there are a few *-ize* verbs in English which are not simple transitives: *agonize* is intransitive, and *theorize* takes a sentential complement, for example. However, all new verbs formed with *-ize* are obligatorily transitive, as the example in (9) suggests:

(9)   They venusianized the Martians.
       *They venusianized.[7]
       *They venusianized that Max was a Martian.

The few nontransitive verbs in *-ize* will be listed in the lexicon. Productive derivations, however, will be uniform in PAS, because the affix imposes a uniform PAS on its output.

This turns out not to be the case for verbs that would have to be zero-derived from nouns, however.[8] Some of the verbs that result from conversion are transitive and others intransitive. A list of such verbs with their PASs is given in (10):

(10) a. German
        pflügen   'plow'   x $<$y$>$
        frühstücken   'breakfast'   x
     b. English
        condition   x $<$y$>$
        culture   x $<$y$>$
        prejudice   x $<$y$>$
        feud   x; x $<$with y$>$
        breakfast   x

In both German and English the output of conversion does not display uniformity of PAS, as we would expect if this process were the result of affixation of a zero morpheme. Thus we have a second argument against analyzing conversion as affixation of zero morphemes in English and German.

The alternative that we are left with in the present theory is the one sketched in (5b), which I have referred to as the relisting analysis. The relisting analysis is in fact consistent with what we have seen so far about conversion in English and German. Since items are relisted in the lexicon more or less at random, we would not expect all nouns formed by conversion to belong to the same gender or declension class or all verbs formed by conversion to exhibit the same PAS. This is indeed what we have observed in the conversion data in (8) and (10). Moreover, there are a number of other reasons to believe that relisting is the correct way to treat conversion in English and German.

First, if items in the lexicon are simply relisted at random, we might expect that speakers of English would have no intuitions about the contents of the lexical entries of newly relisted items. So, for example, if I were to coin a new verb like "to knob" or "to peace" from the corresponding nouns, speakers of English should have no intuitions about the exact meanings of these verbs (except that they should have something to do with knobs and peace respectively), nor any intuitions about their PASs. My impression is that this is in fact the case. Without a context, I can imagine that the verb "to knob" might have any of the meanings in (11a) (among others), and either of the PASs in (11b): [9]

(11) a. meanings   'to imitate a knob'
                     'to assault X with a knob'
                     'to put a knob on X'
      b. PASs   x   'I knobbed all night'
                  x <u>   'I knobbed Fenster'
                           'I knobbed the cabinet'

Second, if conversion is a sort of relisting in the lexicon, then it is a kind of creative coinage (as discussed in the Prologue), rather than a truly productive form of word formation. As such, new instances of conversion should show the characteristics of other creative coinages. We should perceive recent coinages as new or odd. They should strike us as cute or funny or objectionable. They should, in short, be the sort of new words that we notice.

My impression again is that this is true for English. New verbs formed by conversion from nouns often do strike us as odd or outlandish. The verb "to gift," mentioned in note 9, evokes a typical "creative coinage response" for me, as does the verb "to impact" (e.g., *Government policies impact heavily on the poor*), another relatively recent coinage. Similarly, verbs coined from proper nouns are often used in a jocular fashion (e.g., *We Richard Nixoned around the room*). Words formed by conversion should cease to attract attention only when they are firmly entrenched in the lexicon.

Finally, if conversion is relisting of items in the lexicon in English and German, we would expect to find no conversion of complex items derived by productive means of word formation. For example, in English we should find no verbs derived by conversion from nouns in *-ness,* nor any verbs derived by conversion from adjectives in *-less,* since these suffixes are completely productive, and their outputs not listed. Similarly, we should find no nouns derived by conversion from verbs in *-ize* in English. Indeed, the results of trying to subject forms in *-ness, -less,* and *-ize* to conversion sound quite impossible—note, not just funny or odd, but impossible:

(12) a. *We happinessed all night.
          *They happinessed Fenster.
      b. *We hopelessed all night.
          *They hopelessed Fenster.
      c. *We gave the car a Midasize.
          *A Midasize is good for your car.[10]

This is not to say, however, that complex forms which are unproductive, and hence listed in the lexicon, **must** undergo conversion/relisting. Conversion/relisting is a random process. We should expect to find that some complex forms that are listed will be able to undergo relisting, but that of course not every item eligible for relisting does get relisted.[11] Examples which support this are mentioned in Lieber (1980, 1981). For example, verbs in *-ate* in English are not productively derived. As the examples in (13) indicate, *-ate* is generally attached to Latinate stems:

(13) a. associate   b. appreciate
         affiliate   extricate
         initiate   lubricate
         deviate   locate
         estimate   suffocate

The suffix *-ate* does not attach to members of any lexical category to form new verbs: **happiate, *deductate, *productate*. As *-ate* is not productive, we would expect that forms in *-ate* would be listed in the lexicon, and as such, would be available at random for relisting. And in fact, this is the case. Of the verbs in (13), only the ones in the (a) column have been relisted as nouns. Those in (13b) do not have nominal counterparts. Similarly, some but not all nouns in *-eer* in English have verbal counterparts formed by conversion (e.g., *engineer* and *mountaineer* do, *bandoleer* does not); *-eer* is another affix in English which is not productive.

Note that neither the category-changing analysis nor the zero affixation analysis can explain these facts.[12] If a category-changing rule or a zero affix simply takes nouns as inputs and creates verbs, or vice versa, there is nothing to prevent the whole range of items bearing the input category from undergoing the category-changing rule, or taking the zero affix. Simple items, items formed with productive affixes, and items formed with unproductive affixes should all be able to undergo conversion. Since this seems not to be the case for English, we have still another reason to rule out both the category-changing and zero affixation analyses of conversion in this case.

There is one additional sort of observation that we should be able to explain about conversion within our theory. That is, the relisting analysis must be able to explain the sort of intuition that native speakers have that one of a pair of items related by conversion is more basic than its partner, for example, in English that the noun *breakfast* is more basic than the verb *breakfast*. It is indeed possible to explain such intuitions with the relisting analysis. Presumably when a noun like *breakfast* is relisted, a new lexical entry is created. Part of that lexical entry will be a semantic representation, or what we have been calling LCS. Let us say that when a new entry is created turning a noun like *breakfast* into a verb, the LCS of the noun will form the innermost layer in the LCS of the verb, perhaps as illustrated in (14):

(14) a. breakfast, N,   LCS: [EARLY MORNING MEAL]
      b. breakfast, V,   LCS: x EAT [EARLY MORNING MEAL]

Our intuition that the noun is basic and that the verb is derived corresponds in this theory to the generalization that the LCS of the noun forms the basis for the LCS of the verb. This will of course also be true in real cases of derivation; for example, the verb *unionize* will have the LCS of *union* as the basis of its LCS as well.

It seems clear then that the theory being developed here makes available adequate means for explaining the range of conversion data in different languages. A zero affixation analysis is available for cases in which conversion truly acts like affixation, as in French instrumental/agentive nouns. On the other hand, the relisting analysis of conversion is preferable to either the zero affixation analysis or the category-changing analysis for English and German. It is consistent with the observation made here that conversion in these cases does not produce a uniform output, and that only unproductive complex words undergo conversion. It can explain the intuition we have that one of a pair of items related by conversion is more basic than the other. And it does not require the addition of any new rules or principles to the theory outlined in previous chapters. This last is of course the most crucial point. We can explain everything we need to explain about conversion in these languages without going beyond the bounds of Government-Binding theory.

5.3 Mutation and Umlaut

I have argued elsewhere in some detail (Lieber 1983b, 1984b, 1987b) that consonant mutation and Umlaut phenomena can be treated as a form of affixation and need not be accounted for by special morphological rules or processes. Here I will merely review some familiar data, and sketch how the affixation analyses of mutation in Fula and Umlaut in German work. The reader is referred to the works mentioned above for other examples and for discussion of the place of such examples within the theory of autosegmental phonology.

5.3.1 Consonant Mutation

Consonant mutation is a relatively rare morphological phenomenon in which lexical stems exhibit two or more different allomorphs in different morphological environments; the allomorphs differ from one another only in that they have different initial (or less often final) consonants. In Fula, initial consonant mutation is one mark of noun class membership; mutation of initial consonants also occurs in the verbal paradigms, but we will confine ourselves here to a discussion of the noun system. According to Arnott (1970), most stems exhibit either two or three allomorphs: one continuant initial, one stop initial, and for voiced segments, one prenasalized stop initial. The particular allomorph that occurs in each form depends upon the noun class suffix. Certain noun class suffixes require a stem which is stop initial, others a stem which is prenasalized stop initial, and still others a stem which is continuant initial. Part of a Fula noun paradigm is illustrated in (15):

(15) 'monkey'   waa-ndu   Class 11
                 baa-ɗi   Class 25
                 ᵐbaa-kon   Class 6

As illustrated in (15), the noun class 11[13] morpheme *-ndu,* which marks the singular form of this noun requires a continuant initial stem. The class 25 suffix *-ɗi,* a plural class marker, selects a stop initial form of the noun stem. And the class 6 (diminutive) marker *-kon* selects a noun stem which is prenasalized stop initial. Paradis (1986) analyzes the initial mutations of Fula in the following way.[14]

According to Paradis (1986, 1987), the continuant initial allomorphs are generally the underlying forms of Fula nouns. Stop initial and prenasalized stop initial allomorphs result from the affixation of the two prefixes listed in (16):

(16) a. X
      b. X
         n

The prefix in (16a) consists solely of an empty skeleton or timing slot. The one in (16b) contains in addition to an empty timing slot a [+Nasal] feature, abbreviated here as *n.*[15]

The prefixes in (16) have lexical entries which contain the subcategorization frames in (17):

(17) a. X   ＿＿＿ ₙ[Class 25,. . .]
      b. X   ＿＿＿ ₙ[Class 6,. . .]
         n

Lexical entries of suffixes indicate what class they belong to. Note that [+Class N] is a morphosyntactic feature in Fula. Class information in this language is rather like gender in Indo-European languages; agreement inside noun phrases, for example, is determined by the class into which a noun stem falls. I will therefore assume that features like [+Class N] will percolate as other morphosyntactic features do, and therefore that the feature will be "visible" in the morphological tree at the time that a prefix attaches.

Several phonological rules apply to the structures that result from affixing noun class suffixes and the prefixes in (16) to noun stems. Paradis points out, first of all, that the phonology of Fula contains several constraints on geminate segments. Geminate segments cannot appear in the onsets or codas of syllables because neither onsets nor codas may branch in Fula (that is, onset and coda are limited to one consonant each). Moreover, Fula phonology also disallows geminate continuants of any sort. If a continuant such as *f, r, s,* etc., becomes a geminate in the course of a derivation, it is automatically subjected to a phonological process which Paradis (1986, 87) calls "Hardening." In effect, Hardening changes the feature [+Cont] to [−Cont]. A formal statement of this process can be found in Paradis (1986, chap. 5). The class 25 form of the noun *monkey* will therefore be derived as follows:

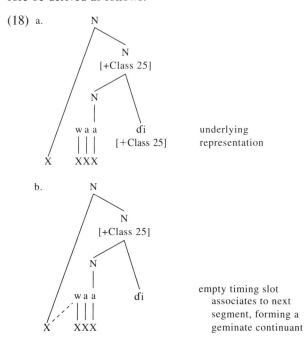

(18) a.   underlying representation

b.   empty timing slot associates to next segment, forming a geminate continuant

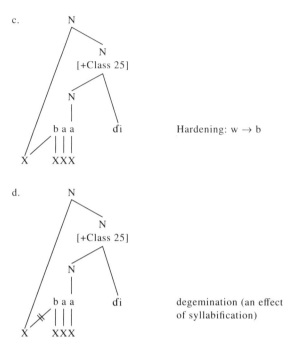

As the derivation in (18) shows, the empty timing slot prefix attaches to the form suffixed with the class 25 noun class marker. The empty timing slot is associated with the closest segment *w*, but since this creates a geminate continuant, the Hardening rule turns *w* to *b*. A second phonological effect then follows: since the rules of syllabification of Fula allow only a single segment in the onset, the initial timing slot is dissociated. The result of these phonological and prosodic rules is then the class 25 form *baa-ɗi*.

Derivation of the class 6 diminutive form *ᵐbaa-kon* runs as follows. The suffix *-kon* is a marker which bears the morphosyntactic feature [+Class 6]. Prefix (16b) attaches to underlying *waa-kon* as shown in (19a):

(19) a.

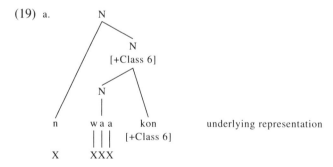

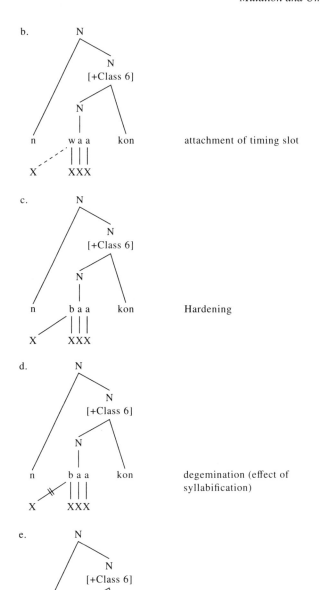

b.   attachment of timing slot

c.   Hardening

d.   degemination (effect of
syllabification)

e.   attachment of floating nasal

The derivation of the class 6 form *ᵐbaa-kon* then proceeds exactly as in the derivation of *baa-ɗi* above. The empty timing slot attaches to the initial segment forming a geminate continuant (19b). This is then subjected to Hardening (19c). Syllabification leaves the first slot prosodically unincorporated, resulting in degemination (19d). Finally, the floating nasal attaches to the initial voiced segment, prenasalizing it. What is significant for our purposes is that in terms of morphological structure, the initial mutations require no special treatment. They are the result of prefixation of phonologically incomplete segments.

5.3.2 Umlaut

The process of Umlaut in German can be treated in a similar fashion. A phenomenon which appears at first glance to require some sort of special morphological rule can in fact again be analyzed as affixation of a floating feature. I will briefly sketch a floating feature analysis of Umlaut, a slightly modified version of the analysis of Umlaut in Lieber (1987b). The reader is referred to that work for a more thorough treatment of Umlaut and for a comparison of the floating feature analysis to earlier analyses.

Lieber (1980) and other works cited therein have argued that Umlaut is not a phonological rule in German, and I will not reiterate those arguments here. Assuming that Umlaut is a morphological phenomenon in which stem vowels are fronted in certain morphological environments, it can be analyzed in the following way. Umlaut-conditioning affixes such as the diminutive *-chen* contain, in addition to the full phonological segments of which they are composed, a floating feature [−Back]. Following a suggestion by Rice (1989), I will assume that lexical representations in German are underspecified, and that only one value of a feature, the marked value, is present in underlying representations. For the feature [Back], the marked value will be [−Back]; [+Back] vowels will receive their specification for this feature late in the derivation by means of a default rule which fills in unmarked values.[16] Affixation of an umlauting suffix to an underspecified stem will result in the linking of the floating [−Back] segment to the underspecified stem vowel, as shown in (20):

(20)
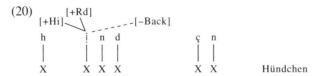

I am assuming here the model of segmental geometry proposed in Sagey (1986), although I represent the structure of relevant segments only partially in (20). Note that assuming underlying representations to be underspecified allows a simplification of the Umlaut analysis in Lieber (1987b); in that work, since it was assumed that stem vowels were fully specified for the feature [Back], it was necessary to assume a rule of Delinking to sever the underlying specification for the feature [Back] before the floating [−Back] feature could attach. With underspecification, it is possible to eliminate the Delinking Rule. Umlaut thus involves nothing more than the association of a floating [−Back] feature to a stem vowel; it is a by-product of affixation.

Umlaut, like consonant mutation, therefore poses no problem for the theory of morphology being developed here. Since Umlaut is analyzed as the by-product of affixing a morpheme bearing the floating feature [−Back] to an underspecified stem, no new sort of morphological rule or process need be added to the theory.

5.4 Reduplication

Reduplication is perhaps the form of word formation that lends itself most strongly to being treated as a process or an operation on a string. It is also a subject that has generated a large literature in recent generative morphology and phonology (among many others Marantz 1982; Broselow and McCarthy 1984; Clements 1985; McCarthy and Prince 1986, 1987), much of which is devoted to showing that this classically nonconcatenative type of word formation is indeed a form of affixation. In this section I first give an illustration of a current affixation analysis of reduplication from McCarthy and Prince (1986). I then focus on two recent claims based on reduplication facts that potentially pose problems for a theory of morphology like the one developed here which allows no independent rules or principles of morphology.

The first claim is that made by Clements (1985) that certain sorts of reduplication require what has come to be called "parafixation," a process whereby reduplicative skeletal material starts out synchronous with part of the stem, and is later reordered. The reordering process is one that would have to be a special morphological rule, and as such it poses a threat to the central claim on which this work is based. However, McCarthy and Prince (1987) propose an alternative to the parafixation analysis which is consistent with the claims of this work, and which I will adopt here.

The second claim is one made by Aronoff (1988) that certain morphological processes, most prominently certain reduplication rules, are what he calls "Head Operations," that is, morphological processes that apply only to the head of a complex word, in a sense reaching inside a word to touch only the innermost part. I will argue below that there are in fact no

Head Operations. In a number of cases in which Aronoff invokes head processes, the affected morpheme is arguably not the head of the word at all. Furthermore, I argue that the examples cited by Aronoff are ones in which a morpheme (most often a reduplicative morpheme) is subcategorized to attach to a prosodic constituent, as well as to a morphological constituent, head or not. Such operations are described in Broselow and McCarthy (1984) and in McCarthy and Prince (1986). I will show in the final part of this section why their sort of analysis is consistent with the framework developed here.

5.4.1 Reduplication as Affixation

Marantz (1982) argues persuasively that processes of reduplication—where a portion of a base word is copied in some morphological environment—can be analyzed as conventional affixation within the theory of autosegmental phonology. Marantz's original idea was that reduplicative morphemes consist solely of skeletal material, in his theory a sequence of CV timing slots that are prefixed or suffixed to a base. The melodic content of these skeletal slots is derived by copying the melody of the base and associating it (left to right for prefixes, right to left for suffixes) to the empty skeletal slots. McCarthy and Prince (1986) motivate a slightly different treatment of reduplication which overcomes some of the technical problems with Marantz's theory; in their theory the reduplicative morpheme is simply a prosodic constituent, for example, a syllable, a foot or a phonological word, rather than a sequence of skeletal slots. I will not reiterate McCarthy and Prince's arguments for substituting phonological constituents for sequences of skeletal segments (see McCarthy and Prince 1986), but will merely present some of their analyses and show why they are consistent with the present theory of word formation.

   McCarthy and Prince (1986, 7) recognize the following sorts of prosodic constituents:

(21) Wd   prosodic word
     F   foot
     σ syllable
     σ_μ light (monomoraic) syllable
     $\sigma_{\mu\mu}$ heavy (bimoraic) syllable
     σ_c core syllable

All of these are phonologically motivated categories, that is, categories independently necessary within the phonology for treatment of stress, syllable structure, or the like. In addition to these McCarthy and Prince (1986, 8) recognize **minimal** versions of some categories; for example, the minimal syllable is σ_c, which consists solely of C V, and the minimal word (Wd^{MIN}), which is a foot.

Within their theory, a reduplicative affix can consist of any one of the prosodic constituents in (21). The lexical entry of the affix, in our terms, states what the constituent is, and whether it is a prefix or a suffix (i.e., whether it subcategorizes something to the right or to the left). For example, according to McCarthy and Prince (1986, 13), Ilokano is a language which has the reduplicative prefix σ. To form the progressive of the verb in Ilokano, the prefix σ is attached to the verb, along with a segmental prefix *ag-*. The verbal melody is copied, and the prefix σ then takes its content from the melodic copy—as many segments as fill out the maximal Ilokano syllable. Some examples are given in (22a), and a derivation in (22b):

(22) a. Base   Progressive

        basa   ag-bas-basa   'be reading'

        dait   ag-da-dait   'be studying'

        adal   ag-ad-adal   'be studying'

        takder   ag-tak-takder   'be standing'

        trabaho   ag-trab-trabaho   'be working'

    b. σ σ σ σ σ σ

       $+$ /\\/\\ $\rightarrow$ /\\ $+$ /\\/\\

            ba sa   bas a   ba sa

As the example in (22b) indicates, the prefix σ takes as many segments as can be fitted into a syllable in Ilokano, regardless of how those segments are syllabified in the base.

One of the various reduplicative affixes in Tagalog is, according to McCarthy and Prince, the phonological constituent σ_c, the core syllable, which consists of at most two segments, a consonant and a vowel. McCarthy and Prince (1986, 16) give the examples in (23):

(23) a. Tagalog recent perfective verbs

       ka-ta-trabaho   'just finished working'

       ka-i-ipon   'just saved'

       ka-ga-galit   'just got mad'

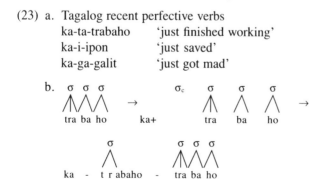

As (23) illustrates, the recent perfective of the verb is formed by prefixing *ka-* plus the core syllable (σ_c) to the verb stem. After copying of the verb stem's melody, the core syllable associates with the first consonant and vowel of the copy (association is assumed to be left to right for prefixes). As the first example in (23a) indicates, a consonant in the onset of the first syllable may be passed over in constructing the prefixal σ_c.

Larger phonological constituents may also be chosen as reduplicative prefixes. For example, Mokilese has a heavy syllable ($\sigma_{\mu\mu}$) as a reduplicative prefix (24), and the Australian language Diyari has a minimal word as shown in (25):

(24) Mokilese (McCarthy and Prince 1986, 21)[17]

Verb Stem	Progressive	
pOdok	pOd-pOdok	'plant'
m^{w}ine	m^{w}in-m^{w}ine	'eat'
dOp^{w}O	dOp^w-dOp^{w}O	'pull'
pa	paa-pa	'weave'
wi.a	wii-wi.a	'do'
kookO	koo-kookO	'grind coconut'

(25) Diyari (McCarthy and Prince 1986, 31)[18]

wila	wilawila	'woman'
kanku	kankukanku	'boy'
napiri	napinapiri	'father'
tilparku	tilpatilparku	'bird type'
nankanti	nankanankanti	'cat fish'

A heavy syllable—that is, two morae—in Mokilese can be CVC or CVV, as the examples in (24) illustrate. The minimal phonological word in Diyari is a foot, which consists of two syllables. Diyari has CV and CVC syllables, although a coda consonant is impossible at the end of a phonological word (thus, *tilparku* reduplicates as *tilpatilparku,* rather than as **tilpartilparku*).[19]

McCarthy and Prince (1986) thus work out a framework for reduplication which is restrictive—the only sorts of reduplicative affixes that exist are those that take the shape of independently needed prosodic constituents—but which nevertheless gives wide empirical coverage. More importantly for our purposes, McCarthy and Prince's theory of prosodic morphology dovetails nicely with the model of morphology being developed here. Reduplication in their theory (as for Marantz 1982) is nothing more than a sort of affixation. Reduplicative affixes have lexical entries just as other affixes do, except that their phonological representations are somewhat skimpier than those of ordinary affixes. We turn next to the two sorts of reduplicative phenomena which have been argued in recent literature to require more theoretical machinery than simple affixation.

5.4.2 Quantity Sensitive Reduplication and the Parafixation Analysis

Clements (1985) points out that some sorts of reduplication processes preserve the distinction between long and short segments as part of the copying process. For example, one of the reduplication processes in Tagalog copies the whole stem, preserving vowel length, so that *li:nis* 'clean' reduplicates as *li:nis li:nis* and *walis* 'sweep' as *walis walis*. Clements dubs this process "quantitative transfer." This phenomenon is somewhat problematic in autosegmental analyses of reduplication for the following reason. If nothing is copied but the phonemic melody, and if the phonemic melody conforms to the Obligatory Contour Principle (OCP) (Leben 1973; Goldsmith 1976; McCarthy 1981, 1986), as is usually assumed, then the phonemic melody copy shows no signs indicating whether its segments were long or short in the original. And yet the reduplicative copy must replicate those quantity patterns. This is illustrated in (26):

(26) Wd   Wd

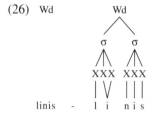

linis   -   l i   n i s

The problem of quantitative transfer appears not only in cases of full reduplication like the Tagalog one above, but also in cases where only part of a word is reduplicated. For example, in the Mokilese example in (24), where we saw that a heavy syllable reduplicates, a long vowel in the first syllable of the base is preserved under reduplication, even though the reduplicative heavy syllable might just as well have been made up by copying the second consonant of the base; so *kookO* 'grind coconut' reduplicates as *koo-kookO* rather than as **kok-kookO*.

Clements (1985) proposes to analyze quantitative transfer as a process of parafixation. For full reduplication, parafixation involves the generation of an exact copy of a stem simultaneous with the stem itself. As the derivation in (27) for the Tagalog full reduplication illustrates, the affix Wd is first parafixed to the Wd node of the base, and then the segments of the base are projected to the new Wd node:[20]

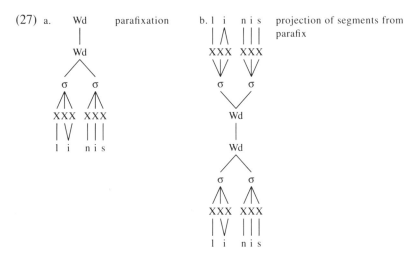

At some point in the derivation the parafix and stem are linearized; in some cases phonological rules may apply to the parafixed representation before linearization takes place.

Partial reduplication works in a similar fashion. Using Clements's (1985) parafixation analysis, Levin (1985) analyzes the Mokilese case as parafixation of a syllable containing three timing slots to the stem:

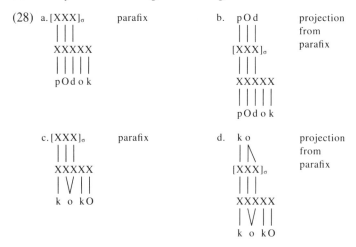

The phonemic melody of the stem is projected or copied via the parafix, preserving length. Again, at a later stage in the derivation the parafixed representation undergoes linearization. Presumably, for partial reduplications like the one in Mokilese, it must simply be stipulated that the parafix precedes the stem after linearization.

McCarthy and Prince (1987) point out a number of problems with the parafixation analysis. First, as just mentioned, the direction of linearization must simply be stipulated. Second, it is not possible to express directly in the parafixation theory that the copy must be adjacent to its base. Third, McCarthy and Prince (1987, 12) point out that linearization is a sort of operation that is unique to reduplication. From our point of view this third criticism is the most serious. If parafixation is necessary in reduplicative word formation, then a new, uniquely morphological process of linearization is necessary. Since linearization of parafixes does not follow from any independent principle of syntax or phonology, we would have to add it to our theory and give up the strong claim it is based upon, that there are no independent principles or rules of morphology.

We are not, however, driven to this extremity. McCarthy and Prince (1987) work out a mechanism for quantitative transfer that is perfectly compatible with the claims of the present theory. Reduplication, as suggested above, involves nothing more than the affixation of a prosodic constituent. Quantitative transfer is an effect of the lexical representation of quantitative phenomena. McCarthy and Prince note that quantity, for example vowel length, is distinctive only in some languages; in those languages in which the length of a vowel is not predictable, there must be some indication of vowel length in lexical entries. Rather than including in a lexical entry a phonemic melody plus the whole skeleton that it goes with (the skeleton of course would encode the length of vowels), McCarthy and Prince propose to annotate phonemic melodies with only enough prosodic information to indicate what is unpredictable. In their theory, this is indicated by linking the mora symbol μ to a long vowel, presumably to show that it covers two morae (one-mora coverage is indicated by default, that is, by no annotation at all). Thus the lexical entry for the Mokilese verb 'to grind coconut' would be as in (29):

(29) μ
        |
       kokO

In cases of reduplication in which there is quantitative transfer the following occurs. After affixation of the prosodic constituent there is no copying of the phonemic melody in the usual sense. Rather, the original lexical representation of the stem is reinserted, complete with annotations indicating distinctive length, as in (30a) (McCarthy and Prince 1987, 30–31). The heavy syllable reduplicative affix is then associated with the heavy syllable template. Although McCarthy and Prince do not show an explicit derivation, the association procedure in (30b, c) gives the intended result. The lexical μ attached to the first vowel of *kokO* indicates that it must fill two morae. It attaches to the second mora of the heavy syllable template (30b), then spreads to associate with the first mora as well (30c):

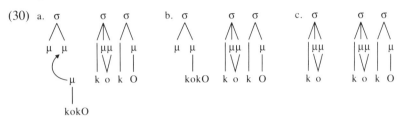

The lexical indication of vowel length must be preserved as long as there is room for it in the target template. Since the reduplicative prefix in Mokilese is a heavy syllable, the distinctive length in the initial vowel of *kookO* is preserved under reduplication. Full reduplication, such as in the Tagalog example, is accomplished in the same way. Underlyingly distinctive length is preserved by reinserting the base from its lexical entry, rather than by copying the phonemic melody.

This alternative to the parafixation analysis is attractive for a number of reasons. Unlike the parafixation analysis, it does not need to stipulate where the reduplicative affix goes; since the mechanism of reduplication is nothing more than affixation of a prosodic category, this is done in the usual way as part of the lexical entry for each reduplicative affix. Nor is there any problem in expressing the observation that the reduplicative copy is always adjacent to what is copied. It could not be otherwise in this theory, since the direction of association is always left to right for prefixes and right to left for suffixes. Finally, McCarthy and Prince's solution to the "transfer" problem does without a rule of linearization, thus eliminating a potential threat to the central claim of this work, that there are no rules or principles unique to morphology.

5.4.3 Against Head Operations: Affixation to Prosodic Structure

Aronoff (1988), on the basis of a number of reduplication and other processes, suggests that there is a class of word formation rules which he calls, following Hoeksema (1985), "Head Operations." Hoeksema defines the notion "Head Operation" as in (31):

(31) Head Operation
    F is a Head Operation if $F(Y) = Z$, and $W = XY$
    (where Y is the head of W) together imply that
    $F(W) = X + F(Y) = X + Z$.

Definition (31) states that a morphological rule is a Head Operation if it reaches into a word W to perform an operation on its head Y, changing Y to Z. Aronoff applies the notion of Head Operation to Tagalog to solve a classic problem of what has been called the "overapplication" of phonological rules. Tagalog has a prefix *pang-* which attaches to nouns. As the data in (32a) show, [ŋ] plus a following stop appears in the derived form as a single nasal homorganic with the underlying stop:

(32) a. atip   'roofing'   pang-atip   'that used for roofing'
        pu:tul   'cut'   pa-mu:tul   'that used for cutting'
     b. pa-mu-mu:tul   'a cutting in quantity'

The example in (32b) shows further that when the second form in (32a) is reduplicated, the stem reduplicates showing the effect of having already undergone affixation; the stem initial *p* has become *m* prior to reduplication. This analysis is of course problematic in traditional frameworks in which morphology strictly precedes phonology, hence the label "overapplication." It is not necessarily problematic in frameworks where morphological rules can apply to the output of phonological rules, and vice versa. But even in frameworks where phonological and morphological rules can be interspersed, it must still be explained why the reduplication rule seems to reach into an already prefixed word.

Aronoff suggests that the derivation of the form in (32b) involves a Head Operation. After affixation of *pang-* which triggers sandhi, reduplication reaches into the word to copy the first two segments of the stem. Aronoff then goes on to analyze several other cases of reduplication and one of conventional affixation as Head Operations.

The notion that certain morphological operations must be "Head Operations" is problematic for us, since it implies once again that there is a class of rules unique to morphology—in this case, a class of rules that can skim a string, looking inside one or more sets of brackets, to apply to some internal constituent. However, there is good reason to believe that there are no Head Operations. It is in any case not clear that such operations apply to heads, as heads are typically defined in morphology. Furthermore, all of Aronoff's data are subject to an alternative analysis: they appear in fact to be examples of what Broselow and McCarthy (1984) and McCarthy and Prince (1986) call affixation to a prosodic constituent.

First, let me give some examples which suggest that the term "Head Operations" is a misnomer in any case for the examples that Aronoff cites. Aronoff himself gives no definition of "head of a word." Still any reasonable definition of head will fail to pick out the correct target in all of his examples. For example, we have seen (section 2.3) that Tagalog word formation is largely left-headed. It is in fact clear that the head in the example (32b) is the reduplicative affix, rather than the stem. *Pang-* attaches to noun or verb stems to form adjectives, according to Schachter and Otanes

(1972). Although the glosses in (32), taken from Bloomfield (1933), suggest that the *pang-* forms are nouns, a native speaker of Tagalog confirms that they are adjectives instead with the glosses 'for roofing' and 'for cutting' in conformity with Schachter and Otanes. Reduplication changes the *pang-* adjective to a noun. If the reduplicative affix changes category, it must be the head. The stem therefore cannot be the head in the Tagalog example.

Similarly, in the Makassarese example that Aronoff cites, there is evidence that the stem to which reduplication applies is not always the head. Consider the data in (33):

(33) a. golla   gollagolla
       manara   manakmanara
     b. i. gássiŋ 'strong'   gassiŋgássiŋ 'somewhat
                                                                 strong'

        ii. gassiŋ+i 'make it strong'   gassikgassiŋi 'make it
                                                                 somewhat
                                                                 strong'

Makassarese reduplication is sensitive to syllable structure. If the stem contains only two syllables, they reduplicate as is. If the stem contains more than two syllables, however, the second syllable of the reduplicative prefix ends in *k*. This is illustrated in (33a). Aronoff then uses the examples in (33b) to show that certain suffixes are syllabified into the stem, so that the stem is treated as if it had three syllables. Under these circumstances the reduplicative prefix in (33bii) ends in *k*, rather than in the *ŋ* of the stem (which has been resyllabified as onset of the following syllable). Reduplication, according to Aronoff, must apply to the "head" after affixation and resyllabification. What the example in (33b) actually shows, however, is that the reduplication applies to the stem which in fact no longer is the **head** in (33bii)—the affix *-i* is category-changing, and therefore must be the head. So the sort of operation that Aronoff is proposing is again not one which applies exclusively to heads.

How can such examples be handled without special "Head" Operations? McCarthy and Prince (1986, 12) suggest that it is sometimes necessary in any case to allow affixes to attach to prosodic constituents (that is, those in (21)), rather than to purely morphological constituents (that is, an X^0 of some sort):[21]

Finally, we will follow Broselow and McCarthy (1984) in assuming that the domain of affixation may be delimited prosodically as well as morphologically. In particular, the notion minWd may be called on to pick out a subsequence of the stem which can serve as a kind of pseudo-stem for purposes of affixation and associated processes.

They argue, for example, that the reduplicative affix in the Australian language Yidiny (Dixon 1977) must attach to Wd^{MIN}, rather than to a simple N^0. Consider the examples in (34):

(34) Yidiny Nominal Reduplication

mulari	'initiated man'	mulamulari	pl.
kintalpa	'lizard species'	kintalkintalpa	pl.
kalamparaa	'March fly'	kalakalamparra	pl.

The Yidiny reduplicative prefix is itself a Wd^{MIN}, which is to say a foot (= two syllables in Yidiny). If this prefix is attached to the stem in the examples in (34), with copying of the phonemic melody, we would expect *mularmulari* alongside *kintalkintalpa*. But the *r* of *mulari* cannot be incorporated into the reduplicative prefix, whereas the *l* of *kintalpa* can.

McCarthy and Prince argue that this pattern of facts follows if the reduplicative prefix attaches to Wd^{MIN} rather than simply to N^0. The most crucial assumption that they make then is that **only the constituent to which a reduplicative affix attaches is available for copying.** For the first example in (34), only the Wd^{MIN} *mula* is available, *r* being the onset in the third syllable. In *kintalpa*, the Wd^{MIN} is *kintal*, since the *l* cannot form part of the onset of the third syllable. Thus in the former case the reduplicated form is *mulamulari*, while in the latter it is *kintalkintalpa*.[22] Note that McCarthy and Prince, following Nash (1980), assume the *mp* of *kalamparra* to be an admissible onset in Yidiny. What is copied in this third example, then, is the Wd^{MIN} *kala*, since both *m* and *p* belong to the onset of the next syllable.

Within the theory being developed here, an affix (reduplicative or otherwise) which has both a conventional morphological subcategorization frame and a prosodic constraint on its attachment will have a lexical entry like that in (35):

(35) Yidiny Reduplication
      Wd^{MIN} $_N[\underline{\hspace{2em}}[_{N/Wd^{\text{MIN}}}$

The notation in (35) should be interpreted as follows. The Yidiny reduplicative prefix is a Wd^{MIN} which attaches to a Wd^{MIN} in prosodic structure and to an N^0 in morphological structure. I assume here, as argued in Booij and Lieber (1989) (cf. also chapter 4), that prosodic and morphological structure are present simultaneously. The derivation of the Yidiny reduplicated forms *kintalkintalpa* and *mulamulari* are given in (36). Note again that McCarthy and Prince crucially assume that only the melody of the prosodic constituent to which an affix attaches is available for copying.

(36) a.

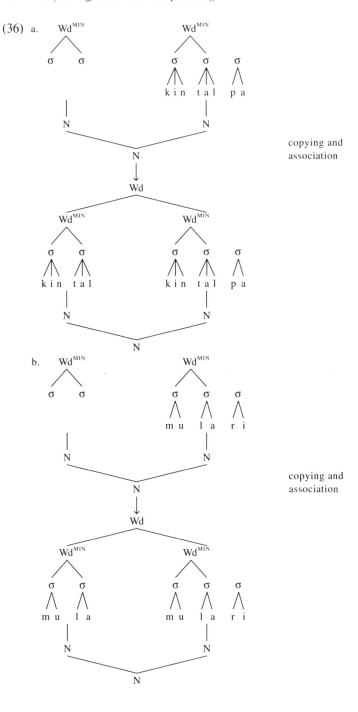

copying and
association

b.

copying and
association

The notion of simultaneous morphological and prosodic subcategorization can now be used to account for the Tagalog case in (32) without the use of a "Head Operation." I will assume that the particular reduplicative prefix in question is a core syllable, σ_c in the notation of McCarthy and Prince (1986), and that it has the lexical entry in (37):

(37) Tagalog Reduplication

$$\sigma_c \qquad [_N \text{———} [_{A/Wd^{MIN}}$$

Lexical entry (37) says that the Tagalog reduplicative prefix σ_c attaches to an A^0 morphologically, and prosodically to the Wd^{MIN}. Let us see what happens when the prefix is attached. I will assume, first, that the prefix *pang-* is attached to a noun or verb stem triggering the phonological sandhi rule. The structure that will result is that in (38), with prosodic structure shown above the segments and morphological structure below:

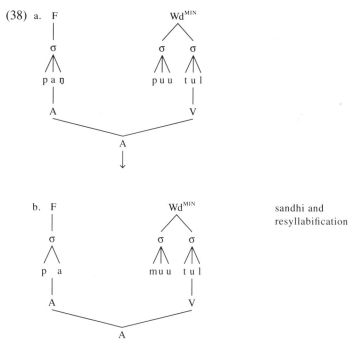

(38) a.

b.   sandhi and resyllabification

If we try to attach the reduplicative prefix σ_c next, however, we find that we cannot fulfill both the morphological and prosodic subcategorizations of the prefix simultaneously. If we insert the σ_c to the left of *pa-* in (38b), the σ_c will not be adjacent to the Wd^{MIN}, as illustrated in (39a). But if we try to insert the reduplicative prefix so that it is adjacent to the Wd^{MIN}, it will not be adjacent to the A, as shown in (39b). Indeed it is unclear how morphological structure could be projected at all in this structure, since to do so would involve creation of morphological structure on top of already existing morphological structure.

(39) a.*

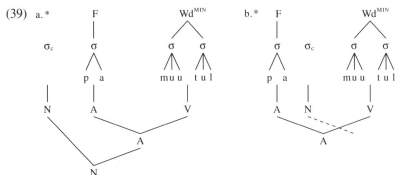

In order to get the reduplicative prefix in Tagalog to fulfill its morphological and prosodic subcategorizations simultaneously, we need to make one further assumption. It is clear that the lexical entry in (37) contains (at least) two sorts of information. The reduplicative prefix consists of phonological information (it is a core syllable lacking any inherent segmental content) and morphosyntactic information (it is a bound noun, which presumably carries all of the morphosyntactic features of nouns in Tagalog). Given the dual content of the reduplicative prefix in Tagalog, I assume that the following occurs. Since it is not possible to satisfy its subcategorization if the prefix remains intact, I assume that a split occurs in the lexical representation of the prefix. The phonological material is inserted into the tree in (38) adjacent to the Wd^{MIN}, thus satisfying the phonological part of the subcategorization, and the morphosyntactic part (that is the category features for N plus concomitant morphosyntactic features) is affixed to the A, thus satisfying the morphosyntactic part of the subcategorization. This is illustrated in (40):

(40) a.

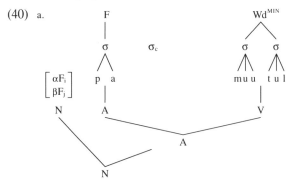

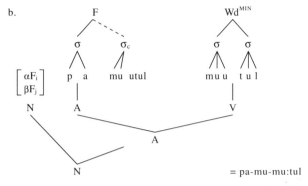

Structure (40a) shows the splitting of the phonological and morphosyntactic parts of the affix. This is then followed by the copying of the phonemic melody of the Wd^{MIN}, and association to the σ_c. I will assume that the σ_c prefix is incorporated into the existing prosodic structure by being absorbed into the preceding foot. This is illustrated in (40b).

Note that this analysis is not meant to imply that the Tagalog reduplicative prefix **moves** from one part of the word structure to another, but rather that the dual subcategorization requirement forces the lexical information on the prefix to split upon insertion, so that the syllable template is severed from its categorial signature. Assuming that prosodic and morphological structure are built in tandem and are present simultaneously, then, there is no need within the present framework to postulate a special category of "Head Operations" or operations which need to reach into and operate on a morpheme inside a word. All of Aronoff's cases of Head Operations are in fact cases of simultaneous morphological and prosodic subcategorization and none of them require any special morphological rules or processes within the present theory.

5.5   Templatic Morphology and the Morphemic Plane Hypothesis [23]

The final sort of word formation to which I turn in this chapter is so-called root and pattern or templatic morphology. This is the sort of morphology for which the Morphemic Plane Hypothesis (henceforth MPH) was originally proposed (McCarthy 1979, 1981). Embedded within the general theory of autosegmental representations, the MPH allowed an explanatory analysis of the morphology of the Semitic languages in which distinct morphemes were projected onto distinct planes. Such multiplanar representations permitted McCarthy to show how, at the same time, the triconsonantal roots of classical Arabic could be distinct morphemes and still be intercalated around vowels in various patterns. Verbal forms were represented as in (41), with the consonantal root, the vocalic melody and the prosodic template or skeleton all occupying distinct planes:

(41)

In terms of current theory, the segments *ktb* and *a* above are shorthand for multitiered representations, and the units C and V of the skeleton for syllable templates, at least in the theory of prosodic morphology developed by McCarthy and Prince (1986), mentioned in the previous section.

More recent work in planar phonology and morphology suggests that morphemes do not remain on different planes throughout the derivation. McCarthy (1986), for example, notes that much of Semitic phonology operates on representations in which vowels and consonants are folded together into the same plane, as illustrated in (42):

(42)
```
k   a   t   a   b
|   |   |   |   |
C   V   C   V   C
```

He proposes, following Younes (1983), that a process of Plane Conflation brings together morphemically distinct planes into a single plane at some stage in the derivation. Cole (1987) also crucially assumes Plane Conflation, and proposes that it occur between the lexical and postlexical levels of the phonology.

While the original support for the MPH came from the root and pattern morphology of the Semitic languages, in recent years the MPH has been invoked in a number of phonological and morphological analyses outside of Semitic. McCarthy (1986) discusses several cases, including phenomena from Rotuman, Afar, and Tonkawa. Cole (1987) extends the domain of the MPH to harmony processes, discussing cases from Coeur d'Alene, Wiyot, and Warlpiri, among others. Finally, Halle and Vergnaud (1987) extend use of the MPH to English, arguing that the cyclic or noncyclic behavior of English affixes can be made to follow from whether they are projected on different planes or not.

The MPH has sparked significant progress in difficult areas of phonology and morphology, but it also raises several questions in the context of the theory of word structure being developed here. We must ask, first, what relation the MPH should have to the sort of hierarchically structured word formation argued here to follow from general principles of the grammar. For example, could the MPH supplant hierarchical word structure entirely? Are all morphemes in all languages introduced onto different planes, or does this happen only in some languages? Conversely, must anything projected onto a distinct plane be a morpheme? And most importantly for the central claim of this work, is the MPH itself a distinct principle of morphology, or does it require other distinct principles of morphology? In this section I will argue that the answers to all three questions are negative.

It is relatively clear that the distribution of morphemes onto different planes could not replace a theory of word structure which assigns hierarchical structure to words, and in fact, no one to my knowledge has explicitly suggested that it should. The only (implicit) indication that distribution of morphemes onto different planes is an alternative to hierarchical structure is a brief suggestion in McCarthy (1986, 228) that the operation of Plane Conflation is the same thing as Bracket Erasure within the framework of Lexical Phonology. Bracket Erasure is the device within Lexical Phonology that obliterates internal structure in words so that the subsequent phonological rules cannot have access to that structure. To say that Plane Conflation has the effect of Bracket Erasure is to suggest that the planar distribution of morphemes is the only structural principle organizing morphemes. There are at least two reasons to believe that this is not the situation, however, one rather specific and another far more general.[24]

A very specific reason for not equating planar distribution with hierarchical structure comes from Modern Hebrew, as argued in Bat El (1988). Bat El (1988) argues persuasively that a rule of Voicing Assimilation in Modern Hebrew must follow Plane Conflation. This rule is stated segmentally in (43b); examples are given in (43a) (Bat El 1988, 480):

(43) a. hit + darder → hiddarder
'he declined, rolled down'

hit + balet → hidbalet
'he became prominent'

b. $[-\text{Son}] \rightarrow [\alpha\text{Voice}] / \underline{\hspace{1cm}} \begin{bmatrix} -\text{Son} \\ \alpha\text{Voice} \end{bmatrix}$

Voicing Assimilation would be a sort of spreading rule in a theory assuming segmental geometry; presumably the laryngeal node of the second $[-\text{Son}]$ segment spreads to the preceding $[-\text{Son}]$ segment. The fact that segments that have been linked by Voicing Assimilation observe Geminate Integrity (a schwa cannot be inserted between the two *d*'s of *hiddarder,* for example) suggests that Voicing Assimilation must follow Plane Conflation. Before Plane Conflation a schwa could be inserted between the linked segments without violating Geminate Integrity; after Plane Conflation, this is impossible:

(44) a. Before Plane Conflation   b. After Plane Conflation

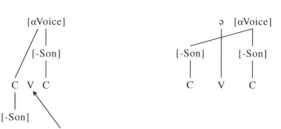

Bat El also notes that certain verb forms in Modern Hebrew undergo a Metathesis rule: "Metathesis applies between the prefixed /t/ of the verb template *hit* + CaC₁eC and a stem-initial sibilant (/c,s,z,š/)" (1988, 480). Her examples are given in (45):

(45) hit + calem → hictalem   'he took pictures of himself'
      hit + sarek → histarek   'he combed his (own) hair'

She further points out that Metathesis applies **only** across a morpheme boundary; in sequences like *hi* + *tsis* 'he fermented', the *t* and *s* do not metathesize, since they are tautomorphemic.

Bat El next shows that Voicing Assimilation must precede Metathesis. From underlying *hit* + *zaken* 'he grew old' and *hit* + *zarez* 'he hurried', we get *hizdaken* and *hizdarez*, rather than **histaken* or **histarez* which would result if Metathesis preceded Voicing Assimilation. By transitivity, then, Metathesis must follow Plane Conflation. If Plane Conflation eliminated all morphological structure, as we would expect to be the case if Plane Conflation were equated with Bracket Erasure, then there would no longer be any morphological structure for Metathesis to be sensitive to. But Metathesis **is** sensitive to morphological structure. Bat El therefore concludes that Plane Conflation does not eliminate morphological boundaries. And here we can draw the further conclusion that words contain morphological structure even if morphemes are also distributed on different planes; presumably that morphological structure is the hierarchical structure that has been the subject of much of this book.

There is another rather general reason to believe that distributing morphemes on different planes could not completely replace hierarchical structure. All present notions of morphological headedness and feature percolation, including the ones proposed in chapters 2 and 3, are based on the assumption that morphemes within words are not only linearly ordered, but also hierarchically structured. A theory which substitutes planar distribution of morphemes for hierarchical structure would be obliged to offer an alternative notion of headedness and to account somehow for the distribution of category and morphosyntactic features. And it is not at all clear how headedness and feature percolation could be accomplished in the absence of hierarchical structure. Nor does it seem likely that such an alternative account of headedness and feature percolation would yield the strong predictions of the theory developed here, namely that the direction of headedness in words is closely connected to the direction of headedness in phrasal syntax. My conclusion then is the same as Bat El's: whether or not morphemes are distributed onto different planes, they still display hierarchical structure.

I turn next to the second question I raised above, whether all morphemes in all languages are introduced onto different planes, and conversely, whether any segment or segments projected on a separate plane must be a morpheme. McCarthy (1989) offers a lucid discussion of this issue, concluding that the MPH, far from being an organizing principle of morphology, is not a principle at all; rather he shows that in a large class of cases, planar segregation between vowels and consonants is required, that these vowels and consonants do not necessarily constitute distinct morphemes, and that vowels and consonants must be distributed on different planes just in case their linear order with respect to each other is entirely predictable. The distribution of vowels and consonants on different planes in Semitic in fact follows from a principle of linear ordering in phonology, rather than from a principle of morphology. I will first briefly sketch McCarthy's arguments and then draw some conclusions from them about the nature of word formation in languages with templatic morphology.

McCarthy (1989, 72) sketches two different versions of the MPH, which he calls the Weak Morphemic Plane Hypothesis and the Strong Morphemic Plane Hypothesis, repeated below in (46):

(46) a. Weak Morphemic Plane Hypothesis (WMPH)
     If separate morphemes, then separate planes.
   b. Strong Morphemic Plane Hypothesis (SMPH)
     Separate morphemes if and only if separate planes.

McCarthy argues first that the SMPH is incorrect; in some cases it is necessary to segregate vowels and consonants onto separate planes even if they do not constitute distinct morphemes; this is the case "when the locality of phonological operations and conditions cannot be otherwise maintained" (1989, 73). The issue is thus one of locality:

"Locality" in phonology is, informally, the requirement that the affected and affecting elements be adjacent somewhere in the representation. A particularly important aspect of locality is expressed by the conjunction of two ideas: (i) all assimilation rules are accomplished by association-line spreading; (ii) association lines do not cross. Thus, biplanar representations are unavoidable when a fundamental violation of locality—crossing association lines—would arise by spreading in a uniplanar representation. (1989, 73)

McCarthy offers as an example here the familiar case of Yawelmani, a language which according to Archangeli (1984) has templatic morphology. Archangeli shows that what superficially seems to be Metathesis in Yawelmani is in fact the result of segments on distinct vocalic and consonantal planes filling different morphologically conditioned skeletal templates, as illustrated in (47):

(47)

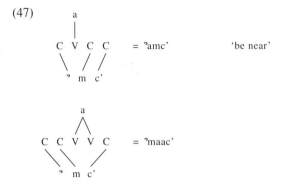

Vowels and consonants in Yawelmani do not constitute distinct morphemes, however.

McCarthy gives a lengthy and careful demonstration that there is no way in which a theory of segmental geometry can be used to allow the spreading of vowels across consonants or consonants across vowels that would be necessary for Yawelmani if, in accordance with the SMPH, vowels and consonants were arrayed on a single plane. As it now stands, the theory of segmental geometry requires that an operation on some set of features actually affects the node dominating those separate features. This means that in Yawelmani the place node dominating vowel features would be spread to the V slots of the template. But in doing so the association line from the neighboring consonant would sometimes be crossed, as illustrated in (48) (same as McCarthy's (9) (1989, 76)):

(48)

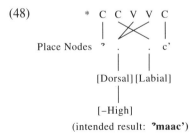

It is theoretically possible to allow spreading from terminal features of the vowel (i.e., [−High] in (47)) "over" the place node ([Labial]) of the consonant, but McCarthy argues that doing so considerably weakens the claims of the theory of segmental geometry. I will not reiterate his proofs here. They do, however, make a convincing case for planar segregation of vowels and consonants in Yawelmani, and therefore for abandoning the SMPH.

McCarthy next argues that the WMPH, although not descriptively incorrect, is not a separate principle either, but rather that it can be made to follow from other assumptions about phonology, as follows (1989, 86):

First, separate planes express the absence of inherent order relations between the two planes. Second, bare morphemes, before word formation, have no linear order relations to one another. Third, at least in systems where word formation is not accomplished by morpheme concatenation, even after word formation separate morphemes have no inherent linear order relations to one another. This lack of inherent linear order relations is exactly what planar segregation expresses.

The upshot of this is that the WMPH is entirely superfluous as an independent principle of the theory. Its effects are obtained by these three premises. In a language like Arabic, planar V/C segregation is morphologically based, but not because of the WMPH. Rather it follows from the fact that vowels and consonants lack linear order relations initially as separate morphemes—because all separate morphemes are unordered with respect to one another—and subsequently because morphemes are not concatenated. The lack of inherent linear order relations across the V/C boundary is exactly what planar segregation expresses.

Planar V/C segregation occurs in Yawelmani and Semitic because the linear order of vowels and consonants is entirely determined by the templates to which they are associated. In Semitic, consonantal strings like *ktb* and vocalic strings like *a* happen to be distinct morphemes having distinct lexical entries. In Yawelmani the strings *ʔmc'* and *a* are separate, inherently unordered strings constituting a single morpheme with a single lexical entry. The order of vocalic and consonantal melody strings may also be predictable, McCarthy points out, in languages without templatic morphology— for example in languages where the structure of roots is always strictly CVC. In such cases as well vowels and consonants will be distributed on different planes although they are not distinct morphemes. Planar segregation therefore follows from a lack of inherent ordering among segments, rather than from their status as morphemes.

The conclusion to be drawn here is that even the templatic morphology of Semitic that seems superficially so different from the affixation and compounding of familiar languages requires no special principles of morphology. Within the present theory, the morphemes of Classical Arabic that appear in the partial paradigm in (49) will have the lexical entries in (50):

(49) Binyan   Perfective Active
     I   katab   'write'
     II   kattab   'cause to write'
     III   kaatab   'correspond'

(50) a. ktb[25]   category and subcategorization: ø
                   LCS: 'write'
     b. a   category and subcategorization:
                   morphosyntactic features: [+Perf, +Act]
                   LCS: perfective active

     c. i. CVCVC[26]   category: [$_V$____]
                         LCS: Binyan I

        ii. CVCCVC   category: [$_V$____]
                         LCS: Binyan II
                         'causative'

       iii. CVVCVC   category: [$_V$____]
                         LCS: Binyan III
                         'reciprocal'

Note that the root *ktb* and the vocalic inflection *a* have neither category nor morphological subcategorization. The latter, like all inflections, has morphosyntactic features belonging to the categorial signature of verbs, but not the whole categorial signature. The former has no category or subcategorization information at all. It follows that Arabic roots take part in nominal word formation as well as verbal word formation. Both of these morphemes are bound, but since they have no morphological subcategorization, they are not affixes. Rather, they are bound because they are in some sense phonologically incomplete. In order to be pronounceable, they must link to the syllabic structure provided by the templates. The templates themselves are stems. That is, they have category (V in (50c)), but no morphological subcategorization. They are still bound, however, because like the root and the inflections, by themselves they are phonologically incomplete.

The Arabic verb forms then are put together as follows. Templates project their categorial signatures by Head Percolation (chapter 3), as in (51a). The root and inflection are inserted, freely, since they have no subcategorization, and the independent principles of linear ordering discussed by McCarthy (1989) ensure that they are arrayed on different planes, as in (51b). Phonological principles of association link the various planes, as in (51c).

Finally, since the inflection *a* has fused with the templatic verb stem, its features become part of the categorial signature of the verb (51d): [27]

(51) a. $\begin{bmatrix} V \\ \text{Perf} \\ \text{Act} \end{bmatrix}$[C V C V C]

b.   k   t   b

$\begin{bmatrix} V \\ \text{Perf} \\ \text{Act} \end{bmatrix}$[C V C V C]

a

$\begin{bmatrix} +\text{Perf} \\ +\text{Act} \end{bmatrix}$

c.   k   t   b

$\begin{bmatrix} V \\ \text{Perf} \\ \text{Act} \end{bmatrix}$[C V C V C]

a

$\begin{bmatrix} +\text{Perf} \\ +\text{Act} \end{bmatrix}$

d.   k   t   b

$\begin{bmatrix} V \\ +\text{Perf} \\ +\text{Act} \end{bmatrix}$[C V C V C]

a

Neither the root nor the inflection adds any layers to the morphological structure since neither has category or subcategorization of its own. The head of the structure is the template, the only element in (51) that possesses a categorial signature. Nevertheless, Arabic verbs have hierarchical structure; they differ from more familiar languages only in that the phonological incompleteness of morphemes allows three morphemes to be composed into a single layer of hierarchical structure.

The sketch of Arabic verbal morphology that I have given here is just that—a sketch. There is obviously much more work that needs to be done on templatic morphology in the framework developed here. Before I conclude, however, I will mention two sorts of templatic morphology that deserve special attention, and show briefly how they fit into the framework developed in this book.

The first is the very interesting case of the Arabic broken plurals discussed by McCarthy and Prince (1990). According to McCarthy and Prince, these plurals are formed by mapping a portion of the singular noun, namely the Wd[MIN], onto a template of a specific shape, namely an iambic foot (that is, a light syllable followed by a heavy syllable). A function which McCarthy and Prince call Φ picks out the minimal word from the singular form, and ordinary processes of association attach the singular melody to the iambic foot template of the plural. Crucially, the remainder of the singular form beyond the minimal word appears unchanged in the plural form. A vocalic melody for the plural is then associated, overwriting the vocalic melody of the singular. The result is that from the singular forms in (52a), the corresponding broken plurals in (52b) are derived:

(52) a. jundub   b. janaadib   'locust'
        sulṭaan   salaaṭin   'sultan'
        nafs   nufuus   'soul'
        jaziir + at   jazaaʔir   'island'

Important for our purposes is the observation that Φ, the operation that picks out the Wd^{MIN} from the singular form, is a phonological operation rather than a morphological one; it is necessary, for example, to delimit the domain of the stress rule in Arabic. Other than this principle, the Arabic broken plurals require no special treatment.

Similarly, the sort of "subtractive" morphology discussed in Martin (1988) requires no special treatment if we assume it to be a species of templatic morphology. Martin considers the data from Koasati illustrated in (53) (data from Martin 1988, 230–31):

(53) Singular   Plural
     pitáf-fi-n   pít-li-n   'to slice up the middle'
     akoláf-ka-n   akol-ká:ci-n   'to erode and collapse'
     tiwáp-li-n   tíw-wi-n   'to open something'
     icoktaká:-li-n   icokták-li-n   'to open one's mouth'
     misíp-li-n   mís-li-n   'to wink'

According to Martin, each form in (53) contains a verb root, an auxiliary (*ka* or *li*), and the suffix *-n*. Martin argues that the process of forming the plural from the singular form of the verb cannot be handled with templatic morphology, and proposes instead two rules, one delinking a final rhyme, and the other a final coda. I would like to suggest to the contrary that the Koasati plural is indeed a case of templatic morphology, and that it can be handled quite elegantly assuming an operation like Φ which identifies the Wd^{MIN} in the verb stem.

I will assume that the Wd^{MIN} in Koasati is a single iambic foot (a light syllable followed by a heavy syllable), as it is in Arabic. Unlike Arabic, however, the Wd^{MIN} in Koasati is isolated by the operation Φ starting at the right edge of the verb stem, rather than at the left edge.[28] The Wd^{MIN} is mapped onto the plural template which is a single syllable, and the remainder of the word, if any, appears to the left of the plural template. This is illustrated in (54):

(54) Singular verb stem: pitáf
     a. Φ parses for Wd^{MIN}: pitáf
     b. Wd^{MIN} mapped onto σ: pit

   c. no remainder
      plural verb stem = pit

Singular verb stem: icoktaká:
a. Φ parses for ·Wd^{MIN}: taká:
b. Wd^{MIN} mapped onto σ: tak
c. remainder added: icoktak
      plural verb stem = icoktak

Subtractive morphology of this sort therefore poses no difficulty for the theory developed here. In general, templatic morphology differs from conventional concatenative morphology only in the extent to which phonological principles play a role in organizing morphological representations.

5.6 Conclusions

In this chapter, I have surveyed a range of word formation types and shown that none of them requires any special independent morphological principle. Circumfixation requires ternary branching trees but nothing further. Nothing in the present theory rules out the generation of ternary-branching trees. The theory developed here forces us to treat conversion either as zero affixation or as relisting of lexical items, rather than as a result of some sort of category-changing morphological rule; in section 5.2 I tried to show that the relisting analysis has a number of positive consequences for conversion data from English and German, whereas zero affixation is more appropriate to French instrumental/agentive compounds. In sections 5.3–5.5 I discuss three sorts of so-called nonconcatenative morphology: consonant mutation and Umlaut, reduplication, and templatic morphology. I have tried to show in these sections that syntactic principles interact with various phonological principles—principles of segmental geometry, underspecification, association, prosodic structure, and linear ordering—to give rise to these more exotic forms of word formation. Consonant mutation, Umlaut, and reduplication are forms of affixation. Even rather problematic sorts of reduplication can be analyzed without special devices such as parafixation or Head Operations. Templatic morphology also involves underspecification of morphemes, along with the principle of linear ordering that segregates vowels and consonants onto separate planes if their linear order is predictable. In no case is any specifically morphological principle needed for these sorts of word formation.

    What these last three sections suggest further is that the syntax of words and the phonology of words interact in quite an intricate fashion. In other words, to maintain the claim that there are no distinct principles of morphology, we have had to look carefully not only at principles of syntax, but also at principles of phonology. But I have not yet discussed in any detail how principles of phonology are to interact with principles of syntax within the present framework. It is therefore to the general issue of the interaction between word syntax and lexical phonology that I turn in the last chapter of this book.

6   The Interface with Phonology

In this book I have primarily been concerned with the relationship between morphology and syntax. I have tried to show that the same general principles of Government-Binding theory constrain the well-formedness of structure both above and below the X^0 level, and that there is no "morphological component" either in the sense of a place where morphology is done, or in the sense of a set of morphology-specific principles. What has become apparent in the last chapter is that although the program I have set here is a plausible one, and one which has a number of attractive consequences, its success also depends upon a number of assumptions about the phonological component. The relationship between morphology/syntax and phonology is of course a subject worthy of a book in itself, and I cannot do it justice here. What I hope to do in this final chapter, then, is merely to sketch the implications of the theory developed here for the theory of phonology.

We have seen in chapter 5 that certain recent advances in phonological theory make it possible to treat classically nonconcatenative types of word formation such as mutation, Umlaut, and reduplication as forms of affixation; these are advances in the theories of segmental geometry and underspecification. Put somewhat differently, the theories of segmental geometry and underspecification are not only compatible with, but actually necessary to the theory under development here. Also necessary to the present theory, as we saw in chapter 5, are assumptions about the theory of prosodic structure. Recall that the analysis of reduplication in chapter 5 necessitated the assumption that certain prosodic categories (σ, F, Wd, etc.) exist, that they are hierarchically structured, and that prosodic structure and morphological structure are available simultaneously, as argued in Booij and Lieber (1989). The theory developed here is thus compatible with and dependent upon those parts of contemporary phonological theory that have to do with phonological representation.

As it stands, however, the organization of the grammar proposed in this book is not entirely compatible with the parts of contemporary phonological theory concerned with the ordering and application of phonological rules. Because I have argued that there is no separate place where morphology is done, rather that both word and phrasal structure are created in a general syntactic component, I have made it impossible for there to exist the sort of temporal and spatial division between lexical and postlexical phonology that is assumed within all present versions of Lexical Phonology. I must therefore sketch in some assumptions about how phonological rules are ordered and how they may apply. I will try to show that all of the crucial claims of Lexical Phonology can in fact be accommodated within the present theory, although certain of the less crucial ones must be abandoned here.

I assume first that phonology **is** a component of the grammar in the sense that it is composed of rules and principles distinct from those of syntax, but not in the sense of being a specific place where phonological rules and principles are applied. In fact, I assume that phonology must consist of a number of subtheories (e.g., theories of segmental geometry, prosodic structure, underspecification, linear order, locality, etc.), and therefore that phonology is modular, as syntax is. Following Bromberger and Halle (1989), I assume that phonology is unlike syntax in also allowing language-particular rules which may need to be extrinsically ordered.

It should already be apparent from the treatment of reduplication in chapter 5 that principles of morphology/syntax and principles of phonology must work in tandem; there we saw that prosodic structures and word structures must be built simultaneously. Thus I will assume that phonological rules of all sorts may be interspersed with the building of morphological (and phrasal) structure. This is the central and perhaps the most crucial claim of Lexical Phonology. It was one of the original motivations for the model in Pesetsky (1979), and it is argued for explicitly in Booij (1981) and Kiparsky (1982).[1] I assume that claim to be correct here.

What cannot be maintained within the present theory of morphology/syntax is the classical way of organizing and applying phonological rules within Lexical Phonology, namely the model in (1) (adapted from Kaisse and Shaw 1985, 9):

(1)

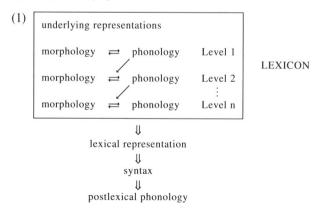

That is, in all versions of Lexical Phonology, phonological rules are split into two basic sorts. Lexical rules apply only to words and only within the lexicon. Postlexical rules apply across words, and only after syntactic operations have ceased. Lexical rules are most often cyclic rules, and are subject to the Strict Cycle Convention (SCC), which says, roughly, that cyclic rules can apply only in derived environments, at least if they are structure-changing rules.[2] Postlexical rules apply across the board and are not subject to the SCC. Booij and Rubach (1987) have also argued for a third class of rules—post-cyclic rules—which apply in the lexicon, but not cyclically and not subject to the SCC. Finally, all lexical rules, cyclic or postcyclic, precede all postlexical rules.

To see how phonological rules might apply in the present theory, let us first consider what our model of grammar now looks like:

(2)

LEXICON
(listed items: primitives and
lexicalized complex words and
phrases)

$$\Downarrow$$

SYNTAX	← P
	← H
productive word formation	← O
	← N
and phrasal structure	← O
	← L
D-structure	← O
↓	← G
S-structure	← Y

Recall that the lexicon in the present theory is merely a list; all productively derived words are built in the syntactic component as are all phrasal structures.[3] (Note that the model in (2) is not meant to imply that all word structure is built before D-structure.) As for the rest of the grammar, as we saw in chapters 1 and 2, phrasal constituents may be contained within X^0s. It is therefore obvious that within a theory like this, all lexical rules—that is, rules applying within X^0—cannot apply before all postlexical rules—that is, those applying to a constituent larger than X^0. In fact, it no longer makes any sense in such a theory even to divide phonological rules into lexical and postlexical rules.

Rather, I would propose that the distinction between lexical and postlexical rules of Lexical Phonology needs to be reconstituted here as a theory of domains. Nespor and Vogel (1986) have already made a good case for stating certain phonological rules in terms of prosodic domains. Further work in this direction can be found in Booij (1987), Cohn (1989), and Inkelas (1989). What I will add to these works is the possibility that phonological rules may be stated in terms of syntactic domains as well. Within the theory developed here, so-called lexical rules will be ones that have X^0 as their domain. Since X^0 is the only recursive node allowed by the X-bar principles, this will be the main structural domain in which phonological rules may apply cyclically (although nothing would rule out cyclic operation of rules with larger domains to the extent that such domains can be nested—cf. Dresher (1983) for a discussion of cyclic operation of postlexical rules). I will assume that this is also the domain of the SCC. Other rules might be stated to apply to all XP or to XP of a certain sort. Presumably, the larger the domain, the more the appearance of across-the-board operation. For example, the quintessential postlexical rules of Lexical Phonology might be recast here as rules with a domain like CP or U (U = phonological utterance, which according to Nespor and Vogel 1986 can be a domain larger than a single sentence under certain circumstances). Such "large domain" rules will not be subject to the SCC.

Rules of different domains will not be extrinsically ordered with respect to each other. Assuming that syntactic construction (lexical and phrasal) occurs from the bottom up, phonological rules will apply as soon as their environments are met. Thus, a phonological rule of the domain YP in this theory can apply before a phonological rule with the domain X^0 just in case the YP occurs structurally inside an X^0, as would be the case, for example, in the phrasal compounds and derivations with which this work started. The lack of extrinsic ordering between rules of different domains does not, however, preclude the possibility that rules with the **same** domain, say X^0, might be extrinsically ordered with respect to one another. The notion of substituting a theory of domains for the lexical/postlexical distinction and of having the nature of domains govern the operation of the SCC is obviously highly speculative, and much work would have to be done to see if such a theory could be worked out in detail. Nevertheless, recent work in the theory of domains (Cohn 1989 and Inkelas 1989) indicates that this may be a promising direction for future research.

There are, however, two areas in which the claims of Lexical Phonology cannot be directly translated into the present theory. The first has to do with so-called Level Ordering, the claim that the lexical component can be divided into several levels or strata as was indicated in (1). In a Level-Ordered morphology, each level consists of a set of affixes or word formation processes which are unordered with respect to each other, and a set of phonological rules which apply cyclically to the morphological forms created at that level. Within a Level-Ordered model, affixes of Level n + 1 are expected to occur only outside of Level n affixes. Level Ordering is impossible within the present theory, however; since the principles that constrain the well-formedness of words are the same as the principles which constrain the well-formedness of sentences (that is, those of Government-Binding theory) and since I have claimed that there are no other specifically morphological principles, there is no way within this theory of segregating morphemes into blocks and ordering those blocks with respect to one another.

There is good reason to believe, however, that the notion of Level Ordering is not a crucial one within Lexical Phonology in any case. Halle and Vergnaud (1987), for example, explicitly reject the principle of Level Ordering, and the idea has been vigorously attacked in both Sproat (1985) and Fabb (1988). The latter in fact attempts to show that the notion of Level Ordering is entirely superfluous for English, the language for which the notion of Level Ordering was originally proposed (Siegel 1974). Fabb (1988) shows that the restrictions on ordering suffixes in English are much more rigid than the Level-Ordering hypothesis would lead us to believe, and that once the proper subcategorization restrictions on affixes are worked out, the Level Ordering in fact becomes superfluous. The ordering of suffixes in English is constrained entirely by the subcategorizations of the suffixes themselves.[4]

Further evidence against the notion of level ordering comes from within Lexical Phonology. That is, several works (e.g., Kiparsky 1982; Halle and Mohanan 1985) have argued that "loops" must be allowed between certain strata so that words formed at Level n can be used as bases for words formed at Level n − m. As Kaisse and Shaw (1985, 14) put it, "Clearly, the invocation of a loop represents a severe compromise of the level-ordering hypothesis." In other words, allowing loops between morphological levels allows us to circumvent the ordering restriction imposed by the Level-Ordering hypothesis in the first place, and essentially evacuates that hypothesis of much of its content. It seems then that rather than being a deficit for the present theory, its inability to accommodate the notion of Level Ordering is an asset.

The other tenet of Lexical Phonology that cannot be maintained in the present theory is the notion of Bracketing Erasure, the most common version of which is stated as in (3) (from Kaisse and Shaw 1985, 9):[5]

(3) Bracketing Erasure Convention (BEC)
     Internal brackets are erased at the end of a level.

Bracketing Erasure eliminates the internal structure of words as they go
from one stratum to another, so that phonological rules at Level n + 1 cannot see the internal structure of words created at or before Level n. The
BEC acts as a sort of locality principle within Lexical Phonology, making
it impossible for phonological rules to look back too far at the derivational
history of certain words.

There are a number of reasons why such a convention could not be a
part of the theory being developed here. The first and foremost is again that
the BEC would have to be stated as an independent principle of morphology, and the present theory claims that no independent principles are
needed. A second reason for discarding the BEC is the following. We saw
in chapter 4 that principles of the Binding theory can explain the patterns
of obligatory disjoint reference in anaphoric island sentences, and of obligatory coreference in *self* compounds if they are allowed to "see" below X^0.
Similarly, the patterns of permissible Head Movement can be explained by
allowing the ECP and the theory of barriers to refer to nodes below X^0 as
well as to nodes above X^0. Both the Binding theory and the theory of ECP
and barriers must, however, be able to see the full internal structure of
words in order to say anything at all about anaphoric islands, *self* compounds, or Head Movement. Internal structure therefore cannot have been
obliterated by the BEC. In other words, not only does the present theory
rule out the BEC in principle, but it could not in fact explain whole classes
of facts that it does explain if a principle like BEC were in effect. Finally,
Fabb (1988) points out that some of the subcategorizations needed for suffixes in his non–Level-Ordered theory require reference to internal structures of words; he argues on these grounds that brackets must not be erased
in the course of the morphological derivation. Since we have assumed here
that Fabb's subcategorization approach to the ordering of affixes is the correct way to capture facts of morphological ordering, we commit ourselves
further on these grounds to the preservation of internal structure in words.

This is not, of course, to say that the present theory should have no principle of locality. It is very likely that a principle of locality will be needed.
Within the present theory we would expect, however, that the principles of
locality will be ones that arise independently in the theories of syntax and
phonology, rather than ones which are stipulated separately, as the BEC
was, for morphology. It remains for further research to determine what the
relevant locality principles might be.

I come here to the end of the task I have set myself—that of deconstructing morphology so that nothing of this component launched in 1970 by Chomsky's "Remarks on Nominalization" remains. This is not, of course, the end of the subject. Rather, what I hope to have shown in this work is that although there are no morphological rules, and there is no morphological component within the theory of grammar, there is still a great deal of work to be done on word formation. Such work can no longer be done in isolation from the theory of syntax and the theory of phonology, however. Further progress in the field depends upon attending to the general web of grammatical principles.

Notes

Prologue

1. That is, I will confine myself to processes which are productive insofar as that can be determined on the basis of the sources available to me.

2. See Baayen and Lieber (1991) for a discussion of the relationship between n_1 and V, and of the linguistic significance of V.

1 The Interface between Morphology and Syntax

1. See Hoeksema (1988) for a discussion of why this proposal is superior to Sproat's (1985) Nonmaximality Constraint which was also proposed to account for the absence of determiners in phrasal compounds.

2. It is perhaps a plausible position to argue within some current version of X-bar theory that modifiers in the prehead position might be phrases of various sorts. Radford (1986) in fact assumes something like this position in his chapter on NPs (without considering the possibility that the constructions he discusses might actually be compounds). That the items in (1) are lexical items rather than phrases of some sort, however, is suggested by the criterion of inseparability: if the maximal phrases on the left were modifiers within N', it ought to be possible to insert another modifier between them and the head. Yet this is not possible: *a pipe and slipper docile husband, etc.

3. Lapointe states his Generalized Lexicalist Hypothesis as follows (1980, 8): "No syntactic rule can refer to elements of morphological structure." Strictly speaking, this version of the Lexicalist Hypothesis does not rule out a morphological rule referring to syntactic structure, for example, a word formation rule of the sort N → XP N to form phrasal compounds. Nevertheless, the Lexicalist Hypothesis has generally been taken to exclude this sort of morphology-syntax interaction as well.

4. This is the case with respect to strictly lexicalist theories, by which I mean those where both inflection and derivation are done within the lexicon, for example, theories such as Lieber (1980), Selkirk (1982), and Williams (1981a). For those theories such as Anderson's (1982) where inflection is done as part of the syntax, the English possessive does not present a problem. But phrasal compounds, as well as the cases of verbal derivation in Tagalog and nominalization in Tamil, to be discussed below, do create problems for theories like Anderson's.

5. Verbs in Tagalog are typically marked with a topic prefix which indicates which of the arguments of the verb is to be focussed. The Subject Topic markers are

those which indicate that the external argument, or the subject is to be focussed. Choice of a particular Subject Topic marker (there are several others in addition to *-um-* and *mag-*) for a given verb is arbitrary, and must be marked in the lexical entry of that verb.

6. According to Subramanian "-VU stands for a set of affixes that behave alike, one member of which is -vu." (1988, 353). Note also that uppercase letters stand for retroflex consonants.

7. Although I disagree with many of Sproat's individual analyses in what follows, I must acknowledge that Sproat's dissertation is ground-breaking work, since it touches upon many of the issues that arise in "deconstructing" the morphological component, for example, the importance of the anaphoric islands data (see chapter 4), and the question of level-ordering in Lexical Phonology (see chap. 6).

8. In chapter 3 I go into some detail about the information contained in lexical entries about category membership. Briefly, there I argue for the existence of what I call the **categorial signature** which lists not only the category features of the item in question, but also the morphosyntactic features which are relevant for that category in that language.

9. In chapter 3 I discuss the relationship between the Lexical Conceptual Structure (LCS) and the Predicate Argument Structure (PAS) as well as the notation which is used in each representation. The LCSs for *run* and *enter* are adapted from Jackendoff (1990).

10. Another possible representation for *un-* will be suggested in section 2.4.

2 Head Theory and Principles of Construction

1. Stowell (1981) points out that it was in principle possible in standard theory to express cross-categorial parallels as the outcome of transformational rules. An example of this might be the work of Lees (1963) on nominalizations.

2. The template in (3) is of course specific to English.

3. Stowell (1981, 281) comments that the order of specifiers and modifiers might have to be set with respect to the head as a parameter of the X-bar system itself, or that conceivably these facts could be made to follow from some other principle of grammar.

4. The three theories under discussion here, Lieber (1980), Selkirk (1982), and Williams (1981a), were worked out during roughly the same period of time.

5. Feature percolation will be discussed in detail in chapter 3.

6. Of course, if a language like English sets the parameter for rightheaded morphology, cases like the prefix *en-* still present a problem.

7. Bauer (1990) points out that a definition of headedness of this sort is problematical. While it may seem plausible for compounds (e.g., a *firetruck* is a sort of *truck*), it does not necessarily yield coherent results when applied to derivation. For example, based on this definition, which morpheme would be head in words like *happiness* and *representation?*

8. The only attempt I am aware of to make the direction of headedness in mor-

phology follow from any principle in syntax occurs in Cutler, Hawkins, and Gilligan (1985), where it is suggested that there is at least a statistical correlation in languages between the order of complement and verb and complement and adposition and the prevalence of prefixing or suffixing morphology. Cutler, Hawkins, and Gilligan show that in languages in which objects precede Vs and Ps, suffixing prevails, but that in languages in which objects follow Vs and Ps, prefixing morphology often occurs. Their hypothesis assumes that all affixes are heads of their words, however, an assumption which is argued in chapters 2 and 3 not to be the case.

9. Pesetsky (1985) argues that *un-* is a categoryless affix, but see section 2.4 below for further discussion of this point.

10. The need for recursion is even clearer when we consider the structure of root compounds. If the head must regularly bear one bar-level less than the node that dominates it, the compounds *rowhouse* and *houserow* would have the structures in (i) and (ii) respectively.

That is, in (i), *house* would have to be a -1-level category, but in (ii) a 0-level category, a result which is very peculiar indeed.

11. Similar proposals have been made in Toman (1983) and Fabb (1984).

12. Whether recursion at higher levels should be possible in base structures is an issue which would go far beyond the scope of this work. As I understand it, it hinges on whether adjunction structures are to be deemed admissible at D-structure.

13. Walinska de Hackbeil (1986) assumes that notions like complement and specifier can have relevance within words (for example, she suggests that the prefix *over-* in *overestimate* is a specifier) without, however, making clear how such terms are to be generally applied.

14. Stowell (1981) is perhaps not correct here that modifiers limit the potential reference only of nouns. It might be the the situation that the reference of a verb like *run* could be fixed by adding an adverbial modifier *quickly,* in which case we must leave open the possibility of restrictive modification of categories other than N. In any event, the examples I give of restrictive modification in what follows will involve nouns.

15. Stowell (1990) raises the possibility that the subject position may in fact be distinct from the position of the specifier. But since he draws no firm conclusion, I will continue here to count subjects as specifiers.

16. Sproat (1985, 203) claims the relationship between the first and second stems in synthetic compounds like *cat lover* to be one of modification rather than complementation. Because he restricts ordinary Theta-role marking to contexts within X′, the first stem cannot be assigned its Theta role via Theta-marking. The only device available within Sproat's theory for assigning Theta-roles within X^0 is

what he calls Theta-identification (taking the term from Higginbotham 1985) which normally links Theta-roles between phrasal modifiers and the items they modify. Thus, by using Theta-identification within synthetic compounds the relationship between stems is at least implicitly claimed to be one of modification. This would seem to obscure the fundamental similarity between the interpretation of synthetic compounds like *truckdriver* and corresponding phrases like *driver of trucks*. Note also that an analysis of synthetic compounds like Sproat's will be hard to reconcile with facts about the acquisition of synthetic compounds to be discussed in 2.4 below.

17. The affix *-ng* is a linking morpheme that occurs after the first element in a modification construction whether that element is the head or the modifier.

18. Schachter and Otanes (1972) note that the *ng* here is not the linker mentioned above, but rather the *ng* subject case marker, which will be discussed below.

19. The topic and nontopic arguments can occur in any order after the verb, according to Schachter and Otanes (1972, 83), but the order verb-nontopic-topic is the most common or neutral order (1972, 84).

20. The boldface in (26) is my own. Clark (1985) actually provides exactly the same translation for the two sentences in (26), although his text supports the difference in meaning that is implied by my use of boldface.

21. See chapter 5 for discussion of the mechanics of reduplication within present autosegmental theory.

22. In addition to the examples in (30) and (31), Schachter and Otanes (1972) list two examples which seem to consist of circumfixes, that is, affixes which consist of both a prefix and a suffix. See chapter 5 for the treatment of circumfixes within the present theory.

23. The connector *-ng* occurs after the first element in the compound if it ends in a vowel.

24. Schachter and Otanes (1972, 360) give *nasa akin* as the base of the verbal derivation *p-um-asa akin*. The preposition *na*, however, does not show up in the resulting verb. I will assume then that the actual base of the derivation is the NP marked with the locative case particle *sa*, rather than the PP as a whole.

25. The infix *-um-* and the prefix *mag-* below are the Subject Topic prefixes that occur with these verbs.

26. Possibly to be added to these are compounds like *hard-hearted* or *long-legged*, which Botha (1984) suggests are derived by affixing *-ed* to a phrase.

27. Actually, *en-* shows up as unproductive in present-day English (see Prologue), so it should probably not be discussed at all. I include it here because it is exactly of the type predicted to be possible, even though it appears not to be living in the synchronic language. Note that words with *en-* are semantically somewhat less regular than words with *de-*, as would be expected for an unproductive affix.

28. There are a few examples of words in *-ize* in which the base does not seem interpretable as predicate: *hospitalize, hyphenize, jeopardize, motorize, notarize, stigmatize*. I assume that words of this sort have lexicalized meanings, but that new words coined in *-ize* and the majority of productively formed examples with this suffix have the meaning in which their base is interpretable as a predicate.

29. My analysis of *de-* and *en-* bears some resemblance to the analysis of *en-* in

Walinska de Hackbeil (1986). There she proposes that denominal verbs like *imprison* and *enchain* are derived by Head Movement from an underlying structure like that in (i):

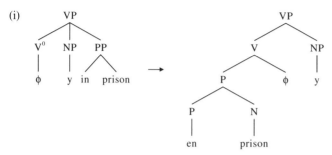

(i)

In other words, Walinska de Hackbeil suggests that the prefix *en-* is a positional allomorph of the preposition *in* and that verbs in *en-* are derived by adjunction of some sort of nonmaximal P constituent to a verbal zero affix. Her analysis incorporates the insight that *en-* is in some sense a Theta-role assigner, but it is problematic in a number of ways. First, it is not clear why the P must always have a bare N (and not a full NP) as its complement (that is, why are there no verbs like **enheavy-chain?*). Second, this analysis does not extend easily to the verb-forming prefix *de-*, which is the productive verb-forming prefix and which has no plausible prepositional allomorph.

30. It has been pointed out that phrasal synthetic compounds like *purple people eater* (= eater of purple people) sound far better than phrasal synthetic compounds like *apple on a stick taster*. This is probably the case if the phrasal part is somewhat lexicalized, as in *purple people eater* or *American history teacher,* since with newly coined phrasal synthetic compounds like *roasted frog eater* or *green car driver* acceptability seems somewhat lower, and with more complex APs modifying the N in the phrase, the compounds seem completely unacceptable: **very green car driver, *deep purple people eater.* The analysis presented here rules out both the unacceptable phrasal synthetic compounds like **very green car driver* and **apple on a stick taster* and the marginal compounds like *purple people eater* and *American history teacher.* To the extent that we wish to allow the grammar to generate compounds like the latter, we must allow phrases like *purple people* to be generated in root phrasal compounds analogous to compounds like *purple people glutton.* Compounds like *purple people eater* will be interpreted as modification structures.

31. Something like this is also suggested in passing in Sproat (1985, 210).

32. See van Kemenade (1987) for a detailed discussion of this subject within a slightly different framework.

33. French also has N-N compounds in which both nouns inflect for the plural, e.g., *chou-fleur* 'cauliflower', *choux-fleurs* (pl.). Even in these cases, however, it is possible to tell that the left-hand noun is head, because it supplies the gender for the compound as a whole (*chou* (m.), *fleur* (f.), *chou-fleur* (m.)).

34. There are also some verb plus adjective compounds of this sort (*gagne petit* 'knife-grinder', *sent-bon* 'tansy') and some verb plus adverb compounds (*couche-tard* 'late bedder', *lève-tôt* 'early riser').

35. The LCS in (68) is the same one proposed by Booij (1989) for English and Dutch agentive/instrumental suffixes *-er*. This LCS indicates that the zero affix binds the external argument in the LCS of the stem verb. See chapter 4 for further discussion of agentive/instrumental affixes.

36. Note that English has a few compounds similar to the instrument compounds of French: *pickpocket, drawbridge, cutpurse,* etc. However, this type of compounding seems never to have become productive in English. See Marchand (1969) for a discussion of this class of compounds.

37. Scalise (1988) has analyzed the Italian counterparts to these prefixes as non-category-changing. In his analysis, the noun base is first converted to a (nonexisting) verb, then prefixed. This analysis has some initial plausibility for French, since *en-* and *dé-* do attach to verbs as well as nouns. The problem that arises, however, is how to explain the nonexistence of verbs such as *pocher* and *bouteiller,* etc.

38. Thanks to Harald Baayen for his ideas on *be-* and *ont-* which follow.

39. Baayen (p.c.) notes that alongside sentences like (i), where N^0 movement has taken place if we are correct, there are sentences like (ii) where the noun *hoofd* occurs unincorporated, with a dummy verb *doen* 'do' as the base for *ont-*. Presumably in this latter sentence *ont-* assigns its Theta-role externally to the NP *zijn hoofd* as predicted by our analysis, with Case being supplied to the NP by the preposition *van:*

(i) De beul onthoofde de koning.
    'The headman beheaded the king.'
(ii) De beul ontdeed de koning van zijn hoofd.
    'The headman took away the king his head.'

3 Feature Percolation and Inheritance

1. And within sentences too, although we will have little to say about this here. Feature percolation must of course be assumed to operate above the X^0 level as well as below. See Cowper (1987) for a discussion of feature percolation in the syntax.

2. Sections 3.1–3.3, and parts of 3.4 are adapted from Lieber (1989), "On Percolation," *Yearbook of Morphology,* vol. 2, with permission of the publisher.

3. Williams (1981a) gives (1b) as his definition of head, but in addition (1b) accounts for feature sharing between a head and a node dominating it.

4. In chapter 5 I will argue that a category-changing analysis is not available within the present theory in any case, because it would have to be a specifically morphological rule.

5. Note that the instrumental/agentive zero affix in French, discussed in section 2.5.1, is an exception here. It does in fact exhibit all the characteristics of overt affixes.

6. I am assuming here that irregular (that is, strong) stems are listed in the lexicon, following Lieber (1980).

7. See also Baker (1987) for discussion of a feature [±Case Assigner] which also seems to have additive properties. See Rappaport and Levin (1988) for another argument against the use of features to encode Theta-roles.

It is not inconceivable that theories of feature structures within other frameworks might handle an example such as the Kinyarwanda one without multivalued features. For example, Shieber (1986, 29–30) proposes a notation for features within "unification-based" theories of grammar which might be adapted to the Kinyarwanda data. It is not clear how his proposal might be adapted to the present framework, however.

8. I am unsure of the origin of this term. Although I cannot find explicit reference to it in any of the published morphological or syntactic literature that I am familiar with, I am fairly sure that this term has been used, at least informally, for some time.

9. See Jackendoff (1987), however, who suggests that selectional restrictions are built directly into the conceptual structure of verbs.

10. The conventions in (24) are in many ways similar to Selkirk's version of feature percolation. The major difference between (24) and Selkirk's conventions is that (24) makes use of the explicit notion of categorial signature that I have developed here.

11. Note that the propagation of the categorial signature will prevent features from percolating across categories.

12. This is not, of course, the first attempt in the literature to do this. Anderson (1982) works out an analysis of P/N marking in Georgian, another language which marks person and number on both subject and object. Anderson's analysis is embedded in a theory of morphology rather different from the one developed here. Indeed, since in his framework inflection is added by postsyntactic rules which insert morphemes into representations already marked for features, there is no mechanism of feature percolation in his analysis. Jensen and Stong-Jensen (1984) reanalyze the Georgian data within a framework that does make use of feature percolation. Still their analysis is based on assumptions that are somewhat different from those used here. In what follows, I will try wherever possible to show how the present assumptions differ from those of Jensen and Stong-Jensen.

13. Evans uses the abbreviation MABL to stand for "Modal-Ablative," that is, the ablative case used in its modal function. Similarly, COBL stands for "Complementizer-Oblique," the oblique case used in its complementizer function.

14. Also number, although I will not illustrate that here. See Lieber (1989) for a complete analysis of the Yavapai verbal paradigm.

15. Jensen and Stong-Jensen (1984) also reject the notion of different features for P/N marking in subject and object, and assume the layered representations that we will adopt here. However, they require that each P/N marker have more than one layer in its lexical feature representation. So, for example, the feature representation of a first person subject affix would differ from that of a first person object

affix in having its [+I] feature lexically represented in a different layer. This sort of representation would not permit a clear generalization to be made if a particular affix were to bear the same person feature as either a subject person marker or object person marker. This situation does not in fact arise in Georgian, but it does in Yavapai, as I have shown.

16. Although I have not given examples, number is also marked separately for subject and object in Yavapai.

17. The position of subject and object P/N features within layers apparently may differ from language to language. For example, in Georgian the inner layer in a two-layer structure contains object features and the outer layer subject features (Anderson 1982; Jensen and Stong-Jensen 1984).

18. One possibility for a system of features for distinguishing cases is suggested in Neidle (1988).

19. The prefix *ñ-* will also merely be specified with the feature [+I]. In Lieber (1989) it is argued that *ñ-* has two different subcategorizations in its lexical entry: one in which it attaches directly to a root, and another in which it attaches to a stem which has already received default features [−I, −II] in its inner feature layer. The reader is referred to Lieber (1989) for the intricacies of these derivations.

20. There are some details of the derivation that I have left out here, namely working out the subcategorization of the prefixes and the suffix, which determines the linear order and hierarchical structure of the whole word. See Lieber (1989) for a discussion of these details.

21. Some of the Vogul data is also discussed in terms of the Extended Word and Paradigm theory of Anderson (1982) in Hammond (1981).

22. Presumably it is used with intransitive verbs as well as with transitive verbs with "undefined" objects, although Kálmán does not give an example of an intransitive verb.

23. The form of these suffixes will be explained below.

24. Note that if *-i* is left underspecified for [Pret] and *-s* for [Pres], *-s* could be attached to *-i* and percolate its feature before the default value is added. However, the result would be independently ruled out, since [+Pres, +Pret] is an impossible combination of features.

25. Liimola points out that the other subject suffixes (that is, the first and second person ones), although superficially close to the first and second person possessives as well, actually developed from the personal pronouns (1968, 317). If so, we are justified in assuming that they do not have the feature [+Poss].

26. One fact which suggests that this analysis may be along the right lines is that the *l* has been generalized as the singular object suffix throughout the third person paradigms in the Tavda dialect of Vogul (Liimola 1968, 313).

27. A similar observation is made in Jensen and Stong-Jensen (1984, 478) and in Selkirk (1982, 75–77). Selkirk in fact claims that inflectional affixes are not heads and that features are percolated from inflectional affixes in the event that the head of the word is unmarked for those features. Her justification for this claim is rather different from that offered here, since her model lacks an explicit notion of categorial signature.

28. The Oblique cannot be used Adnominally, according to Evans (1985, 63).

29. The case system of Vogul has six cases, and three numbers. The possessive is not counted as one of the six cases by Kálmán (1965).

30. On the other hand, a suffix like -*ish* in English which can attach to a phrase like *old maid* will have a categorial signature specifying that it is an A^0.

31. Pollock (1989) argues that Infl should be decomposed into two phrases— AgrP and TP (T = tense). AgrP takes VP as its complement, and TP takes AgrP as its complement. In Pollock's framework, TP = IP. In addition, he argues that Head Movement of V to AgrP occurs only in languages which are inflectionally rich, for example, French. Presumably, the sort of languages that have been discussed in this chapter would count as inflectionally rich for Pollock. Inflectionally poor languages, like English, involve movement of affixes to V, along the lines of the standard Affix Hopping analysis.

32. Note that the traditional Affix Hopping analysis is also compatible with the results we have obtained here. Since in the Affix Hopping analysis affixes adjoin to verbs, the verb determines the category of the word as a whole (that is, the verb stem is the head), and provides the categorial signature by Head Percolation.

33. Carrier and Randall (1989) use the predicate INC (inchoative BE) for GO. I substitute the more transparent name for this primitive here.

34. Carrier and Randall (1989) refer to this representation as the Argument Structure.

4 Binding, Barriers, and X^0

1. An earlier version of this section appeared as Lieber (1984a).

2. However, in Sproat and Ward (1987) and Ward, Sproat, and McKoon (in press) this judgment is reversed.

3. Words like *she-wolf* are not productively formed, of course.

4. Since my stated goal here is to explain the facts of word formation within a specific syntactic theory, namely Government-Binding theory, I will leave aside the larger issue of whether the Binding theory is the best possible way of handling the facts of co- and disjoint reference within linguistic theory. Specifically, I will leave aside the issue of whether Binding theory is superior to pragmatic or discourse-based theories of anaphora such as Hankamer and Sag (1977) and Reinhart (1983). See Sproat and Ward (1987) and Ward, Sproat, and McKoon (in press) for a discussion of some of the anaphoric islands facts within a pragmatic theory of coreference.

5. I am assuming that the main clause subject is *pro*. Note also that third person subject is not marked on verbs in Yavapai. Also, I use S′ and S in (7) instead of CP and IP, because in some details Finer's structure cannot be translated into the framework that uses CP and IP. As far as I can tell, nothing in what follows hinges on these details.

6. For details of why the matrix clause is the governing category and also why -*k* and -*m* are positioned in the Comp of the lower S′, see Finer (1985).

7. Again, see Finer (1985) for details.

8. Sproat (1988a) argues that the sort of indexing used in agreement (especially in agreement between Agr and pro in pro-drop languages) is not the same as the indexing of arguments relevant to Binding theory. The analysis of Switch Reference in Finer (1985), however, suggests that Sproat's conclusion is incorrect.

9. But see 4.1.3, where this idea is made more precise.

10. Some of the conditions under which successful sublexical reference occurs are discussed in Sproat and Ward (1987) within a rather different framework.

11. It is not clear to me whether the device that effects this passing of indices up the head projection is percolation; nothing in what follows hinges on this issue, however.

12. The P values for *-ary, -ship,* and *-age* are respectively 0, 0.0003, and 0.0011, according to Baayen (p.c.). In other words, *-ary* appears to be completely unproductive, since it falls below the P value for simplex nouns (0.0001), and *-ship* and *-age* are of only marginal productivity.

13. A question of course arises whether this claim can be maintained with respect to the phonology. In other words, do phonological rules or principles need to analyze these words? This is a question, however, which must await further research.

14. The idea that *self* is a sublexical anaphor has been pursued several times in recent literature, first, to my knowledge in Lieber (1984a), and following that in Sproat (1985). Farmer (1987) also discusses some of the data involving *self,* although more in terms of argument structure than in terms of Binding theory.

15. I assume that the verb *self-destruct* is an exception here and that it was created as a backformation from the noun *self-destruction.* Sproat's reasons for claiming that *self* attaches to Vs are entirely internal to his analysis. In order to get *-er* in *self-admirer* to c-command the reflexive *self,* he must assume that *self* is lower in the tree than *-er;* that is, *self* must attach to the V *admire* first, and *-er* to *self-admire.*

16. Note that the choice of predicate in sentences like (24) affects whether the arbitrary or coindexed reading is more likely or more prominent. For example, in a sentence like *Fenster is guilty of self-contempt,* the coindexed reading is more prominent, whereas in the sentence *Fenster despises self-contempt,* the arbitrary reading is the dominant one. I assume that further study of the LCSs of these predicates will shed light on why they influence the readings of *self* nouns.

17. Note that the phrase is fine with the indexing: *his$_j$ self$_i$-admirer,* as long as this is taken to mean "the self-admirer that he possesses." We will return to this odd fact below.

18. She argues that *-er* binds (in a different sense than that of Binding theory) the external argument of its base verb. *Self* fixes the direct internal and external arguments as being the same. *His* then cannot be interpreted as the internal argument of *admire,* since it is already bound by *self.* Farmer thus explains why *his* cannot be interpreted as the internal argument of *admire,* but she cannot explain why the indexing in (25a) is ruled out even where *his* is interpreted as possessive, rather than as internal argument. We will see below that the impossibility of the latter interpretation receives a reasonable explanation within Binding theory.

19. According to Booij (1989), *-er* binds the external argument, where binding

is meant in the sense that a logical operator binds a variable. I avoid using the word binding in this way here so as not to confuse it with the binding of Binding theory.

20. A reviewer points out that an aribtrary reading of *self* is possible in the phrase *self-criticism promoter*. If *promoter* governs both the N^0 *self-criticism* and the reflexive *self* within the compound, this reading should not be possible (*self* should be obligatorily coindexed with *-er*, as in (32)). One possible explanation for the arbitrary reading is the following, namely that the definition of government needs more refinement when referring to elements within words; specifically, should X be said to govern a nonhead morpheme of Y if X governs Y? If not, then *promoter* arguably does not govern *self*, and therefore cannot bind *self*. *Self* might then be bound by a PRO_{arb} in the specifier of NP (or by a possessive NP in this position).

21. The same will be true in (26a) and (26b): since neither the affix *-ion* nor *-al* counts as a subject, the MGC of *self* in both these examples will be NP rather than N'.

22. I use the word "nominal" here in a loose sense to cover anaphors, pronominals, names, and common nouns.

23. Note that X, the node immediately dominating t, doesn't count for the calculation of barriers: since X^0s are not L-marked, they would be BCs, and would automatically block antecedent government. An X^0 would never be able to move anywhere if its own X^0 were relevant to the calculation of barriers.

24. This case is also discussed briefly in Strauss (1987), although under a somewhat different set of assumptions.

25. It would also eliminate the case where Move-Alpha moves a stem away from an affix.

26. Note that we must assume that morphological subcategorization must be met only at S-structure. It is not enough for an affix like *-er* to be coindexed with a trace at S-structure that meets its subcategorization.

27. Note that this same story would also independently preclude the movement of affixes out of words.

28. See also Hoeksema (1987) for arguments against Pesetsky's analysis of Bracketing Paradoxes.

29. See chapter 6 for further discussion of the Bracket Erasure Convention.

30. This is a question which of course can be raised independently for any given syntactic framework—GPSG, relational grammar, lexical functional grammar, etc.

31. Of course, such analyses have been proposed. See DiSciullo and Williams (1987), Bok-Bennema and Groos (1988), Sadock (1980, 1986, 1991) for non-movement analyses of incorporation.

5 Beyond Affixation and Compounding

1. Bauer (1988) also discusses cases that seem to consist of two consecutive prefixes or two consecutive suffixes, neither of which pose any problem for the the-

ory being developed here. He also mentions examples of word formation which consist of a prefix or suffix plus some internal modification of the stem, or prefixation/suffixation plus reduplication. Cases like these will be discussed respectively in sections 5.3 and 5.4. Within the framework developed here, the latter cases have nothing in common with circumfixation.

2. Schachter and Otanes also give an example of a circumfix consisting of a reduplicative prefix plus a suffix which creates nouns designating an imitation of the noun base. Anticipating the results of section 5.4, I can say that this circumfix consists of a syllable template prefix, plus the suffix *-an*.

3. Note that it is not clear that the circumfix *ge. . .te* needs to be dealt with as part of productive word formation at all. Schultink (1987, 483–484) states that "Belonging to the lexicon of Dutch are approximately fifteen nouns of the so-called neuter *het* gender, with the structure *ge* + NOUN + *te,* and with a 'collective' connotation. . . ." He adds that neologisms like *getwijgte* 'shrubs' from *twijg* 'twig' seem to be the result of "deliberate coining with a connotation intended as literary or comical." The latter is of course the hallmark of unproductive (creative) coining. So it seems likely that the issue of the headedness of the circumfix does not really arise. In any case, if *ge. . .te* were a productive circumfix in Dutch, or if another language had a similar productive circumfix, the issue of headedness would be dealt with as suggested below.

4. It is of course a classical problem shared by all zero affixation analyses whether the zero affix is a prefix or a suffix.

5. Presumably in languages that have conjugation and declension classes, if there is a default class, a native speaker might assume that the newly converted item would fall under the default case.

6. In Lieber (1980), I argued that stem allomorphs could be distinguished on the basis of a diacritic feature. Particular inflectional affixes were then subcategorized to attach only to stems bearing the appropriate diacritic. In addition, phonological rules (schwa insertion, degemination, schwa deletion) may apply to particular combinations of stem allomorph and inflection to produce a surface form. See Lieber (1980) for further details of this analysis and for derivations.

7. This sentence is possible only with an obligatorily reflexive reading. This indicates that the verb really does have two arguments, the first of which must be coindexed with the second if the latter is not to be present overtly.

8. Note that it is often difficult to decide whether a noun is zero-derived from a verb, or vice versa. In the examples in (10), I assume on semantic grounds that the verbs are derived from the nouns.

9. Some verbs formed by conversion from nouns can of course have more complex PASs. For example, the verb "to gift," which has been appearing in American magazines around Christmastime for a number of years, can have a PAS like: x <$\underline{y}$, with z>; *I gifted Fenster with a silver dogbowl.*

10. Note that there is nothing wrong with the meanings that the sentences in (12c) are trying to convey; one can indeed convey this meaning by forming the *-ing* noun form of the verb: *We gave the car a Midasizing, A Midasizing is good for your car.*

11. This is, of course, true of monomorphemic items. We must count it as purely accidental that the noun *peace* in English has never been relisted as a verb.

12. Kiparsky (1982) tries to explain these facts using Level Ordering. If conversion is ordered before Level II, where affixation of *-less, -ness,* and other productive native suffixes is performed, such words would not be eligible for conversion. However, there is good reason to believe that English morphology should not be Level Ordered. See Fabb (1988) for persuasive arguments to this effect. And if English morphology is not Level Ordered, then Kiparsky's explanation for these facts will not hold. See chapter 6 for some discussion of Level Ordering.

13. The class numbering system used here comes from Arnott (1970).

14. I adopt Paradis's (1986) analysis here, rather than that of Lieber (1987b), because Paradis embeds the analysis of consonant mutation in Fula within a thorough analysis of Fula phonology. This allows her to dispense with some of the more ad hoc features of my earlier analysis.

15. Here I differ from Paradis in detail. Paradis works out her analysis of Fula within the Charm and Government framework of Kaye, Lowenstamm, and Vergnaud (1985). For Paradis the segment *n* in the prefix does not consist of a distinctive feature but of what Kaye and Lowenstamm call "elements." Nothing in her analysis hinges on the choice of terminology. I therefore present the analysis assuming the more familiar autosegmental framework. I also differ from Paradis (1986) in the notation for indicating subcategorizations of morphemes. The notation in (17) has been made consistent with that proposed in earlier chapters of this work. In addition, the particular features I use in the subcategorizations of (17) are different from those used in Paradis's analysis.

16. The assumption that [−Back] is the marked value for the feature [Back] in German is also made by Hall (1989) in an analysis of the phonological rule of Fricative Assimilation.

17. Mokilese also allows the initial syllable of a vowel initial base to acquire an onset from the reduplicative prefix so that the base *uruur* 'laugh' reduplicates as *ur-r-uruur*. As McCarthy and Prince point out, reduplication processes may vary in whether the syllabification of the base is changed after reduplication or not.

18. McCarthy and Prince do not state what the morphological function of this reduplication is.

19. McCarthy and Prince (1986) discuss cases of reduplicative suffixes as well.

20. Clements's notation is somewhat different in detail from the one used in (27), but nothing hinges on these minor differences.

21. Recall that we have already seen an example of this in our analysis of Bracketing Paradoxes in section 4.2.4.

22. Note that there is an inconsistency in McCarthy and Prince's theory in that it must really be the phonemic melody that is copied here, rather than a new lexical entry being inserted, as was required for the quantitative transfer cases discussed above. A temporary solution to their problem would be to stipulate that where there is no lexical entry equal to the base of affixation, that base itself is copied. The latter will happen only where the base is a phonological constituent that happens not to be coextensive with a morphological constituent.

23. The Morphemic Plane Hypothesis was originally called the Morphemic Tier Hypothesis. Since the advent of theories of segmental geometry which reserve the notion "tier" for the position of a feature in segmental structure, it has become common to refer to the positions of morphemes in space as "planes" rather than "tiers." I will adopt this terminology here and apply it consistently, even where its use is somewhat of an anachronism, as in the description of McCarthy's early work, immediately below.

24. McCarthy (1989) in any case retracts his 1986 suggestion that Plane Conflation and Bracket Erasure are the same thing.

25. The strings *ktb* and *a* are shorthand for phonological segments (or sequences of segments), perhaps underspecified.

26. The CV skeleta in (50c) are shorthand for some sort of syllabic template, as suggested by McCarthy and Prince (1986).

27. I use labeled bracketing rather than trees for the hierarchical structure here in order to be able to show morphological structure and phonological structure simultaneously.

28. The reason for this is that historically the remainder (after the Wd^{MIN} has been isolated) consisted of a prefix, or a sequence of prefixes, according to Martin (1988).

6 The Interface with Phonology

1. Booij in fact came to the conclusion that morphological and phonological rules must be allowed to apply to each other's outputs independently of Pesetsky and Kiparsky (Booij p.c.).

2. Structure-building rules—for example, rules building prosodic structure—are not restricted to derived environments.

3. It is of course possible that there is some set of phonological rules that applies within the lexicon in this sense. Such rules might, for example, be the sort of lexical rules that are subject to idiosyncratic exceptions (like Trisyllabic Laxing). I will not pursue this idea further here, however.

4. Fabb (1988) actually refers to these restrictions as selectional restrictions, but in terms of the present theory they would be part of the subcategorizations of individual morphemes. I therefore refer to this information as subcategorizational information.

5. I am assuming in what follows that Bracketing Erasure applies to syntactic (morphological) brackets rather than to the brackets of prosodic structure. Within the present theory, there would in fact be no problem with a phonological principle of Bracketing Erasure that eliminated prosodic structure under certain conditions.

References

Abney, S. 1987. The English Noun Phrase in Its Sentential Aspect. Ph.D. diss., MIT, Cambridge.

Allen, M. 1978. Morphological Investigations. Ph.D. diss., University of Connecticut, Storrs.

Anderson, S. 1977. "On the Formal Description of Inflection." In W. A. Beach, S. E. Fox, and S. Philosoph, eds., *Papers from the Thirteenth Regional Meeting of the Chicago Linguistic Society*, 15–44. Chicago: Chicago Linguistic Society.

———. 1982. "Where's Morphology?," *Linguistic Inquiry* 13: 571–612.

Aoun, J. 1981. The Formal Nature of Anaphoric Relations. Ph.D. diss., MIT, Cambridge.

———. 1982. "A Symmetric Theory of Anaphoric Relations." In C. Jones and P. Sells, eds., *The Proceedings of NELS XIV*, 1–10. Distributed by the GLSA, Department of Linguistics, University of Massachusetts, Amherst.

Archangeli, D. 1984. Underspecification in Yawelmani Phonology and Morphology. Ph.D. diss., MIT, Cambridge.

Arnott, D. W. 1970. *The Nominal and Verbal Systems of Fula*. Oxford: Oxford University Press.

Aronoff, M. 1976. *Word Formation in Generative Grammar*. Cambridge: MIT Press.

———. 1988. "Head Operations and Strata in Reduplication: A Linear Treatment." *Yearbook of Morphology* 1: 1–16.

Baayen, H. 1989. A Corpus-Based Approach to Morphological Productivity: Statistical Analysis and Psycholinguistic Interpretation. Dissertation, Free University, Amsterdam.

———. 1990. "Corpusgebaseerd onderzoek naar morfologische produktiviteit." *Spektator* 19: 213–233.

Baayen, H., and R. Lieber 1991. Productivity and English Derivation: A Corpus Based Study. *Linguistics* 29: 801–843.

Baker, M. 1985. Incorporation: A Theory of Grammatical Function Changing. Ph.D. diss., MIT, Cambridge.

———. 1987. How Complex Words Get Their Properties. MS, McGill University, Montreal.

———. 1988a. *Incorporation: A Theory of Grammatical Function Changing*. Chicago: University of Chicago Press.

————. 1988b. "Morphological and Syntactic Objects: A Review of A. M. DiSciullo and E. Williams, *On the Definition of Word*. *Yearbook of Morphology* 1: 259–284.

Baltin, M. 1990. "Heads and Projections." In M. Baltin and A. Kroch, *Alternative Conceptions of Phrase Structure*. Chicago: University of Chicago Press.

Bat El, O. 1988. "Remarks on Tier Conflation." *Linguistic Inquiry* 19: 477–485.

Bauer, L. 1978. *The Grammar of Nominal Compounding with special reference to Danish, English, and French*. Odense: Odense University Press.

————. 1988. "A Descriptive Gap in Morphology." *Yearbook of Morphology* 1: 17–28.

————. 1990. "Be-heading the Word." *Journal of Linguistics* 26: 1–31.

Bloomfield, L. 1933. *Language*. New York: Henry Holt.

Bok-Bennema, R., and A. Groos. 1988. "Adjacency and Incorporation." In M. Everaert, A. Evers, R. Huybregts, and M. Trommelen, eds., *Morphology and Modularity*. Dordrecht: Foris.

Booij, G. 1977. *Dutch Morphology*. Dordrecht: Foris.

————. 1981. "Rule Ordering, Rule Application, and the Organization of Grammars." *Phonologica 1980:* 45–56.

————. 1987. "On the Relation Between Lexical and Prosodic Phonology." In P. M. Bertinetto and M. Loporcaro, eds., *Certamen Phonologicum, Papers from the 1987 Cortona Phonology Meeting*, 63–75. Torino: Rosenberg and Sellier.

————. 1988a. "The Relation Between Inheritance and Argument Linking: Deverbal Nouns in Dutch." In M. Everaert, A. Evers, R. Huybregts, and M. Trommelen, eds., *Morphology and Modularity*, 57–74. Dordrecht: Foris.

————. 1988b. Review article of M. Nespor and I. Vogel, *Prosodic Phonology*. *Journal of Linguistics* 24: 515–525.

Booij, G. 1989. "Morphology, Semantics, and Argument Structure." Vrije Universiteit Working Papers in Linguistics, no. 33. Amsterdam: Department of Linguistics, Vrije Universiteit.

Booij, G., and T. van Haaften. 1988. "On the External Syntax of Derived Words: Evidence from Dutch." *Yearbook of Morphology* 1: 29–44.

Booij, G., and R. Lieber. 1989. On the Simultaneity of Morphological and Prosodic Structure. MS, Free University, Amsterdam.

Booij, G., and J. Rubach. 1984. "Morphological and Prosodic Domains in Lexical Phonology." *Phonology Yearbook* 1: 1–28.

————. 1987. "Postcyclic and Postlexical Rules in Lexical Phonology." *Linguistic Inquiry* 18: 1–44.

————. 1989. "Lexical Phonology." To appear in *The Oxford Encyclopedia of Linguistics*.

Borer, H. 1988. "On the Morphological Parallelism between Compounds and Constructs." *Yearbook of Morphology* 1: 45–66.

Botha, R. 1980. "Word-Based Morphology and Synthetic Compounding." Stellenbosch Papers in Linguistics, no. 5, University of Stellenbosch.

————. 1984. *Morphological Mechanisms.* Oxford: Pergamon Press.

Bromberger, S., and M. Halle. 1989. "Why Phonology is Different." *Linguistic Inquiry* 20: 51–70.

Broselow, E., and J. McCarthy. 1984. "A Theory of Internal Reduplication." *The Linguistic Review* 3: 25–88.

Brousseau, A.-M. 1989. Les Noms composés en Haitien: Évidence pour une définition intrinsèque de tête morphologique. MS, UQAM, Montreal.

Browne, W. 1974. "On the Topology of Anaphoric Peninsulas." *Linguistic Inquiry* 5: 619–620.

Canale, W. 1978. Word Order Change in Old English: Base Reanalysis in Generative Grammar. Ph.D. diss., McGill University, Montreal.

Carrier, J., and J. Randall. 1989. From Conceptual Structure to Syntax. MS, Harvard University, Cambridge and Northeastern University, Boston.

Carrier-Duncan, J. 1985. "Linking of Thematic Roles in Derivational Word Formation." *Linguistic Inquiry* 16: 1–34.

Chomsky, N. 1965. *Aspects of the Theory of Syntax.* Cambridge: MIT Press.

————. 1970. "Remarks on Nominalization." In R. Jacobs and P. Rosenbaum, eds., *Readings in English Transformational Grammar.* Waltham, MA: Ginn.

————. 1981. *Lectures on Government and Binding.* Dordrecht: Foris.

————. 1982. *Some Concepts and Consequences of the Theory of Government and Binding.* Cambridge: MIT Press.

————. 1986a. *Barriers.* Cambridge: MIT Press.

————. 1986b. *Knowledge of Language: Its Nature, Origin, and Use.* New York: Praeger.

Clark, E., B. Hecht, and R. Mulford. 1986. "Coining Complex Compounds in English: Affixes and Word Order in Acquisition." *Linguistics* 24: 7–29.

Clark, R. 1985. "The Syntactic Nature of Logical Form: Evidence from Toba Batak." *Linguistic Inquiry* 16: 663–669.

Clements, G. N. 1985. "The Problem of Transfer in Nonlinear Phonology." *Cornell Working Papers in Linguistics,* vol. 7. Ithaca, N.Y.: Dept. of Linguistics, Cornell University.

Cohn, A. 1989. "Stress in Indonesian and Bracketing Paradoxes." *Natural Language and Linguistic Theory* 7: 167–216.

Cole, J. 1987. Planar Phonology and Morphology. Ph.D. diss., MIT, Cambridge.

Collinder, B. 1957. *Survey of the Uralic Languages.* Stockholm: Almqvist and Wiksell.

Corbett, G. 1987. "The Morphology/Syntax Interface." *Language* 63: 299–345.

Corum, C. 1973. "Anaphoric Peninsulas." In C. Corum et al., eds., *Papers from the Ninth Regional Meeting of the Chicago Linguistic Society.* Chicago: Chicago Linguistic Society.

Cowper, E. 1987. "Pied Piping, Feature Percolation and the Structure of the Noun Phrase." *Canadian Journal of Linguistics* 32: 321–338.

Cutler, A., J. Hawkins, and G. Gilligan. 1985. "The Suffixing Preference: A Processing Explanation." *Linguistics* 23: 723–758.

Darmesteter, A. 1875. *Formation des mots composés en français*. Paris: N.P.

Dell, F., and E. Selkirk. 1978. "On a Morphologically Governed Vowel Alternation in French." In S. J. Keyser, ed., *Recent Transformational Studies in European Linguistics*. Cambridge: MIT Press.

Dench, A., and N. Evans. 1988. "Multiple Case Marking in Australian Languages." *Australian Journal of Linguistics* 8: 1–47.

DeVooys, C. G. N. 1967. *Nederlandse Spraakkunst*. Groningen: J. B. Wolters.

DiSciullo, A.-M. 1988. "Formal Relations and Argument Structure." Third International Congress in Morphology, Krems, Austria.

DiSciullo, A.-M., and E. Williams. 1987. *On the Definition of Word*. Cambridge: MIT Press.

Dixon, R. M. W. 1977. *A Grammar of Yidiɲ*. Cambridge: Cambridge University Press.

Donaldson, B. C. 1987. *Dutch Reference Grammar*. Leiden: Martinus Nijhoff.

Dresher, B. E. 1983. "Postlexical Phonology in Tiberian Hebrew." In M. Barlow, D. Flickinger, and M. Wescoat, eds., *Proceedings of the West Coast Conference on Formal Linguistics*, 67–78. Stanford: Stanford Linguistics Association.

Emonds, J. 1985. *A Unified Theory of Syntactic Categories*. Dordrecht: Foris.

Evans, N. 1985. Kayardild, The Language of the Bentinck Islanders of North West Queensland. Ph.D. diss., Australian National University, Canberra.

Evers, A. 1975. The Transformational Cycle in Dutch and German. Ph.D. diss., University of Utrecht, Utrecht, Netherlands.

Fabb, N. 1984. Syntactic Affixation. Ph.D. diss., MIT, Cambridge.

———. 1988. "English Suffixation Is Constrained Only by Selectional Restrictions." *Natural Language and Linguistic Theory* 6: 527–539.

Fanselow, G. 1988. "'Word Syntax' and Semantic Principles." *Yearbook of Morphology* 1: 95–122.

Farmer, A. 1987. "On the Analysis of Deverbal Adjectives and Nouns with Self-." Paper presented at the annual meeting of the LSA, San Francisco, CA.

Finer, D. 1985. "The Syntax of Switch-Reference." *Linguistic Inquiry* 16: 35–55.

Giurescu, A. 1975. *Les Mots composés dans les langues romanes*, The Hague: Mouton.

Goldsmith, J. 1976. *Autosegmental Phonology*. Ph.D. diss., MIT, Cambridge.

Haegeman, L., and H. van Riemsdijk. 1986. "Verb Projection Raising, Scope, and the Typology of Rules Affecting Verbs." *Linguistic Inquiry* 17: 417–466.

Hall, T. A. 1989. "Lexical Phonology and the Distribution of German [ç] and [x]." *Phonology* 6: 1–17.

Halle, M., and K. P. Mohanan. 1985. "Segmental Phonology of Modern English." *Linguistic Inquiry* 16: 57–116.

Halle, M., and J.-R. Vergnaud. 1987. "Stress and the Cycle." *Linguistic Inquiry* 18: 45–84.

Hammond, M. 1981. "Some Vogul Morphology: A Hierarchical Account of Multiple Exponence." In T. Thomas-Flinders, ed., *Inflectional Morphology: Introduction to the Extended Word-and-Paradigm Theory*, 84–166. UCLA Occasional Papers no. 4, Los Angeles, CA.

Hankamer, J., and I. Sag. 1977. "Syntactically versus Pragmatically Controlled Anaphora. In R. W. Fasold and R. W. Shuy, eds., *Studies in Language Variation*. Washington, D.C.: Georgetown University Press.

Higginbotham, J. 1985. "On Semantics." *Linguistic Inquiry* 16: 547–594.

Hoeksema, J. 1985. *Categorial Morphology*. New York: Garland Publishing Inc.

———. 1987. "Relating Word Structure and Logical Form." *Linguistic Inquiry* 18: 119–125.

———. 1988. "Head-Types in Morpho-Syntax." *Yearbook of Morphology* 1: 123–138.

Hoekstra, T. 1984. *Transitivity*. Dordrecht: Foris.

———. 1986. "Deverbalization and Inheritance." *Linguistics* 24: 549–584.

Hoekstra, T., and F. Van Der Putten. 1988. "Inheritance Phenomena." In M. Everaert, A. Evers, R. Huybregts, and M. Trommelen, eds. *Morphology and Modularity*, 163–186. Dordrecht: Foris.

Inkelas, S. 1989. Prosodic Constituency in the Lexicon. Dissertation, Stanford University, Stanford, CA.

Jackendoff, R. 1977. *X′ Syntax: A Study of Phrase Structure*. Cambridge: MIT Press.

———. 1987. "The Status of Thematic Relations in Linguistic Theory." *Linguistic Inquiry* 18: 369–412.

———. 1990. *Semantic Structures*. Cambridge: MIT Press.

Jensen, J., and M. Stong-Jensen. 1984. "Morphology Is in the Lexicon." *Linguistic Inquiry* 15: 474–498.

Kaisse, E., and P. Shaw. 1985. "On the Theory of Lexical Phonology." *Phonology Yearbook* 2: 1–30.

Kálmán, B. 1965. *Vogul Crestomathy*. Indiana University Publications, Uralic and Altaic Series, vol. 46. The Hague: Indiana University and Mouton.

———. 1984. "Beiträge zum Konsonantismus der wogulischen Sprache." In O. Gschwantler, K. Rédei, and H. Reichert, eds. *Linguistica et Philologica, Gedenkschrift für Björn Collinder*. Wien: Wilhelm Braumuller.

Kaye, J., J. Lowenstamm, and J.-R. Vergnaud. 1985. "The Internal Structure of Phonological Elements: A Theory of Charm and Government." *Phonology Yearbook* 2: 305–329.

Kayne, R. 1984. *Connectedness and Binary Branching*. Dordrecht: Foris.

Kemenade, A. van. 1987. *Syntactic Case and Morphological Case in the History of English*. Dordrecht: Foris.

Kendall, M. 1976. *Selected Problems in Yavapai Syntax*. New York: Garland Publishing, Inc.

Kiparsky, P. 1982. "From Cyclic Phonology to Lexical Phonology." In H. van der Hulst and N. Smith, eds., *The Structure of Phonological Representations*. Dordrecht: Foris.

Koopman, H. 1984. *The Syntax of Verbs*. Dordrecht: Foris.

Koster, J. 1975. "Dutch as an SOV Language." *Linguistic Analysis* 1: 111–136.

Lakoff, G., and J. R. Ross. 1972. "A Note on Anaphoric Islands and Causatives." *Linguistic Inquiry* 3: 121–125.

Lapointe, S. 1980. A Theory of Grammatical Agreement. Ph.D. diss., University of Massachusetts, Amherst.

Leben, W. 1973. Suprasegmental Phonology. Ph.D. diss., MIT, Cambridge.

Lees, R. 1963. *The Grammar of English Nominalizations.* Bloomington: Indiana University; The Hague: Mouton.

Levi, J. 1977. *The Syntax and Semantics of Complex Nominals.* New York: Academic Press.

Levin, B., and M. Rappaport. 1986. "The Formation of Adjectival Passives." *Linguistic Inquiry* 17: 623–662.

Levin, J. 1985. A Metrical Theory of Syllabicity. Ph.D. diss., MIT Cambridge.

Lieber, R. 1980. On the Organization of the Lexicon. Ph.D. diss., MIT, Cambridge. [Reproduced by IULC, 1981; page numbers refer to IULC version.]

———. 1981. "Morphological Conversion within a Restrictive Theory of the Lexicon." In M. Moortgat, H. van der Hulst, and T. Hoekstra, eds., *The Scope of Lexical Rules.* Dordrecht: Foris.

———. 1982. "Allomorphy." *Linguistic Analysis* 10: 27–52.

———. 1983a. "Argument Linking and Compounds in English." *Linguistic Inquiry* 14: 251–286.

———. 1983b. "New Developments in Autosegmental Morphology." In M. Barlow, D. Flickinger, and M. Wescoat, eds., *Proceedings of the West Coast Conference on Formal Linguistics,* vol. 2. Stanford: Stanford University Linguistics Association.

———. 1984a. "Grammatical Rules and Sublexical Elements." In D. Testen, V. Mishra, and J. Drogo, eds., *Papers from the Parasession on Lexical Semantics,* 187–199. Chicago: Chicago Linguistic Society.

———. 1984b. "Consonant Gradation in Fula: An Autosegmental Approach." In M. Aronoff and R. Oehrle, eds., *Language Sound Structure.* Cambridge: MIT Press.

———. 1987a. "Review of S. Scalise, *Generative Morphology. Canadian Journal of Linguistics* 32: 398–405.

———. 1987b. *An Integrated Theory of Autosegmental Processes.* Albany: SUNY Press.

———. 1988. "Phrasal Compounds in English and the Morphology-Syntax Interface." In D. Brentari, G. Larson, and L. MacLeod, eds. *CLS-24-II, Papers from the Parasession on Agreement in Grammatical Theory,* 202–222. Chicago: Chicago Linguistic Society.

———. 1989. "On Percolation." *Yearbook of Morphology* 2: 95–138.

Liimola, M. 1968. "Das l der objektiven Konjugation des Wogulischen." In P. Ravila, ed., *Congressus secundus internationalis Fenno-Ugristarum, Acta Linguistica,* 313–318. Helsinki.

Marantz, A. 1982. "ReReduplication." *Linguistic Inquiry* 13: 435–482.

———. 1984. *On the Nature of Grammatical Relations.* Cambridge: MIT Press.

———. 1988. "Apparent Exceptions to the Projection Principle." In M. Everaert, A. Evers, R. Huybregts, and M. Trommelen, eds., *Morphology and Modularity,* 217–233. Dordrecht: Foris.

Marchand, H. 1969. *The Categories and Types of Present-Day English Word-Formation*. München: C. H. Beck'sche Verlagsbuchhandlung.

Marle, J. van. 1985. *On the Paradigmatic Dimension of Morphological Creativity*. Dordrecht: Foris.

Martin, J. 1988. "Subtractive Morphology as Dissociation." In H. Borer, ed., *Proceedings of the Seventh West Coast Conference on Formal Linguistics*, 229–240. Stanford: Stanford Linguistics Association.

May, R. 1977. The Grammar of Quantification, Ph.D. diss., MIT, Cambridge.

McCarthy, J. 1979. Formal Problems in Semitic Phonology and Morphology. Ph.D. diss., MIT, Cambridge.

———. 1981. "A Prosodic Theory of Nonconcatenative Morphology." *Linguistic Inquiry* 12: 373–418.

———. 1986. "OCP Effects: Gemination and Antigemination." *Linguistic Inquiry* 17: 207–263.

———. 1989. "Linear Order in Phonological Representation." *Linguistic Inquiry* 20: 71–99.

McCarthy, J., and A. Prince. 1986. Prosodic Morphology. MS, University of Massachusetts, Amherst, and Brandeis University, Waltham, MA.

———. 1987. Quantitative Transfer in Reduplicative and Templatic Morphology. MS, University of Massachusetts, Amherst, and Brandeis University, Waltham, MA.

———. 1990. "Foot and Word in Prosodic Morphology: The Arabic Broken Plural." *Natural Language and Linguistic Theory* 8: 209–284.

Mohanan, K. P. 1982. Lexical Phonology. Ph.D. diss., MIT, Cambridge.

Nash, D. 1980. Topics in Warlpiri Grammar. Ph.D. diss., MIT, Cambridge.

Neidle, C. 1988. *The Role of Case in Russian Syntax*. Studies in Natural Language and Linguistic Theory. Dordrecht: Kluwer Academic Publishers.

Nespor, M., and I. Vogel. 1986. *Prosodic Phonology*. Dordrecht: Foris.

Paradis, C. 1986. Phonologie et Morphologie lexicales: Les classes nominales en Peul (Fula). Ph.D. diss., University of Montreal.

———. 1987. "Strata and Syllable Dependencies in Fula: The Nominal Classes." *Journal of African Languages and Linguistics* 9: 123–139.

Pesetsky, D. 1979. "Russian Morphology and Lexical Theory." MS, MIT, Cambridge.

———. 1985. "Morphology and Logical Form." *Linguistic Inquiry* 16: 193–248.

Pollock, J.-Y. 1989. "Verb Movement, Universal Grammar, and the Structure of IP." *Linguistic Inquiry* 20: 365–424.

Postal, P. 1969. "Anaphoric Islands." In *Papers from the Fifth Regional Meeting of the Chicago Linguistic Society*, Chicago: Chicago Linguistic Society.

Radford, A. 1986. *Transformational Grammar, A First Course*. Cambridge: Cambridge University Press.

Randall, J. 1988. "Inheritance." In W. Wilkins, ed., *Syntax and Semantics*, vol. 21, 129–146. New York: Academic Press.

Rappaport, M., and B. Levin. 1988. "What to do with Θ-Roles." In W. Wilkins, ed., *Syntax and Semantics*, vol. 21, 7–36. New York: Academic Press.

Reinhart, T. 1983. *Anaphora and Semantic Interpretation*. Chicago: University of Chicago Press.

Renouf, A. 1987. "Corpus Development." In J. Sinclair, ed., *Looking Up: An Account of the Cobuild Project in Lexical Computing*. London: Collins.

Rice, K. 1989. Review of Lieber, *An Integrated Theory of Autosegmental Processes*. *Canadian Journal of Linguistics* 34: 59–78.

Riemsdijk, H. van 1978. *A Case Study in Syntactic Markedness: The Binding Nature of Prepositional Phrases*. Dordrecht: Foris.

Roeper, T. 1987. "Implicit Arguments and the Head-Complement Relation." *Linguistic Inquiry* 18: 267–310.

———. 1988. "Compound Syntax and Head Movement." *Yearbook of Morphology* 1: 187–228.

Roeper, T., and M. Siegel. 1978. "A Lexical Transformation for Verbal Compounds." *Linguistic Inquiry* 9: 197–260.

Rohrer, C. 1977. *Die Wortzusammensetzung im modernen Französisch*. Tübingen: TBL Verlag Gunter Narr.

Ross, J. R. 1967. Constraints on Variables in Syntax. Ph.D. diss., MIT, Cambridge.

———. 1971. "On the Superficial Nature of Anaphoric Island Constraints." *Linguistic Inquiry* 2: 599–600.

Sadock, J. 1980. "Noun Incorporation in West Greenlandic." *Language* 56: 300–319.

———. 1986. "Some Notes on Noun Incorporation." *Language* 62: 19–31.

———. 1991. *Autolexical Syntax: A Theory of Parallel Grammatical Representations*. Chicago: University of Chicago Press.

Safir, K. 1987. The X-zero Complementation Theory: An Outline for Further Research. MS, Rutgers University, New Brunswick, N.J.

Sagey, E. 1986. The Representation of Features and Relations in Nonlinear Phonology. Ph.D. diss., MIT, Cambridge.

Savini, M. 1983. Phrasal Compounds in Afrikaans. M.A. thesis, University of Stellenbosch, Stellenbosch, Republic of South Africa.

Scalise, S. 1984. *Generative Morphology*. Dordrecht: Foris.

———. 1988. "The Notion of 'Head' in Morphology." *Yearbook of Morphology* 1: 229–246.

Schachter, P., and F. Otanes. 1972. *Tagalog Reference Grammar*. Berkeley: University of California Press.

Schultink, H. 1961. "Produktiviteit als morfologisch fenomeen." *Forum der Letteren* 2: 110–125.

———. 1987. "Discontinuity and Multiple Branching in Morphology." In N. Arhammar, ed., *Aspects of Language*, vol. 2, 481–491. Amsterdam: Rodopi.

Selkirk, E. 1982. *The Syntax of Words*. Cambridge: MIT Press.

———. 1984. *Phonology and Syntax*. Cambridge: MIT Press.

Shieber, S. 1986. *An Introduction to Unification-Based Approaches to Grammar*. CSLI Lecture Notes, no. 4. CSLI, Stanford University, Stanford, CA.

Siegel, D. 1974. Topics in English Morphology. Ph.D. diss., MIT, Cambridge.

Simpson, J. 1983. Aspects of Warlpiri Morphology and Syntax. Ph.D. diss., MIT, Cambridge.

Smith, C. 1964. "Determiners and Relative Clauses in a Generative Grammar of English." *Language* 40: 37–52.

Sproat, R. 1985. On Deriving the Lexicon. Ph.D. diss., MIT, Cambridge.

———. 1988a. "On Anaphoric Islandhood." In M. Hammond and M. Noonan, eds., *Theoretical Morphology.* New York: Academic Press.

———. 1988b. "Bracketing Paradoxes, Cliticization and Other Topics: The Mapping between Syntactic and Phonological Structure." In M. Everaert, A. Evers, R. Huybregts, and M. Trommelen, eds., *Morphology and Modularity.* Dordrecht: Foris.

Sproat, R., and G. Ward. 1987. "Pragmatic considerations in Anaphoric Island Phenomena." In B. Need, E. Schiller, and A. Bosch, eds., *Papers from the Twenty-third Annual Regional Meeting of the Chicago Linguistic Society.* Chicago: Chicago Linguistic Society.

Steriade, D. 1988. Reduplication, Ablaut and Syllabicity in Sanskrit. MS, MIT, Cambridge.

Stowell, T. 1981. Origins of Phrase Structure. Ph.D. diss., MIT, Cambridge.

———. 1990. "Subjects, Specifiers, and X-bar Theory." In M. Baltin and A. Kroch, eds., *Alternative Conceptions of Phrase Structure.* Chicago: University of Chicago Press.

Strauss, S. 1982. "On 'Relatedness Paradoxes' and Related Paradoxes." *Linguistic Inquiry* 13: 694–700.

———. 1987. "Word Formation with Lexical Insertion and Filters." In E. Gussman, ed., *Rules and the Lexicon, Studies in Word-Formation,* 137–167. Lublin: Wydawnictw.

Subramanian, U. 1988. "Subcategorization and Derivation: Evidence from Tamil." In D. Brentari, G. Larson, and L. MacLeod, eds., *Papers from the Twenty-fourth Annual Regional Meeting of the Chicago Linguistic Society,* 353–361. Chicago: Chicago Linguistic Society.

Surridge, M. 1985. "Le genre grammatical des composés en français." *Canadian Journal of Linguistics* 30: 247–271.

Toman, J. 1983. *Wortsyntax.* Tübingen: Max Niemeyer Verlag.

———. 1987. "Issues in the Theory of Inheritance." Paper delivered at the Round Table on Word-Structure Theories, Fourteenth International Congress of Linguists, Berlin.

Travis, L. 1984. Parameters and Effects of Word Order Variation. Ph.D. diss., MIT, Cambridge.

———. 1990. "Parameters of Phrase Structure." In M. Baltin and A. Kroch, eds., *Alternative Conceptions of Phrase Structure.* Chicago: University of Chicago Press.

Trommelen, M., and W. Zonneveld. 1986. "Dutch Morphology: Evidence for the Right-hand Head Rule." *Linguistic Inquiry* 17: 147–169.

Walinska de Hackbeil, H. 1986. The Roots of Phrase Structure: The Syntactic Base of English Morphology. Ph.D. diss., University of Washington, Seattle.

Ward, G., R. Sproat, and G. McKoon. In press. "A Pragmatic Analysis of So-Called Anaphoric Islands." To appear in *Language.*

Williams, E. 1981a. "On the Notions 'Lexically Related' and 'Head of a Word'." *Linguistic Inquiry* 12: 245–274.

———. 1981b. "Argument Structure and Morphology." *Linguistic Review* 1: 81–114.

Wurzel, W. 1970. *Studien zur Deutschen Lautstruktur.* Studia Grammatica VIII. Berlin: Akademie Verlag.

Younes, R. 1983. "The Representation of Geminate Consonants." MS, University of Texas, Austin.

Author Index

Abney, S., 12, 28, 39, 49, 50, 53
Allen, M., 19
Anderson, S. R., 19, 96, 205, 211, 212
Aoun, J., 125
Archangeli, D., 190
Arnott, D. W., 166, 217
Aronoff, M., 1, 2, 3, 28, 151, 154,
  171–72, 178–80, 185

Baayen, H., 2, 4–6, 8, 13, 74–75, 131,
  205, 210, 214
Baker, M., 19, 20, 21, 37, 60–61, 115,
  121, 140–42, 145, 211
Baltin, M., 37
Bat El, O., 187–89
Bauer, L., 12, 13, 66, 67, 155, 206, 215
Bloomfield, L., 180
Bok-Bennema, R., 215
Booij, G., 72, 73, 116, 117, 118, 119, 136,
  149, 150, 181, 197, 198, 199, 200, 210,
  214, 218
Borer, H., 19–20
Botha, R., 12, 208
Bromberger, S., 198
Broselow, E., 171, 172, 179, 180
Brousseau, A.-M., 32, 68
Browne, W., 24, 122
Budenz, J., 110

Canale, W., 63
Carrier, J., 118, 213
Carrier-Duncan, J., 43
Chomsky, N., 14, 20, 21, 27, 28, 30, 49,
  60, 115, 121, 124, 126, 138, 140, 141,
  143, 144, 145, 203
Clark, E., 61
Clark, R., 42, 43, 208
Clements, G. N., 154, 171, 175–76, 217
Cohn, A., 150, 200

Cole, J., 186
Collinder, B., 102, 110
Corbett, G., 15
Corum, C., 24, 122
Cowper, E., 210
Cutler, A., 207

Darmesteter, A., 66
Dell, F., 82–85, 158
Dench, A., 94
DeVooys, C. G. N., 74
DiSciullo, A.-M., 14, 21, 23, 32, 66, 68,
  77, 79, 91, 117, 215
Dixon, R. M. W., 181
Donaldson, B., 68
Dresher, B. E., 200

Emonds, J., 37, 39
Evans, N., 94, 95, 211, 213
Evers, A., 70

Fabb, N., 12, 19, 20, 149, 201–02, 207,
  217, 218
Fanselow, G., 119
Farmer, A., 135, 137, 214
Finer, D., 124–25, 213, 214

Gilligan, G., 207
Giurescu, A., 66
Goldsmith, J., 175
Groos, A., 215

Haaften, T. van, 116, 117, 118, 119
Haegeman, L., 86
Hall, T. A., 217
Halle, M., 186, 198, 201
Hammond, M., 212
Hankamer, J., 213
Hawkins, J., 207

Hecht, B., 61
Higginbotham, J., 208
Hoeksema, J., 11, 12, 73, 178, 205, 215
Hoekstra, T., 70, 86, 116

Inkelas, S., 200

Jackendoff, R., 22, 27, 51–53, 118, 206, 211
Jensen, J., 211, 212

Kaisse, E., 198, 201
Kálmán, B., 102, 103, 107, 108, 110, 212, 213
Kaye, J., 217
Kayne, R., 156
Kemenade, A. van, 63, 70, 209
Kendall, M., 95, 124
Kiparsky, P., 12, 19, 151, 198, 201, 217, 218
Koopman, H., 69, 70
Koster, J., 70

Lakoff, G., 24, 122
Lapointe, S., 14, 151, 205
Leben, W., 175
Lees, R. E., 151, 206
Levi, J., 12
Levin, B., 22, 117, 118, 211
Levin, J., 176
Lieber, R., 5, 6, 8, 12, 14, 19, 21–23, 29–32, 36, 57, 62, 77–80, 82, 84–87, 91, 97, 131, 149–151, 158–60, 162, 164, 165, 171, 179, 181, 197, 205, 206, 210, 211, 212, 213, 214, 216, 217
Liimola, M., 102, 110, 212
Lowenstamm, J., 217

McCarthy, J. J., 24, 25, 150, 154, 171–75, 177–81, 183, 185–87, 189–93, 217, 218
McKoon, G., 213
Marantz, A., 24, 45, 87, 149, 171, 172, 174
Marchand, H., 56, 58, 63, 210
Marle, J. van, 3
Martin, J., 194, 218
May, R., 149

Mohanan, K. P., 151, 210
Mulford, R., 61

Nash, D., 14, 181
Neidle, C., 212
Nespor, M., 150, 200

Otanes, F., 16, 40–42, 44, 45, 48, 155, 179, 180, 208, 216

Paradis, C., 166–67, 217
Pesetsky, D., 23, 56, 122, 147–49, 151, 198, 207, 215, 218
Pollock, J.-Y., 87, 115, 121, 140, 213
Postal, P., 24, 121–23, 129
Prince, A., 25, 150, 171–74, 177–81, 183, 186, 193, 217, 218

Radford, A., 205
Randall, J., 24, 117, 118, 213
Rappaport, M., 22, 117, 118, 211
Reinhart, T., 213
Renouf, A., 5
Rice, K., 170
Riemsdijk, H. van, 69, 70, 87
Roeper, T., 59–60, 62, 86, 88, 117
Rohrer, C., 65, 66, 67
Ross, J. R., 24, 122, 152, 153
Rubach, J., 149, 150, 199

Sadock, J., 215
Safir, K., 59
Sag, I., 213
Sagey, E., 170
Savini, M., 11, 12
Scalise, S., 32, 36, 210
Schachter, P., 16, 40–42, 44, 45, 48, 155, 179, 180, 208, 216
Schultink, H., 3, 4, 216
Selkirk, E., 14, 19, 23, 29–31, 55, 58, 62, 66, 77–80, 82–85, 91, 149–51, 158, 205, 206, 211, 212
Shaw, P., 198, 201
Shieber, S., 211
Siegel, D., 201
Siegel, M., 60, 62
Simpson, J., 14–15
Smith, C., 51

Sproat, R., 12, 19–21, 122, 123, 130, 132, 135, 137, 139, 149, 201, 205, 206, 207, 208, 209, 213, 214
Steriade, D., 45
Stong-Jensen, M., 211, 212
Stowell, T., 27, 28, 33, 37–39, 50–54, 62, 206, 207
Strauss, S., 149, 215
Subramanian, U., 17–18, 206
Surridge, M., 65, 66, 67

Toman, J., 12, 19–21, 24, 85, 87, 88, 115, 207
Travis, L., 28, 34, 60, 63, 71, 141
Trommelen, M., 32, 72

Van der Putten, F., 116
Vergnaud, J.-R., 186, 201, 217
Vogel, I., 150, 200

Walinska de Hackbeil, H., 20, 39, 207, 209
Ward, G., 213, 214
Williams, E., 2, 14, 19, 21, 23, 29–32, 38, 49, 55, 57, 66, 77–79, 87, 91, 117, 149, 151, 205, 206, 210, 215
Wurzel, W., 86, 160

Younes, R., 186

Zonneveld, W., 32, 72

Language Index

Afar, 186
Afrikaans, 11
Arabic, 185–86, 191–94

Chinese, 34, 89, 90
Coeur d'Alene, 186

Diyari, 124, 174
Dutch, 1, 23, 26, 64; agentive/instrumental
suffixes in, 210; circumfixes in, 155–57,
216; headedness in, 32, 76; inheritance
in, 117; Licensing Conditions in, 68–71;
phrasal compounds in, 11–13, 72; position of complements with respect to
heads, 69–71; position of modifiers with
respect to heads, 69; position of specifiers
with respect to heads, 68–69; prefixes in,
73–75; root compounds in, 72; synthetic
compounds in, 73; word formation in, 72

English: ablaut verbs, 85; anaphoric islands,
121–24, 126–32; argument structure,
88, 117; assignment of Theta-roles, 136;
categorial signature, 89–90, 213;
cliticization analysis of prenominal adjectives, 51–52; comparative suffix, 148;
comparison to Dutch, 69, 71–73,
75–76; comparison to French, 65,
67–68, 76; compounds, 58; conversion,
157–58, 160–65, 195, 217; criteria for
identifying compounds, 12–13; indexing
in, 126; Level Ordering and, 201; Licensing Conditions, 64; Morphemic Plane
Hypothesis and, 186; parameter settings,
34–35; percolation in, 93; phrasal compounds, 11, 56; phrase structure in, 26;
position of complement with respect to
head, 49; position of specifier with respect to head, 49; position of modifier

with respect to head, 50–53; possessive
marking in, 14, 114–15, 205; prefixes,
31–32, 46, 55–57, 208; productivity of
affixes in, 5–9; root compounds, 56;
self-compounds, 132–39; suffixes, 55;
synthetic compounds, 23, 30, 36, 39,
59–62, 210; word structure in, 54; X-bar
template for, 206

French: derivational word formation,
67–68; Head Movement in, 213; instrumental compounds, 63, 66–67; Learned
Backing, 82–85; left-headed morphology, 32; percolation in, 93; phrase
structure, 26, 35; position of complement
with respect to head, 64; position of modifier with respect to head, 64; position of
specifier with respect to head, 65; prefixes, 68, 210; root compounds, 65–66,
209; word structure, 23, 76; zero-affixation in, 158, 160, 165, 195
Fula, 165–68, 170, 217

Georgian, 211, 212
German: categorial signature, 89–90; circumfixes, 155–56; conversion in,
157–58, 160–63, 165, 195; feature
[back] in, 217; percolation in, 93, 114;
phrasal compounds, 11–12; specifiers in,
33; strong verbs, 85–86; Umlaut in,
170–71
Greek, 66

Hebrew, 19, 187–88

Ilokano, 173
Italian, 32

Japanese, 33

233

Kayardild, 94–95, 97, 112–13
Kinyarwanda, 87–88, 211
Koasati, 194
Kpelle, 34

Latin, 66, 80–82

Makassarese, 180
Mohawk, 140
Mokilese, 174–78, 217

Old English, 62–63, 71

Potawatomi, 95

Rotuman, 186
Russian, 92, 93, 112

Tagalog: circumfixes, 155–57; compounds, 39; left-headed morphology in, 23, 76; phrasal derivation, 16–17, 47, 205; phrase structure in, 26; position of complement with respect to head, 40; position of modifier with respect to head, 41; position of specifier with respect to head, 41; reduplication, 173–76, 179–80, 183–85; sentence structure, 42–43; topic prefixes in, 205–6; word structure, 44–48, 55, 64, 152
Tamil, 17–18, 205
Toba Batak, 42–43
Tondano, 155–57
Tonkawa, 186

Upper Sorbian, 15–16

Vietnamese, 31
Vogul, 1, 101–14, 212, 213

Warlpiri, 14–15, 186
Wiyot, 186

Yavapai, 1, 95–101, 112, 116, 124–25, 211, 212, 213
Yawelmani, 190–91
Yidiny, 181

Subject Index

Adjectival possessives in Upper Sorbian, 15–16
Affixation, 154
Affixes: adjective forming, 5, 8; noun forming, 5, 8; productivity of English, 6–7; restrictions on, 4; verb-forming, 6, 8
Affix Hopping, 140, 213
Agentive nominals, 135–38
Allomorphy, 20
Anaphoric islands, 24, 121–24, 126, 128–30, 152, 202, 206
Anaphors, sublexical, 132, 214
Antecedent government, 142, 143, 147
Argument structure, 4, 24, 77, 86–88, 116–19, 135
Autosegmental morphology, 185
Autosegmental phonology, 165, 172

Backformations, 58, 214
Backup Percolation, 120; circumfixes and, 157; definition of, 92; inflection and, 112, 116; in Vogul, 106, 109, 111; in Yavapai, 98–101; operation of, 92–93
Barriers, 140–44, 147, 152–53, 202, 215
Base component, 27
Binding theory, 21, 24, 140, 152, 202, 213, 214, 215; anaphoric islands and, 121, 126–32; disjoint reference and, 124; generalized, 125; sublexical anaphors and, 133, 135, 138–39
Blocking Category, 141, 142, 147, 215
Bracketing Erasure, 151, 187, 188, 201–2, 218
Bracketing Erasure Convention, 202, 215
Bracketing Paradoxes, 122, 140, 147–50, 215, 217
Broken plurals, Arabic, 193–94

Case-assignment, direction of, 34
Case marking, 28, 60; Warlpiri, 14–15
Case theory, 21, 33, 62
Categorial signature, 23, 77, 88–91, 101, 119–20, 123, 206, 213; in Arabic word formation, 192–93; inflection and, 106, 112–15, 212; in Tagalog reduplication, 185; multiply marked features and, 97–98; percolation and, 92–93, 109–11, 211; V-Movement and, 116; Vogul, 104
c-command, 127
CELEX, 5, 8, 74
Charm and Government theory, 217
Circumfixation, 24, 154–57, 195, 208, 216
Clitics, Romance, 52
Complements: application of term to sublexical elements, 39; definition of, 38; Dutch, 70; English, 49; French, 64
Component of grammar, 1, 197–98; morphological, 1, 121; separation of, 14, 19–21, 33
Compounds, 112, 154, 205; acquisition of, 161; criteria for identifying, 12–13; instrumental, 66–67; phrasal, 12–13, 20–21, 33, 56, 59, 60, 72, 73, 76, 205, 209; root, 56, 65–66, 72, 73, 76, 207; *self*, 132–39, 142, 202; synthetic, 59–63, 66, 75–76, 136, 140, 142, 143, 207, 208, 209
Concatenative morphology, 154
Condition A, 126, 128, 133, 135, 138, 139
Condition B, 126, 127, 129, 138
Condition C, 126, 128, 129
Consonant mutation, 24, 154, 165–68, 170, 195
Conversion, 24, 154, 157–58, 195; category changing analysis of, 158, 164; relisting analysis of, 158–65

Coreference, 123, 124, 132
Creativity, morphological, 3

Derivation, 24, 77, 111–13, 120, 159, 205;
    phrasal, 16
Disjoint reference, 123, 124, 132

Empty Category Principle, 24, 122,
    140–47, 149, 152–53, 202
Extended Word and Paradigm theory, 212

Feature percolation, 23–24, 77, 92, 121,
    206; above word level, 210; for multiply
    marked features, 94; early statements of,
    78–79; Head and Backup, 91–92; head
    theory and, 31; inheritance and, 116,
    119; nonconcatenative morphology and,
    188–89; what features percolate, 80–88
Feature Percolation Conventions, 30,
    91–92
Features: case, 89, 94, 95; default, 101,
    104; diacritic, 77, 79–86, 119; morpho-
    syntactic, 77, 79, 87–91, 96–97, 101,
    104, 114, 116, 119, 156–57, 159, 167,
    192, 206; multiply marked, 93–94, 120;
    person/number, 96, 104, 107; semantic,
    90; tense/aspect, 106
First Sister Principle, 62
Foot, prosodic, 150, 172, 174

Generalized Phrase Structure Grammar, 215
Generative Semantics, 122, 123, 151
Government, 141, 215
Government-Binding theory, 197; category-
    changing rules and, 158; disjoint refer-
    ence in, 213; Incorporation in, 141;
    modules of, 21, 24, 121, 152; Licensing
    Conditions in, 35; phonology and, 201;
    prenominal modifiers in, 53; projection
    in, 30; semantic representation in, 123;
    use in previous work on morphology,
    20–21; V Movement analyses in, 115;
    X-bar principles of, 33

Hapax legomena, 4
Head: of phrase, 20, 30; of word, 20, 26,
    30–32, 179
Headedness, direction of, 32–33

Head Initial/Final parameter, 34–35
Head Movement, 60, 75, 115, 202, 209,
    213
Head Movement Constraint, 141, 145
Head Operations, 154, 171–72, 178–80,
    183, 185, 195
Head Percolation, 120; Affix Hopping and,
    213; circumfixes and, 157; definition of,
    92; inflection and, 112; in Arabic, 192; in
    Vogul, 106, 109, 111; in Yavapai,
    98–101; operation of, 92–93
Heavy NP Shift, 54
Hyponyms, 32

Incorporation, 19, 140–41, 215
Indexing, 121, 131, 139, 214; sublexical,
    124, 139
Inflection, 24, 77, 111–15, 120, 205, 212
Inheritance, 24, 78, 87–88, 116–19
Internal arguments, 38
Island Constraints, 153
Islands, 152

Learned Backing, 82–85
Level Ordering, 200–201, 217
Lexical Conceptual Structure, 22, 206;
    conversion and, 159–62, 165, 210;
    inheritance and, 24, 118–20; relation of
    categorial signature to, 90; *self*-com-
    pounds and, 136
Lexical entries, 30
Lexical Functional Grammar, 215
Lexicalist Hypothesis, 14, 18–19, 24,
    121–22, 151–52, 205
Lexical Phonology, 25, 151, 187, 198–
    202, 206
Lexical semantics, 118
Lexical structure, 44, 54
Lexicon, 21
Licensing Conditions, 35, 38–40, 55–56,
    58–59, 62, 64; Dutch, 69–71; English,
    49–50, 54; French, 64–65; Old English,
    63; Tagalog, 43–44, 48–49
Linear order, 198
Listemes, 21
L-Marking, 141–44, 146–47, 215
Locality, 140, 153, 189, 198, 202
Logical Form, 147

M-command, 127
Minimal Governing Category, 126, 133, 135–38, 215
Modifiers: definition of, 38; Dutch, 69; English, 50–53; French, 64
Morphemic Plane Hypothesis, 154, 185–89, 218; Strong, 189–91; Weak, 189, 191
Move-Alpha, 24, 63, 121, 140–47, 152, 158, 215

No Stray Affix Principle, 145–46
Nominalizations, Tamil, 17–18
Nominative Island Constraint, 153
Nonconcatenative morphology, 154, 197
Nonmaximality Constraint, 205

Obligatory Contour Principle, 175

Parafixation, 154, 171, 175–78, 195
Parameterization, 26, 28, 31, 34–35
Phonological word, 150
Plane Conflation, 186, 187, 188, 218
Possessives, in English, 14, 114–15
Pragmatic theory of anaphora, 213
Predicate Argument Structure, 22, 206; conversion and, 159–60, 162–63, 216; inheritance and, 24, 118–19; *self*-compounds and, 136
Productivity, 3–9, 74, 121, 129, 131, 214; definition of, 3; degree of, 4; dictionaries and, 5; index of, 2; measures of, 3–5; morphological, 1–3
Projection Principle, 28, 30
Prosodic categories, 149
Prosodic constituents, 172
Prosodic domains, 200
Prosodic structure, 149–50, 197–98, 218
Prosodic word, 172

Quantifier Rule, 149

Redundancy rules, 104
Reduplication, 20, 24, 149, 154, 195, 198, 208; affixation analysis of, 172–75, 217; Head Operations and, 179–85; problems concerning, 171–72; quantity-sensitive, 175–78; Tagalog, 45, 173, 175–76, 179, 183–85

Reflexives, 133, 139
Relational grammar, 215
Right-hand Head Rule, 19, 30–32, 57
Root and pattern morphology. *See* Templatic morphology

Segmental geometry, 170, 187, 190, 197, 198, 218
Selectional restrictions, 90
Specified Subject Condition, 153
Specifiers: definition of, 38–39; Dutch, 69; English, 49–50; French, 65
Strict Cycle Convention, 199, 200
Strong verbs, 85–86
Subcategorization, morphological, 22, 30, 146
Subjacency, 140, 153
Subtractive morphology, 194–95
Switch Reference, 124–25, 214
Syllable, 149, 172, 173; core, 150, 172–74, 183; heavy, 172, 174; light, 172; minimal, 173

Templatic morphology, 24, 154, 185–86, 190–95
Tensed S Condition, 153
Theta-government, 141, 142, 143
Theta grids, 118, 119
Theta-identification, 63, 71, 73, 208
Theta-marking, 207; direction of, 34
Theta role, 118, 136, 137; assignment, 28, 57
Theta theory, 20, 21, 32, 152
Truncation, 20

Umlaut, 24, 154, 165, 170–71, 195
Underspecification, 197, 198
Unification-based grammar, 211
Uniformity of Theta Assignment Hypothesis, 61

Visibility Condition, 60
V Movement, 115–16
Vocalic ablaut, 85

Word formation rules, 28
Word, minimal, 173, 174, 181, 193, 194

Word structure rules, 29
Word structure trees, 30

X-bar template, 34–36; revised, 37
X-bar theory, 19–21, 77, 121, 140, 152;
   circumfixes and, 156; conversion and,
   158; modifiers in, 51; movement and, 62;
   parameterization of, 23, 75, 206; phonology and, 200; position of maximal
phrases in, 37; prehead position in, 205;
principles of, 26–28, 33–35, 37; revised
principles of, 38; Tagalog and, 40

Zero-affixation, 154, 216; conversion and,
   158–62, 164–65; in French, 67, 83–84

.